Kickstart Database Management System Fundamentals

Key Concepts, Principles, and Advanced Techniques for Modern Database Design, Management, and Optimization

Dr. Jagdish Chandra Patni

Dr. Latika Pinjarkar

www.orangeava.com

First Published: December 2024

Published By: Orange Education Pvt Ltd, AVA®

Address: 9, Daryaganj, Delhi, 110002, India

275 New North Road Islington Suite 1314 London,

N1 7AA, United Kingdom

ISBN (PBK): 978-93-48107-77-0

ISBN (E-BOOK): 978-93-48107-71-8

Scan the QR code to explore our entire catalogue

www.orangeava.com

Dedicated To

My Parents:

Prayag Datt Patni

Haripriya Patni

My Parents-in-law:

Bhagwati Sharan Sharma

Bimla Sharma

- Dr. Jagdish Chandra Patni

My Parents:

Vasantrao Bhorkar

Asha Bhorkar

- Dr. Latika Pinjarkar

About the Authors

Dr. Jagdish Chandra Patni is a Professor at the Alliance School of Advanced Computing, Alliance University, Bengaluru, India. His research interests include Artificial Intelligence, Database Systems and Optimizations, Machine Learning, Deep Learning, High-Performance Computing, and Software Engineering. Before joining Alliance University, he held positions at Symbiosis International University, Pune, Jain University, Bengaluru, and the University of Petroleum and Energy Studies, Dehradun. He has authored over 100 research articles published in nationally and internationally recognized journals and conferences of repute, as well as 8 books and more than 12 book chapters with international publishers.

Dr. Patni is an active Guest Editor and Reviewer for various peer-reviewed international journals, serving as a reviewer for over 20 reputable international journals. He has delivered keynote and guest speeches in India and abroad, and has organized multiple conferences/seminars/workshops/Faculty Development Programs (FDPs) globally. He has been awarded the Eminent Engineers Award, Outstanding Performance Award, Guru Siromani Award, Professor of the Year, Researcher Excellence Award, Young Scientist Award, Teacher of the Year, and Best Paper Award by Hosei University, Tokyo, Japan. He is a Fellow Member of the Institution of Engineers (India), a Senior member of IEEE, and a member of ACM, MIE, IEANG, IACSIT, and Vigyan Bharti.

Dr. Latika Pinjarkar obtained her PhD in Computer Science and Engineering from CSVTU, Chhattisgarh, India, in 2019. She completed her M.Tech in Computer Technology and Application from CSVTU, Chhattisgarh, India, in 2008, and her BE in Computer Technology from Nagpur University, Maharashtra, in 1999. With over 22 years of experience in research and teaching, she is currently an Associate Professor and Academic Head in the CSE Department at Symbiosis Institute of Technology, Nagpur, part of Symbiosis International (Deemed University) Pune, Maharashtra, India.

Latika has presented more than 40 papers in international and national journals, and conferences, with 5 patents to her credit. She has also completed a research project sponsored by TEQIP-III. Her research interests include Image Processing, Computer Vision, Content-Based Image Retrieval (CBIR), and Machine Learning.

About the Technical Reviewer

Sachin Gupta has over 15 years of experience in the IT Industry. He has a proven track record of innovation and a commitment to driving technological advancements. He has successfully led multi-million-dollar projects and managed global teams, consistently delivering high-quality solutions in Database, Security, and Cloud technology. He is a member of various prestigious organizations, including IEEE (Senior Member), Sigma XI (Full Member), and IETE (Fellow Member). He has authored numerous scholarly articles in the field of Database and Cloud Computing.

His experience in managing global teams has equipped him with a unique perspective on technology challenges and opportunities worldwide. With a strong track record of innovation, he has designed and implemented cutting-edge solutions that have significantly improved the organization's efficiency, security, and performance.

Currently, Sachin works as a Technical Architect in the Database and Cloud Computing department at Paramount (Paramount Global), New York, USA. He has been a dedicated IT professional at Paramount since 2010, contributing significantly to the evolution and maintenance of its IT infrastructure.

Acknowledgements

I would like to express my heartfelt gratitude to each one who supported me throughout the journey of this book on Database Management System.

First and foremost, my family has been my greatest source of encouragement. Their unwavering belief in my vision kept me motivated through both challenging and happy moments. A special thanks to my wife, Priyanka Patni, my children, Shrey Patni and Parisha Patni, and my mother, Haripriya Patni, for their patience and understanding, and for always being my sounding board.

I am deeply grateful to my reviewers and well-wishers, whose insightful feedback and guidance helped shape this book. Thank you to Dr. Mahendra Singh Aswal, Dr. Ravi Tomar, Dr. Tanupriya Choudhury, Dr. Nilesh Bahadure, Dr. Amit Agarwal, and Dr. Hitesh Kumar Sharma, and all other experts who made this possible with their continuous support – your expertise made all the difference. Special thanks to Mahesh Pant and Suman Pant for their continuous encouragement to do good things.

I hope this book resonates with you as much as it has with me.

- Dr. Jagdish Chandra Patni

I am deeply thankful to everyone who supported me throughout the journey of creating this book on Database Management Systems.

Firstly, I owe my heartfelt gratitude to my family, who have been my greatest source of strength and encouragement. Their unwavering belief in my vision kept me motivated during both challenging and joyful moments. A special mention to my husband, Shyam Pinjarkar, my son Vedant and daughter Kavya and my parents, Vasantrao Bhorkar and Asha Bhorkar for their constant support, they have always been my pillars of inspiration.

I extend my sincere thanks to my esteemed reviewers and well-wishers, whose valuable feedback and guidance were instrumental in shaping this book. I am especially grateful to Dr. Jagdish Chandra Patni along with many other experts whose continuous encouragement and expertise made this endeavor possible.

I truly hope this book vibrates with you as deeply as it has with me.

- Dr. Latika Pinjarkar

Preface

Organizations increasingly rely on data to build their strategies and planning, making effective database management essential to manage the vast amount of data generated every second. This book aims to define the basics of Database Management Systems (DBMS) and provide readers with a comprehensive understanding of their principles and best practices. It also covers the advanced topics of database management systems that will lead towards the latest technologies and trends in the form of applications.

Data is a very crucial term that is used in all organizations, whether it is research, industry, education, or any other. This book not only covers the theoretical aspects of DBMS but also offers practical insights with real-world examples. It is designed for students, professionals, researchers, and anyone willing to learn database systems.

This book is divided into 10 unique and well-organized chapters that cover database basics and advanced topics in database management systems. It comprises database examples written in SQL that will help readers easily understand the concept by implementation.

The details are as follows:

Chapter 1. Introduction to Database Systems: This chapter introduces readers to the basics of database systems, including their advantages and best practices.

Chapter 2. Data Modeling and Design: This chapter provides detailed descriptions of various data models and their relationships, such as the ER Model.

Chapter 3. Relational Database Management Systems: This chapter describes one of the most widely used database management systems: the relational database management system, where data is organized in the form of rows and columns.

Chapter 4. Query Optimization: This chapter describes the concepts of query processing and explains how to optimize queries for effective processing.

Chapter 5. Database Normalization and Normal Forms: This chapter emphasizes database design, offering guidelines for database design and applying normalization where necessary.

Chapter 6. Transaction Management and Concurrency Control: This chapter elaborates the concepts of transaction management and concurrency control to execute the transactions concurrently.

Chapter 7. Data Warehousing and Business Intelligence: This chapter discusses the concepts of data warehousing and examines how it will affect the business by applying intelligence.

Chapter 8. Distributed Databases and NoSQL: This chapter explains the concepts of distributed database systems and how it is implemented in NoSQL.

Chapter 9. Data Security and Privacy: Security is a significant concern for any database system. This chapter addresses how to tackle the various security challenges.

Chapter 10. Database Administration and Cloud Services: This chapter discusses the administration and various cloud services that are helpful for managing a huge database.

Get a Free eBook

We hope you are enjoying your recently purchased book! Your feedback is incredibly valuable to us, and to all other readers looking for great books.

If you found this book helpful or enjoyable, we would truly appreciate it, if you could take a moment to leave a short review with a 5 star rating on Amazon. It helps us grow, and lets other readers discover our books.

As a thank you, we would love to send you a free digital copy of this book, and a **30%** discount code on your next cart value on our official websites:

www.orangeava.com

www.orangeava.in (For Indian Subcontinent)

☑ **Here's how:**

Leave a review for the book on Amazon.

Take a screenshot of your review, and send an email to **info@orangeava.com** (it can be just the confirmation screen).

Once, we receive your screenshot, we will send you the digital file, within 24 hours.

Thank you so much for your support – it means a lot to us!

Colored Images

Please follow the links or scan the QR codes to download the ***Images*** of the book:

You can find code bundles of our books on our official Github Repository. Go to the following link to and QR code to explore the further:

https://github.com/orgs/ava-orange-education/repositories

Please follow the link to download the Colored Images of the book:
https://rebrand.ly/4yaxbcz

In case there's an update to the code, it will be updated on the existing GitHub repository.

Errata

We take immense pride in our work at **Orange Education Pvt Ltd,** and follow best practices to ensure the accuracy of our content to provide an indulging reading experience to our subscribers. Our readers are our mirrors, and we use their inputs to reflect and improve upon human errors, if any, that may have occurred during the publishing processes involved. To let us maintain the quality and help us reach out to any readers who might be having difficulties due to any unforeseen errors, please write to us at :

errata@orangeava.com

Your support, suggestions, and feedback are highly appreciated.

DID YOU KNOW

Did you know that Orange Education Pvt Ltd offers eBook versions of every book published, with PDF and ePub files available? You can upgrade to the eBook version at **www.orangeava.com** and as a print book customer, you are entitled to a discount on the eBook copy. Get in touch with us at: **info@orangeava.com** for more details.

At **www.orangeava.com**, you can also read a collection of free technical articles, sign up for a range of free newsletters, and receive exclusive discounts and offers on AVA® Books and eBooks.

PIRACY

If you come across any illegal copies of our works in any form on the internet, we would be grateful if you would provide us with the location address or website name. Please contact us at **info@orangeava.com** with a link to the material.

ARE YOU INTERESTED IN AUTHORING WITH US?

If there is a topic that you have expertise in, and you are interested in either writing or contributing to a book, please write to us at **business@orangeava.com**. We are on a journey to help developers and tech professionals to gain insights on the present technological advancements and innovations happening across the globe and build a community that believes Knowledge is best acquired by sharing and learning with others. Please reach out to us to learn what our audience demands and how you can be part of this educational reform. We also welcome ideas from tech experts and help them build learning and development content for their domains.

REVIEWS

Please leave a review. Once you have read and used this book, why not leave a review on the site that you purchased it from? Potential readers can then see and use your unbiased opinion to make purchase decisions. We at Orange Education would love to know what you think about our products, and our authors can learn from your feedback. Thank you!

For more information about Orange Education, please visit **www.orangeava.com**.

Table of Contents

Chapter 1
Introduction to Database Systems

Introduction

Defining a database entails defining the kinds of data that will be kept in it, as well as their formats and limitations. The term 'meta-data' refers to the descriptive information or database definition that the database management system (DBMS) stores as a database catalog or dictionary. Storing the data on a storage device under DBMS control is the building process of a database.

A database is created and manipulated using the programs, and these changes are permanent in the database. We can also retrieve the data with the help of other similar programs. A database system supports multiple users and multiple programs to access the database.

A database management system is a collection of linked data and a group of software applications used to define, create, maintain, and work with databases.

Structure

In this chapter, we will cover the following topics:

- Definition and Characteristics of Databases
- Importance of Databases in Business and Technology
- Evolution of Database Management Systems
- Roles and Responsibilities of Database Administrators (DBAs)
- Types of Database Models (Relational, NoSQL, and so on)

History of Database

The data can be defined as unprocessed, uncontextualized bits or pieces of information; it can be quantitative and qualitative. While qualitative data is descriptive, quantitative data is typically numerical.

The data can also be numerical and qualitative. Numerical results from measurements, counts, or other mathematical computations form quantitative data. When data is contextualized, it provides information that may be further compiled and examined to aid in decision-making, leading to knowledge creation. As an illustration: values like 20, 30, 40, and 60 are meaningless until we clarify that they represent the number of students enrolled in particular classes. As a result, it is now knowledge that a university can use to establish rules, policies, and so on. Transforming data into information is the primary objective of an information system, which creates knowledge and aids in decision-making. Databases are intended for uses like these. A database is characterized as a well-organized set of connected data. Everything kept in a database has a connection. For instance, information on the airline reservation system shouldn't be stored in the students' database. Database Management System refers to the general-purpose software program that is used to manage the data in databases.

Punch cards were utilized for data input, output, and even data storage in the early days of computers. The databases arrived later. The first computer programs were created in the 1950s. The information was viewed as unimportant or merely a by-product of processing information, but as computers became widely accessible, businesses began using the previously unimportant data for practical needs.

Charles W. Bachman created the first database management system (DBMS) in the 1960s. During the same period, IBM also developed a database system known as IMS. These two databases were considered the forerunners of navigational databases, which located records or objects by following links from other objects. The invention of discs, as opposed to the previously used punched cards and magnetic tapes, made these databases possible. In these systems, access to data could only be made sequentially.

As computers became more powerful and versatile over time, numerous general-purpose database systems were introduced. Due to the need for standardization, Bachman established the Database Task Group, which was tasked with standardizing and designing databases. In 1971, the group presented the "CODASYL approach" standard. The method was intricate and necessitated both physical assistance and instruction. The following methods could be used to retrieve or search the records:

- Using the primary key (CALC key)
- Navigating relationships between records (Sets)
- Scanning the records in chronological order

In A *Relational Model of Data for Large Shared Data Banks*, Edgar Codd proposed a novel approach to the processing and storing huge databases. He used a table with fixed-length records instead of CODASYL's linked list form because he was dissatisfied with the searching capabilities of both IBM's IMS and CODASYL. In 1974, as part of the INGRES project, Michael Stonebraker and Eugene Wong of UC Berkeley expressed their interest in the project and researched relational database systems. The Project proved that the model is both effective and useful. Because of their work with the QUEL query language, systems, such as Ingres Corp., MS SQL Server, Sybase, Wang's PACE, and Britton-Lee were developed. A different relational database system prototype, known as System R, was developed by IBM. It used the SEQUEL query language and aided in the creation of Non-Stop SQL, Allbase, SQL/DS, and DB2. IBM developed SQL in 1974, replacing QUEL and numerous other functional query languages. The popularity of network and hierarchical database models decreased as a result of the success of relational database models in the database industry. The flagship product was IBM DB2, which also paved the way for creating other products including Watcom SQL, OS/2 database manager, PARADOX, RBASE 5000, RIM, Dbase III, and IV. Along with the development of Object Database Management systems in the early 1990s, client tools for Application Development were also launched. Released tools include VB, PowerBuilder, Oracle Developer, and others. Many Internet database connectors were released in response to the growing popularity of Internet databases in the late 1990s. Among the open-source solutions made available for the internet were Apache, MySQL, GCC, and CGI.

Relational Database Management Systems (RDBMS) efficiently process and store structured data. However, as time went on and the internet was used more often for social media, unstructured data, such as images, music, and videos became more prevalent. Traditional Relational Database Management Systems (RDBMS), were primarily designed to manage structured data with well-defined schemas and often faced challenges handling non-relational or schema-less data. NoSQL databases have emerged to address these limitations. NoSQL databases offer flexible data models, scalability, and often distributed architectures, making them well-suited for managing diverse data types, including unstructured and semi-structured data. Although they have gained a lot of popularity recently due to their high levels of flexibility, scalability, affordability, and ability to handle any type of data, they also have certain drawbacks. For example, they are very resource intensive, requiring a large memory and CPU resources for execution.

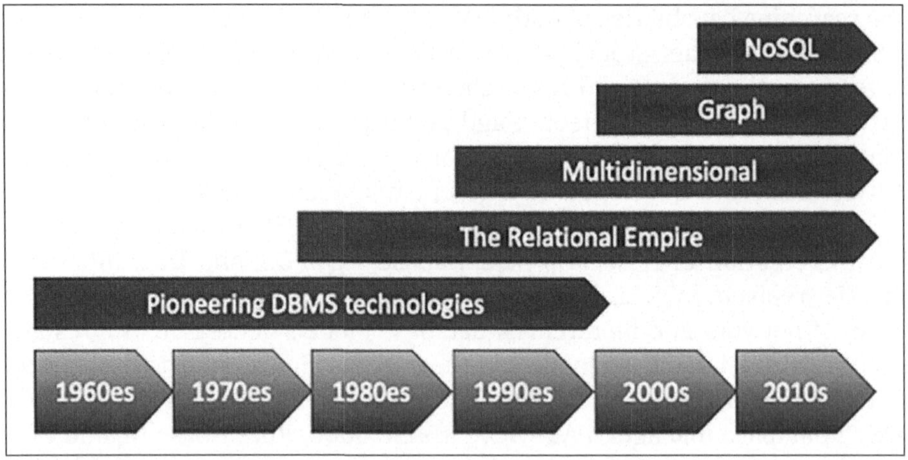

Figure 1.1: *History of Database Systems*

The preceding figure shows the progress of data and data-related technologies starting from 1960 and till present, as we now enter the world of big data.

Data and Information

Data and information are two basic building blocks of a database system. Let us discuss in detail:

Data

Data is any form of raw facts and figures that can be processed to get the Information. In the relational database paradigm, data is often arranged in rows and columns. Let's use a bank database including client information, for example, names, addresses, phone numbers, and other details. These characteristics or columns in the Bank database are only data; they don't contribute to anything that can aid in decision-making or the acquisition of any kind of crucial information.

The following traits and features are connected to the database data:

- **Shared:** As the database's contents will be utilized to provide users with certain insights, it should therefore be shared by users and programs alike.
- **Persistence:** The information in a database is stored indefinitely, so even after the operation that created or used it has ended, the information remains in the database and is not deleted.
- **Integrity:** Information kept in a database needs to be accurate about the outside world.
- **Security:** Unauthorized users shouldn't be able to access data stored in databases.

- **Consistency:** The values that are recorded in the database and related to the actual world must also match in terms of their relationships.
- **Non-Redundancy:** No two pieces of data should be the same representation of a global thing.
- **Independence:** Internal, conceptual, and external data representations should be separate from one another. One level of change shouldn't have an impact on another.

Information

Information is a very important resource, when we are constantly being inundated with too much data. Organizations and businesses that process and use this data to inform their decision-making will have a competitive advantage in today's cutthroat market. William Pollard once stated, "Information is a source of learning." However, it is a burden rather than an advantage if data is not sorted, processed, and made available to the appropriate parties in a format that allows decision-making. Information is refined data. Data manipulation and modification are now possible, thanks to the sophisticated technology in place. As a result, information systems that use these devices can operate in several fields, for example, information can be used for Artificial Intelligence and Machine Learning, recommender systems, engineering solutions, diagnosis, and more.

Information is made up of text, audio, documents, pictures, and data. Models are used to process data and extract information. The recipient receives the created knowledge well in advance and uses it again to make judgments. The cycle continues as a result of these decisions, which may also set off more incidents and activities that produce copious amounts of dispersed data that are then collected and transmitted as input.

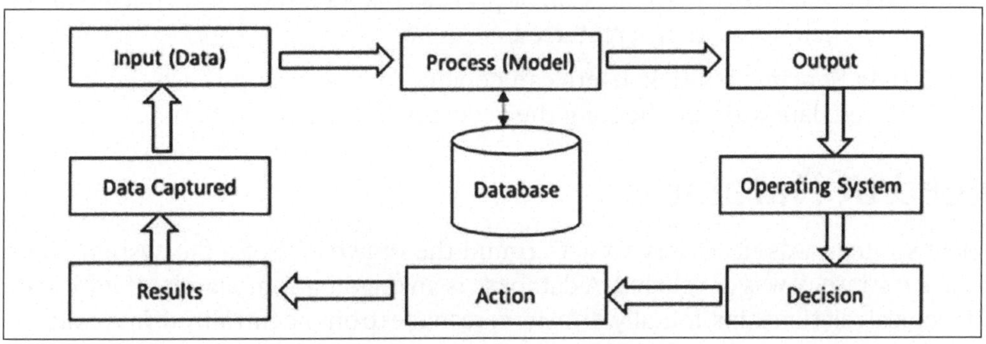

Figure 1.2: *Information Cycle*

The masses are inundated with false information. Therefore, high-quality information is necessary. Sufficient information is precise, up-to-date, and pertinent.

- **Accuracy:** If information is accurate in terms of its correctness, it implies that information shouldn't be altered or twisted. The significance of the facts it is based on should be evident.

- **Time-Bound:** The recipient must receive the information within the required time range.

  Information relevance refers to the idea that even though the information may have been timely and correct, it may not be relevant for another user. For instance, someone requesting the computer model's configuration would be told, "The model costs ₹ 40,000." Despite being accurate and timely, the information is useless.

Database and Database Systems

Computer usage is increasing, and database technology plays a significant role. It is reasonable to argue that databases are essential in every field that uses computers, including genetics, business, engineering, electronic commerce, medicine, law, and library science. A grouping of linked data is called a database. We refer to known facts with implicit meaning that can be captured as data. Think about the names, phone numbers, and addresses of the people you know, for instance.

A database is a systematically arranged set of linked organizational data prepared and shared by several users. A database should be securely kept, easily accessed, connected, and well-organized. Take into account, for instance, a student's name, address, and roll number that are kept in a student file. It is a grouping of connected information with a suggested meaning. The database may contain shared, integrated, and persistent data.

- **Persistent:** Data that remains stored in the database and can be retrieved and used even after the application or process that created it has ended and is not lost when the system is restarted.
- **Data Sharing:** Multiple users can concurrently access and use the database's stored data without affecting the accuracy of the information.

Need of Database

A new strategy was necessary to get around the drawbacks of a file system. Thus, a database strategy was developed. A database is an ongoing compilation of information with logical relationships. Initially, efforts were made to offer centralized data collection. A database is inherently self-explanatory. It includes more than just an organization's data integration and sharing into a single database. While a small database can be maintained manually, managing a large database with several users is challenging. A computerized database is helpful in that situation.

A database system has the following benefits over more conventional, paper-based record-keeping techniques:

- **Compactness**: Minimal requirement for several paper files.
- **Speed**: A machine can retrieve and modify data quicker than a human.
- **Less laborious tasks:** The effort needed to maintain files manually is less.
- **Accuracy**: Current and precise information is retrieved whenever the user requests it.
- A database can have any size or level of sophistication. For instance, the previously mentioned list of names and addresses might simply include a few hundred records, each with a straightforward format. Amazon.com is an illustration of a sizable business database. More than 20 million books, CDs, movies, DVDs, games, electronics, clothes, and other products are stored in its database.
- **Manual vs. computerized:** There are two ways to create and manage a database: manually and automatically. A basic database, such as a phone directory, could be made and updated by hand. A database management system or a collection of application programs designed especially for that purpose may construct and manage large and complicated databases. Data are the foundational resource of an organization in a computerized information system. Thus, for an organization to function well, data must be properly managed and organized. The understanding of database management systems pertains to the storage and management of data on computerized information systems. Any organization needs accurate and trustworthy data to make better decisions, protect data privacy, and manage data effectively. Examples include bank transactions, hotel, airline, or railway reservations, purchases, and inventory management.

Database Management System (DBMS)

A group of applications called a database management system (DBMS) gives users the ability to build and administer databases. To be more precise, a database management system (DBMS) is a type of general-purpose software by which we can easily create and manipulate the database as per the users' requirements.

A database management system (DBMS) consists of a collection of applications that access linked data and the data collection itself. Given that, it is an implicitly meaningful collection of related data; this is a database. The data collection, often known as the database, contains information relevant to an organization. A database management system's primary goals are to store and retrieve database data conveniently and efficiently (DBMS). We speak about facts that carry implicit meaning and can be recorded as data.

The management system is essential since database maintenance is impossible without rules and regulations. To establish a relationship between two tables, we must choose which common attributes to include in each table, which tables to handle when a new record needs to be added or removed, and other considerations. To fix these problems and preserve the database's integrity, there needs to be some sort of guidelines.

Large data sets are managed by database systems by design. Establishing frameworks for information storage and offering tools for information manipulation are both components of data management. Furthermore, in the event of a system failure or an attempt at unauthorized access, the database system must guarantee the security of the data kept. If multiple users are to share data, the system has to prevent unexpected outcomes.

Since most organizations rely heavily on information, computer scientists have created a vast corpus of ideas and methods for handling data.

Functions of DBMS

It must provide the ability to define the structure of the database and grant access rights to authorized users.

- The database management system (DBMS) provides features, such as adding records to the database, updating data, removing data, and retrieving data.
- A DBMS must support CRUD operations (Create, Read, Update, Delete) to enable comprehensive data management.
- To ensure data consistency, a Database Management System (DBMS) must manage concurrent access to shared data objects.
- Database Management System (DBMS) must have the capability to perform database recovery in case of system failure

Purpose of Database Systems

The database systems were developed in response to early approaches to computerized business data management. Take a look at a department inside a university that maintains data on all of its instructors, students, departments, and course offerings, as an illustration of such 1960s-style procedures. Operating system files are one place on a computer where data can be kept. The system includes several application programs that manipulate the files to give users the ability to alter the information. These programs include those that:

- Add new records may be students, faculty, and courses.
- Registration of students for courses and create class groups.
- Manage students' grades, analyze results, and print.

These application programs were created by system programmers to satisfy the demands of the university.

When the need arises, new application programs are added to the system. Let's say, for instance, that a university decides to offer a new major. The university establishes a new department and generates new permanent files (or adds information to existing files). It is necessary for the university to create new application procedures to handle regulations unique to the new major and new application programs to accommodate the university's new regulations. Consequently, the system accumulates more data and application programs with time.

A more traditional operating system provides support for this type of file-processing mechanism. The system keeps permanent records in several files, and to retrieve records from and add records to the relevant files, it requires a variety of application programs. Before the introduction of database management systems (DBMSs), organizations often used these systems to store information. Maintaining organizational data in a file-processing system comes with several significant drawbacks:

- **Redundant and inconsistent data**: The numerous files and application programs may have diverse formats and be written in many programming languages since different programmers generate them over an extended period. Furthermore, the same data could be repeated across multiple locations. For instance, a student pursuing a double major in music and mathematics may find their address and phone number in two different files: one containing the student records from the music department and the other from the mathematics department. Storage and access expenses are increased as a result of this redundancy. Furthermore, it could result in data inconsistency, that is, different versions of the same data might no longer agree. A modified student address, for instance, might show up in the Music department records but not anywhere else in the system.
- **Difficulty in accessing data**: Let's say, a university clerk needs to know the names of all the pupils that attend school in a specific postal code. The clerk requests that such a list be created by the data processing department. There isn't an application program available to fulfill this requirement because it was not anticipated by the system's original creators. Nonetheless, a program for applications exists to create a list of every student.

  The university clerk now has two options: hire a programmer to create the required application program or get the list of all students and manually extract the essential data.

  Assume that after writing such a program, the clerk must remove students who have taken fewer than 60 credit hours from the list within a few days. Naturally, there isn't a program available to create this kind of list. Once more, the clerk has the two possibilities that came before, neither is ideal. The key takeaway is that traditional file-processing environments make it difficult to extract necessary data quickly and effectively. For widespread use, more responsive data-retrieval technologies are needed.

- **Integrity issues**: Certain consistency criteria must be met by the data values kept in the database. Let's say, the university keeps track of the balance in each department's account and records it. Furthermore, assume that the university mandates that a department's account balance never drop below zero. Developers impose these restrictions on the system by including the necessary code in the different application programs. It is challenging to modify the programs to implement additional restrictions. When limitations contain many data items from separate files, the issue is exacerbated.
- **Atomicity issues**: Similar to any other item, computer systems can malfunction. For many applications, it is essential that in the event of a failure, the data be returned to its consistent state from before the failure.

  For example, one needs to transfer $500 from department A's account balance to department B's account balance. It is possible that the $500 was taken out of Department A's balance but not credited to Department B's balance in the event of a system failure during program execution, leading to an inconsistent database state. It is obvious that either the debit and credit occur simultaneously or they occur neither, to maintain database consistency.

  In other words, the money transfer needs to be atomic–either it happens completely or not at all. Atomicity in a traditional file-processing system is hard to guarantee.
- **Unusual concurrent access**: Many systems allow numerous users to change the data at once for improved system performance and faster response times. Millions of consumers may access the data of the biggest online merchants daily. It is conceivable for concurrent changes to interact in such an environment, which could lead to inconsistent data. Take department A, which has a $10,000 account balance. The concurrent executions may result in an inaccurate (or inconsistent) budget if two department clerks debit department A's account balance (by say, $500 and $100, respectively) at almost the same moment. Assume that the programs that process each withdrawal read the previous balance, subtract the withdrawal amount from that amount, and then write the outcome back. Should the two programs execute simultaneously, they may each read the value of $10,000 and return $9500 or $9900, in that order. The account balance of department A could include either $9500 or $9900 instead of the right amount of $9400, depending on who writes the figure last. The system has to have oversight in place to prevent this from happening. However, because data may be accessed by numerous application programs that have not been previously coordinated, oversight might be challenging to supply.

As an additional illustration, let's say that a registration program keeps track of the students enrolled in a course to enforce registration caps. Upon a student's registration, the program retrieves the current number of courses, confirms that it hasn't reached its maximum, adds one, and then saves the count back into the database. Assume that two students sign up simultaneously, making a total of nine.

Even though two students successfully enrolled for the course and the count should have been eleven, the two program executions may both read the value nine and then write back ten. This would result in an inaccurate rise of just one. Moreover, if there was a 10-student maximum for course registration, both students would be allowed to register, exceeding the cap.

- **Security issues**: All data should not be accessible to every user of the database system. Payroll staff at a university, for instance, only needs to view the portion of the database containing financial data. They don't require access to academic record information. These challenges led to the creation of database systems, among other things. The ideas and methods that allow database systems to resolve issues with file-processing systems will be covered in the sections that follow.

Database Management System Applications

A system used for maintaining and manipulating records is called a database management system. It serves as a collection point or container for digital data files. Allowing users to define, store, retrieve, and change database content on demand is the main goal of database management systems (DBMS). Anything important to a person or an organization might be considered information.

Every part of our lives is impacted by databases. The following are a few of the main application areas:

- Banking Systems
- Railway/ Airline Reservation System
- College/University System
- Production and Manufacturing
- HR and Marketing

Business Data:

- **Sales:** For details on customers, products, and purchases.
- **Accounting:** For assets, account balances, payments, receipts, and other accounting data.

- **Human resources:** For data on workers, pay, benefits, payroll taxes, and wages; also to create payroll.
- **Manufacturing:** For supply chain management, monitoring production in factories, inventory management in warehouses and retail locations, and tracking item orders.
- **Online retailers:** For the previously mentioned sales data in addition to online order tracking, suggestion list creation, and upkeep of online product reviews.

Finance and Banking:

- **Banking**: For accounts, loans, client data, and banking operations.
- **Credit card transactions**: For credit card purchases and monthly statement creation.
- **Finance**: For keeping records of financial instrument holdings.
- **Universities:** For keeping all the data related to students, faculty, courses, and other supporting data required for a university.
- **Airlines:** To track, book, and manage booking for an Airline system.
- **Telecommunication:** To keep track of call records, billing, and recharge information for the customers.

Example:

To keep track of student information, grades, and courses in a university setting, think of a **`UNIVERSITY`** database. Five files, each containing identical data records, make up the structure of the database.

1. **`STUDENT`**: It contains the student details.
2. **`COURSE`**: It contains the details of the courses offered.
3. **`SECTION`**: This has the data about sections of the students.
4. **`GRADE_REPORT`**: It contains the grades of the students.
5. **`PREREQUISITE`** file: Have the information of the courses required earlier.

Database Definition

Define the various fields for each of the databases.

For example:

- **`STUDENT`** table have **`student's_Name`**, **`Roll_ number`**, and **`Class_Major`**, **`DOB`**, **`Mobile_no`**
- **`COURSE`** table have **`Course_name`**, **`Course_number`**, **`Credit_hours`**, and **`Department`**

- **`Section`** includes **`section_name`**, **`faculty_name`**, **`Classroom`**, **`duration`**
- **`Grade_Report`** includes **`roll_no`**, **`Name`**, **`Marks`**, **`Grade`**
- **`Prerequisite`** includes the **`subject_name`**, **`Subject_ID`**

Each record has a suitable datatype. For example, student is a string of alphabetic characters and **`Student_number`** is an integer type.

Student_Name	Roll_Number	Class_Major	DOB	Mobile_no

***Table 1.1**: Student*

Course_Name	Course_Number	Credit_hours	Department

***Table 1.2:** Course*

Section_Name	Faculty_Name	Classroom	Duration

***Table 1.3**: Section*

Roll_No	Name	Marks	Grade

***Table 1.4**: Grade*

Subject_name	Subject_ID

Table 1.5: *Prerequisite*

University Database

Store information to represent every student, course, section, grade report, and prerequisite as a record in the relevant file to create the UNIVERSITY database.

Documents found in different files might be connected. Jatin's record in the STUDENT file, for instance, is connected to two records in the GRADE_REPORT file that list Jatin's grades in two different sections. In a similar vein, every entry in the PREREQUISITE file has a relationship with two course records: one for the course and one for the prerequisite.

Now we can enter the records, delete the records that are not required, and update the records with the data manipulation languages. Data definition and data manipulation languages will be discussed in the next section.

The requirements specification and analysis phase start with the design of a new database or a new application for an existing database, like the software in general. These specifications are thoroughly recorded and converted into a conceptual design that can be represented and altered with the aid of computer tools, making it simple to maintain, alter, and convert into a database implementation.

Once a logical design has been created, it can be defined in a data model that is used with a commercial database management system. Physical design is the last phase, in which more details regarding database access and storage are offered. The database design is put into practice, real data is added, and ongoing maintenance is done.

Database Approach versus File Processing Approach

Think of a company that is set up as a group of offices or departments. There are specific data processing 'needs' for every department, many of which are department-specific. Under the file processing method, every department would be in charge of a grouping of pertinent data files and software programs for working with that data. For instance, the grade reporting office is one user that might maintain student and grade-related files. The application incorporates programs to print a student's transcript and enter new grades. The accounting office, a second user, might monitor student data and payments. Users are interested in student data, but because each user needs certain data from the other users' files, users keep separate files and programs to alter these files. In addition to wasting storage space, this redundancy in defining and storing data also results in duplicate attempts to preserve common, up-to-date data.

In the database model, data is defined once and then accessed by multiple users from a single repository. File systems allow data items to be named independently by each program. On the other hand, in a database, queries, transactions, and applications utilize the names or labels of the data frequently after they are defined once.

The following are the primary differences between the file-processing and database approaches:

- The self-explanatory character of a database system
- Data abstraction and program-to-data insulation
- Support for various data views
- Data sharing and multiuser transaction handling
- **Self-describing Nature:**

  The database system includes a full definition or description of the database structure and restrictions in addition to the database itself. This is a crucial feature of the database approach. The system catalog which houses a description of each file's structure, each field's type and storage format, and the different constraints on the data (that is, requirements that the data must meet), is where this meta-data, that is, data about data is kept.

  Users are not the only ones who utilize the system catalog; the DBMS software also has to "know" how the data is organized and structured to interpret it in a way that makes sense.

- **Data Abstraction:**

  Program-Data Independence: In conventional file processing, an application's source code contains "hard-coded" information about the structure of the data files it can access. Any application where a hard-coded description of a file's structure exists has to be updated if, for whatever reason, the data structure changes.

  However, because the structure of the data is described independently from the programs that access it and such programs consult the catalog to determine whether the structure of the data is interpreted properly or not, DBMSs provide a level of abstraction that makes managing changes easier; significant changes to the data structure may still require some level of modification to the applications, though less as compared to file systems. It gives application programs a conceptual or logical representation of the data so that changes to the underlying implementation can be made without affecting the programs.

- **Multiple Views**

  There are typically several users in a database, and each user may require a different viewpoint or understanding of the database. A view may be a subset of the database or virtual data taken from the database files but isn't explicitly saved. A multiuser database management system (DBMS) whose users employ a variety of unique applications has to have multiple view definition features.

- **Multiuser Transaction Processing:**

  A multiuser database management system (DBMS), as the name implies, must enable multiple users to access the database at once. This is essential if data from multiple applications needs to be updated and merged into one database. Concurrency control software is a prerequisite for database management systems (DBMSs) to guarantee that many users updating the same data do so in a controlled manner and that the modifications produce the desired results. For instance, the DBMS should ensure that only one reservation agent at a time can access each seat to assign it to a passenger when multiple agents attempt to assign seats on an airline flight. Online transaction processing (OLTP) applications are the common term for these applications.

  Ensuring the proper and efficient operation of concurrent transactions is a core function of multiuser database management systems. Many database applications now revolve around the idea of a transaction. An executing program or process that involves one or more database accesses, including reading or modifying database records, is referred to as a transaction.

Advantages and Disadvantages of DBMS

Advantages:

- **Controlling Redundancy:** Unnecessary data duplication in a database system is prevented by having a centralized database and centralized DBA management over data.
- **Better Data Sharing**: A user can exchange data across multiple application programs, thanks to DBMS.
- **Data integrity:** It refers to the accuracy of the data stored in the database. Integrity requirements for data in the database can be defined by the administrator with the assistance of centralized data control. For example: we can enforce based on the choice like customers only from Mumbai and Bengaluru will be entertained.
- **Security:** The DBA may ensure that only authorized users have access to the

database by exercising total control over the operational data. The permission checks that are performed each time someone tries to access sensitive data can be specified by the DBA.

- **Data Consistency:** We significantly lower the chances of inconsistency by getting rid of redundant data. For instance, we cannot disagree on the stored values if a customer address is only ever stored once. When all values are kept in one location, updating data values is also much easier. Lastly, by avoiding redundant data storage, we can prevent storage waste.
- **Effective Data Processing:** In a database system, the DBMS is responsible for managing the data and granting all access to it. This makes the DBMS a crucial component of efficient data processing.
- **Enforcement of Standards:** DBAs can create and implement data standards, such as naming conventions and data quality standards, by using centralized data.
- **Data Independence:** The database management system in a database system acts as an interface between the data and the application programs. The metadata that the DBMS obtains is altered when modifications are made to the data representation, but the DBMS nevertheless delivers the data to application programs in the manner that was previously employed. When necessary, the DBMs take care of the data transformation task.
- **Cut Down on Application Creation and Maintenance Time**: Database management systems (DBMSs) help the rapid creation of applications by supporting a multitude of crucial functions shared by many applications, such as accessing data stored in the database.
- **Resolution of Conflicts:** DBAs settle disputes regarding the needs of different users and applications. To obtain optional performance for the application, the DBA selects the optimal file structure and access technique.

Disadvantages:

- It's a little complicated. The underlying software has grown complicated because it supports different features to provide the greatest experience for the user. To get the most out of the program, the engineers and designers should be well-versed in it.
- It requires a lot of RAM due to its usefulness and complexity. Large memory is also necessary for it to function well.
- The DBMS system is centralized, that is, users from all around the world can access it. Therefore, all users will be impacted by any DBMS failure.
- DBMS is generalized software, that is, it is built to operate on a system as a whole rather than a single one. As a result, parts of the application may run slowly.

Database Architecture

A database system is made up of several programs that facilitate user access to and modification of linked data sets. Giving people an abstract view of the data is one of a database system's main goals. In other words, specifics about the data's maintenance and storage are concealed by the system. The system needs to retrieve data quickly to be functional. Complex data structures are used by designers to represent data in databases due to the necessity for efficiency. Because many users of database systems lack computer skills, developers hide the complexity from users by using multiple levels of abstraction to make it easier for users to engage with the system:

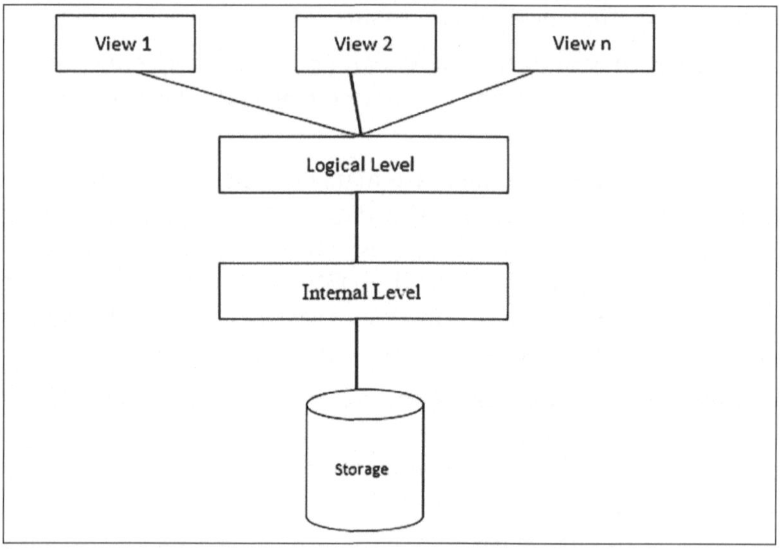

Figure 1.3: *Abstraction in a Database System*

- **Physical level, also known as Internal View / Schema:** This level of abstraction explains the real data storage. Complex low-level data structures are detailed at the physical level.

  The next level of abstraction, known as the logical level (sometimes called the conceptual view or schema), explains the types of data kept in the database and the relationships that exist between them. Thus, the logical level expresses the whole database in terms of a limited number of rather straightforward structures. The user of the logical level does not have to be aware of the intricacy involved in implementing the simple structures at the logical level, even though it may include sophisticated physical-level structures. We call this physical independence of data. Database administrators employ a logical level of abstraction when determining what data to retain in the database.

- **View level, Also known as External View / Schema**: The maximum level of abstraction only covers a portion of the database. Because of the variety of data held in a large database, complexity persists even when using simpler structures at the logical level. Many database system users just require access to a portion of the database; they do not require all the information. The purpose of the view level of abstraction is to make their interactions with the system simpler. The same database may have multiple views available via the system. To better understand the differences between the various degrees of abstraction, consider an analogy to the idea of data types in programming languages. For example, a record is defined by the following:

```
Student record
Roll_no  : varchar (15);
Student_name : char (20);
dept : char (20);
DOB : date;
end;
```

This code defines a new record type called student with four fields. Each field has a name and a type associated with it. A university organization may have several such record types, including department, have fields **dept_name**, **block**, and **chair** course, have fields **course_number**, **name**, **dept_name**, **credit** student, have **roll_no**, **Student_name**, **dept**, and **Grade** A teacher, department, or student record can be conceptualized as a block of successive storage spaces at the physical level. Programmers are not exposed to this degree of information via the compiler. In a similar vein, database programmers are not given access to many of the lowest-level storage specifics by the database system. Conversely, database managers could know specifics about how the data is physically arranged.

Like in the preceding code section, each of these records is logically specified by a type definition, which also defines the relationships between these record types. This level of abstraction is where programmers who use a programming language operate. Likewise, this level of abstraction is typically where database administrators operate. Lastly, computer users encounter a collection of application programs that conceal data type specifics at the view level. A database user can see some or all of the views that have been defined at the view level. The views offer a security feature that stops users from accessing specific areas of the database in addition to concealing logical-level facts. For instance, registrar office clerks at universities are only able to view the portion of the database containing student data; they are unable to view information regarding faculty wages.

Instances and Schemas

A database instance is the collection of data kept in the database at a specific time. The database schema refers to the overall layout of the database. Schemas are rarely, if ever, modified. One way to understand database schemas and instances is to compare them to programs written in programming languages. The variable declarations in a program, along with the corresponding type definitions, match the database schema. Every variable has a specific value at any given time. A program's variable values at any one time relate to a particular instance of a database schema. Several schemas are present in database systems, which are divided based on the abstraction layers.

The database design is explained at the physical level by the physical schema and at the logical level by the logical schema. Additionally, a database may have many view-level schemas, often known as subschemas; each describes a distinct database view. Since programmers use the logical schema to develop applications, the logical schema has the greatest impact on application programs of all of them. Underneath the logical schema lies the physical schema, which is typically easily modifiable without disrupting application programs. When application programs are not dependent on the physical schema and do not require rewriting if the physical schema changes, they are said to demonstrate physical data independence.

Data Independence

Three levels of data abstractions are discussed in the previous section:

- **Internal level:** The internal level is essentially the physical database storage and includes a lower level of data abstraction. It describes how the database stores data and how data structures are used by the database.
- **Logical level:** Describes the kinds of entries stored in the database and their relationships; the conceptual level is the higher degree of data abstraction than the Internal degree. The logical structure of the entire database is contained in this level.
- **External or View level:** This level facilitates viewing the user's desired material within the database, rather than the full database. A database has one conceptual level and one physical level, but it might have multiple external levels depending on what the users require.

The ability to modify the database schema at one level of the database system without affecting the schema at a higher level is known as data independence in database management systems. Additionally, this feature helps to separate data from other apps. A database stores data in addition to the data it contains. Metadata is the term for this type of data or data about data. Additionally, after metadata is saved in a database, it would be very challenging to modify. However, when the database grows, the metadata must be adjusted to satisfy the user's needs. Modifying the metadata would be challenging if all the data depended on one another. Furthermore, because the metadata adheres to the tiered design, changes made to one layer of data do not impact the preceding or the following layers. We can better understand the idea of data independence by using the three schema/level architectures covered in the preceding section. Two ideas are used to define data independence:

- **Logical Data Independence:** Logical data independence is the ability to modify the conceptual schema of a database, which defines the logical structure and relationships of data, without requiring changes to the external schemas or views used by the applications. It means that operations, such as adding or removing tables, modifying constraints, or altering relationships can be performed without impacting the functionality of existing applications. While changes to view definitions and mappings may be necessary to maintain consistency, the related application programs should ideally remain unaffected or require minimal adjustments.
- **Physical Data Independence:** It alludes to the ability to alter the physical schema without affecting the logical data or conceptual schema. Thus, there is no change in the external schema either. When files are rearranged on storage devices or new access paths are provided to implement faster access strategies, the underlying structure may be altered. Physical data independence is most prevalent because file settings conceal information about the precise placement of data on storage devices as well as the use of encoding, compression, and splitting techniques to separate and combine records. These details are usually hidden from users and applications are unaware of these details.

  Logical data independence, though often more challenging than physical data independence, is a key goal in database design. It allows modifications to the conceptual schema with minimal impact on applications. While some adjustments may be needed, mappings between schemas help minimize disruption. Modern DBMSs employ techniques like views to enhance logical data independence, offering flexibility and maintainability despite potential minor inefficiencies.

Importance of Database Independence:

- It contributes to raising the caliber of the info that the user is shown.
- The database system's maintenance expenses drop.
- Enhanced database security strengthens data security.
- Simple physical adjustments can be performed to enhance the system's performance.
- It contributes to the improvement of the state of any damaged system components.

Data Models

The data model, a set of conceptual tools for characterizing data, data relationships, data semantics, and consistency requirements, forms the foundation of a database's structure. A data model offers a means of characterizing a database's logical, physical, and view designs. Four categories can be used to group the data models:

- **Relational Model:** In the relational model, a collection of tables represents data and the relationships among them. Each table has many columns with unique names for each column. Tables are also known as relations. The relational model is one kind of record-based model. Record-based models receive their name because the database is arranged into fixed-format records of different types. Each table contains records of a particular type. For every type of record, a fixed number of fields or characteristics are established. The columns of the table reflect the attributes of the record type. The relational data model is the most widely used data model and the foundation of most contemporary database systems.

Student_Name	Roll_Number	Class_Major	DOB	Mobile_no
Amit	12	CSE	12 Apr 2001	898999
Sumit	13	ECE	11 Aug 2001	789876
Jatin	14	CSE	11 Aug 2000	788877
Shrey	15	CSE	21 Oct 2002	678768

Table 1.6: *Student details*

Here in the above relation, four records for the student relation and each record shares the same attributes. Each row represents the record and each column represents the attribute for the records.

- **Entity-Relationship Model:** The entity-relationship (E-R) data model makes use of relationships between a set of fundamental items known as entities. In the actual world, an entity is a "thing" or "object" that can be distinguished from other objects. In database architecture, the entity-relationship model is frequently applied. The entity-relationship model is also known as ER model where each entity set contains several entities. An entity will be any real-world object, such as a table, a chair, a student, a faculty, a laptop, and so on. Similar kinds of entities form an entity set and different entity sets have the relationship and entities of the entity sets are participating in the relationship.

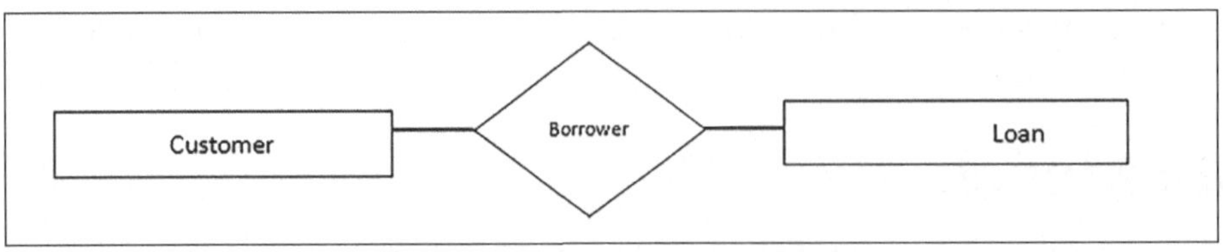

Figure 1.4: E-R *Model for Loan*

In the preceding E-R diagram, two entity sets, that is, customers and loans are participating in the borrower relationship which means the customers are the borrowers for the specific loans.

- **Data Model Based on Objects**: Object-oriented programming has taken over as the most popular approach for developing software, particularly in Java, C++, and C#. As a result, an object-oriented data model was created, which is comparable to an extension of the E-R model that includes concepts of object identity, methods (or functions), and encapsulation. The relational and object-oriented data models' characteristics are combined in the object-relational data model.
- **Network Model:** Even though this model may have multiple parent segments, there is a logical relationship between the segments that belong to any level. These sections are divided into tiers. Any two segments often have a many-to-many logical link. Graphs are the logical connections that exist between the segments. As a result, this model replaces the hierarchical tree with a graph-like structure, enabling nodes that are more widely related. It may possess M: N, or many-to-many, relations.

Here, a relationship is referred to as a set, and each set consists of the two types of records listed below, at least one of which is present:

- o An owner record in the hierarchical model that is identical to that of the parent
- o A member record in the hierarchical model that is identical to that of a kid

- **Semi-structured Data Model**: Data, where distinct data items of the same kind may have varying sets of attributes, can be specified using the semi-structured data model. This is not the case with the previously discussed data models, where each data item of a specific kind needs to contain the same set of properties. Semi-structured data can be represented broadly using the Extensible Markup Language (XML). The relational data model was historically preceded by the network and hierarchical data models. These models made data modeling more difficult and were intimately linked to the underlying implementation. As a result, they are hardly utilized anymore, except for outdated database code that is occasionally still in use.

Database Languages

Once we finish the schema, we start implementing the database with the help of database languages.

Data Definition Language (DDL)

When there is no rigorous level separation maintained, the DBA and database designers define both schemas using the data definition language (DDL). A DDL compiler built into the database management system (DBMS) will process DDL statements to find schema construct descriptions and put them in the catalog.

Declarative DMLs, also known as nonprocedural DMLs, ask the user to identify the data that are required without outlining the method for obtaining those data.

A unique language known as a data-definition language (DDL) is used to express a set of definitions that specify a database schema. Additional data characteristics can also be specified using the DDL.

DSDL and DDL are not typically considered subcategories of each other. These statements specify the database schemas' implementation specifics, which are often not visible to users. There are consistency restrictions that must be met by the data values contained in the database. Let's say, the university mandates that a department's account balance never be negative. The DDL offers tools for defining these restrictions. Declarative DMLs, also known as nonprocedural DMLs, ask the user to identify the data that are required without outlining the method for obtaining those data.

Every time the database is updated, the database system verifies these limitations. Generally speaking, a constraint can be any random condition related to the database. Arguably, testing arbitrary predicates could be expensive. Therefore, integrity restrictions that can be tested with little overhead are implemented by database systems.

- **Restrictions by Domain**: For each sort of attribute (integer, character, date/time, and so on.), there must be a domain of possible values. An attribute's possible values are limited when it is declared to belong to a certain domain. The most basic type of integrity constraint is a domain constraint. Every time a new piece of data is added to the database, the system tests them with ease.

  Declarative DMLs, also known as nonprocedural DMLs, ask the user to identify the data that are required without outlining the method for obtaining those data.

- **Integrity of Reference**: Referential integrity is the need to guarantee that a value that occurs in one relation for a certain set of characteristics likewise appears in a particular set of attributes in another relation. For example, each course must have a department name that is an actual department. To be more exact, the department name value from a course record needs to show up in the department name attribute of some department-related record. Referential integrity problems may result from database updates. Rejecting the activity that violated a referential-integrity requirement is standard procedure when one occurs.

  An assertion is any requirement that the database must consistently meet. Two types of specific assertions are domain constraints and referential-integrity constraints. Still, there are a lot of limitations that these particular forms are unable to convey. An example of a claim would be, "Every department needs to offer at least five courses each semester." The system verifies an assertion as soon as it is produced. If the statement is true, any further database changes will only be permitted, provided they do not result in the allegation being refuted.

- **Permission**: When it comes to the numerous types of access that users are allowed on distinct database data values, we might want to distinguish between them. The most common way to express these differentiations is through authorization: read authorization permits reading of data but not modification; insert authorization permits adding of new data but not modification of preexisting data; update authorization permits modification of data but not deletion of data; and delete authorization permits data deletion. The user may be given all, none, or a mix of these kinds of authorization.

  Similar to other programming languages, the DDL takes statements as input and outputs certain statements. The DDL output is stored in the data dictionary, which holds metadata or information about information. It is believed that the data dictionary is a unique kind of table that can only be changed and accessed by the database system itself, not by ordinary users. Before accessing or altering real data, the database system looks for information in the data dictionary.

Storage Definition Language (SDL)

The DDL is only used to define the conceptual schema; storage definition language is utilized when there is a clear division between the conceptual and internal levels. The internal schema is specified using SDL or storage definition language. One of these languages may be used to specify the mappings between the two schemas.

View Definition Language (VDL)

The mappings between user views and the conceptual schema are specified using the view definition language. SQL is used in relational database management systems (DBMSs) as a VDL to define user or application views that are the output of predefined queries.

Data Manipulation (DML)

Data manipulation tasks such as data retrieval, insertion, deletion, and modification are carried out using data manipulation languages (DML).

There are two main types of DMLs:

- **Nonprocedural DML** can be used alone to succinctly describe intricate database operations. High-level DML statements can be integrated into a general-purpose programming language or typed interactively from a display monitor or terminal by many DBMSs. In the latter scenario, DML statements need to be located within the program for a precompiler to extract them and the DBMS to handle them. High-level DMLs are referred to as set-at-a-time or set-oriented DMLs since they, like SQL, can specify and retrieve several records in a single DML expression. In high-level DMLs, a query typically indicates which data to retrieve instead of how to retrieve it; for this reason, these languages are also known as declarative.

- **Procedural DML** has to be integrated into a programming language with a broad purpose. Typically, this kind of DML pulls specific records or objects out of the database and handles them one at a time using linguistic constructions like looping to get and handle every record in a collection of records. Because of this characteristic, low-level DMLs are sometimes known as record-at-a-time DMLs. Low-level DML DL/1, created for the hierarchical model, is used to browse between records in a database hierarchy using commands. The general-purpose programming language that has embedded DML commands, whether high-level or low-level, is referred to as the host language, and the DML is referred to as the data sublanguage.

A query language is a high-level DML used in standalone interactive applications.
A language that lets users access or work with data that is arranged according to the right data model is known as a data manipulation language (DML).

The many forms of access include:

- Accessing data that is kept in the database
- Updating the database with fresh data
- Information is removed from the database
- Alterations made to data kept in the database
- The user must indicate which data are required and how to obtain them when using procedural DMLs. Declarative DMLs, also known as nonprocedural DMLs, ask the user to identify the data required without outlining the method for obtaining those data. Generally speaking, declarative DMLs are simpler to understand and utilize than procedural DMLs. However, the database system needs to come up with an effective way to access data because the user does not need to indicate how to retrieve the data.
- A statement asking for information to be retrieved is called a query. A query language is the part of a DML that deals with information retrieval. It is customary to refer to a query language as a data manipulation language, even if this is strictly inaccurate.

Data Dictionary

A data dictionary is a part of a database system that contains definitions of the properties and connections of data. Such "data about data," as you may remember, were known as metadata. The self-descriptive feature of the DBMS is provided by the DBMS data dictionary. The data dictionary is an essential component of the data administration function and is akin to an X-ray of the complete company's data collection.

There are two primary categories of data dictionaries: stand-alone and integrated. A built-in data dictionary is part of the database management system. An integrated data dictionary or system catalog, for instance, is present in all relational database management systems and is regularly consulted and updated by the RDBMS. The DBA may employ third-party stand-alone data dictionary systems in place of other DBMSs, particularly older models, which lack an integrated data dictionary.

Active and passive data dictionaries are further classifications for them. Every time a database is accessed, the DBMS immediately updates an active data dictionary, maintaining the most recent version of its access metadata. A batch operation is typically needed to update a passive data dictionary since it is not updated automatically. The DBMS typically uses data dictionary access information for query optimization.

The primary purpose of the data dictionary is to hold the descriptions of every object that communicates with the database. Integrated data dictionaries typically only store metadata for data that is under DBMS management. Whether or not the organization's data is computerized, the DBA can describe and manage it all with the help of stand-alone data dictionary systems, which are typically more versatile. Regardless of the structure of the data dictionary, having it makes communication between database designers and end users considerably easier. The data dictionary is another tool that the DBA uses to assist in resolving data conflicts.

While the information contained in the data dictionary does not have a uniform format, there are a few features that are shared. As an illustration, the data dictionary normally contains descriptions of every:

- Bits of data are specified in every table throughout every database. Names, datatypes, display formats, internal storage formats, and validation criteria are all kept in the data dictionary. Where, by whom, and other details about an element's usage are provided by the data dictionary.
- Every database has defined tables. The name of the table creator, the creation date, the number of columns, access authorizations, and so on, are likely to be included in the data dictionary.
- Indexes are defined for every table in the database. The DBMS keeps track of each index's name, attributes used, location, unique properties, and creation date, at the very least.

- Identify databases by stating who generated them, when they were produced, and where they are kept.
- DML queries to access and modify the database.
- Permissions to the users as per their role.
- Relationships among the various relations and their types with all other constraints.

Database Architecture

The underlying computer system that a database system operates on has a significant impact on the architecture of the database system. Database systems can be client-server or centralized, that is, a single server computer handles tasks for several client computers. Additionally, database systems can be made to utilize parallel computer architectures. Distributed databases are spread across several geographically dispersed computers.

Modules within a database system handle every aspect of the system's overall responsibility. A database system's functional parts can be separated generally into two categories: query processor and store manager components. The storage manager is crucial because databases often need a lot of storage space. The query processor is crucial because it makes the database system simpler and easier to use.

The database system's job is to convert queries and updates written at the logical level in a nonprocedural language into an effective physical sequence of actions.

Typically, database applications are divided into two or three sections, as shown in *Figure 1.5*. In a two-tier architecture, the program runs on the client computer and uses query language statements to access database system functionality on the server computer. To facilitate communication between the client and the server, application program interface standards like ODBC and JDBC are utilized. On the other hand, the client computer in a three-tier design just serves as a front end and doesn't make any direct database requests. Rather, an application server and the client end communicate, typically via an interface.

To access data, the application server converses with a database system. Rather than being spread over several clients, the application's business logic, which determines what actions to do under what circumstances, is contained in the application server. Larger programs and those that operate on the World Wide Web are better suited for three-tier applications.

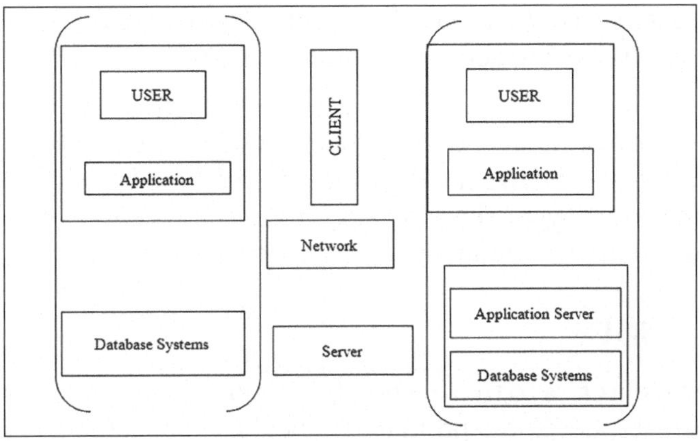

Figure 1.5: *Two-tier and three-tier architectures*

- **Query Processor:** The DDL interpreter, which decodes DDL commands and stores the definitions in the data dictionary, is one of the query processor's components.

  The DML compiler is responsible for converting DML statements in a query language into an evaluation plan that is comprehensible to the query evaluation engine using low-level instructions.

  Generally, a query can be converted into any of several different evaluation schemes, all of which produce the same outcome. In addition, the DML compiler optimizes queries, that is, it selects the option with the lowest cost evaluation plan among the available options.

  The query evaluation engine is responsible for carrying out the DML compiler's low-level instructions.

- **Storage Manager**: A storage manager is a program module that acts as an interface between the application programs and queries that are submitted to the system and the low-level data kept in the database. The communication between the storage manager and the file manager is under its purview. The file system, which is often offered by a traditional operating system, is used to store the raw data on the disc. The different DML statements are converted into low-level file-system commands by the storage manager. For this reason, the database's data must be updated, retrieved, and stored by the storage manager.
  - Among the components of the storage manager are the authorization and integrity manager, which verifies user access permissions and assesses if integrity restrictions are met.
  - The transaction manager guarantees that concurrent transaction executions occur without conflict and that the database stays in a consistent (correct) state even in the event of a system failure.

- File manager controls how disc storage space is allotted and data structures that are utilized to represent information on the disc.
- The buffer manager is in charge of selecting which data to cache in the main memory and retrieving data from disc storage into the main memory. As it allows the database to accommodate data amounts that are significantly bigger than the size of the main memory, the buffer manager is an essential component of the database system.

Database Users

"Actors on the scene" refers to those who utilize and manage database content as well as people who create, develop, and manage database applications. "Workers behind the scenes" refers to those who create DBMS software, associated tools, and computer systems operators.

- **Database Administrator (DBA):** Chief administrator, in charge of supervising and administering the database system (software and data included). Among the responsibilities include granting users access to the database, arranging and supervising its usage, purchasing hardware and software for updates, and so forth. Issues like inadequate system response times and security breaches are the DBA's responsibility. A support staff may be available to the DBA in large organizations.
- **Database Designers:** Accountable for determining whether data needs to be stored and for selecting the best method of organization. Database designers usually work with every possible user group to create database views that satisfy their needs for processing and data. All user groups' needs must be able to be supported by the final database design.
- **End Users:** These are the people who can query, update, and generate reports from the database. There are various end-user categories:
    - **Casual Users** use databases infrequently, requiring distinct information each time; they usually work with middle-or high-level managers; they express their requirements using a query language.
    - **Naive Users** are the largest user base; regularly update the database with standard prepared transactions that have been well-verified and developed beforehand.
        - **Examples**: Clerks or officers at the bank check the account balance and other account-related activities. Reservation of airline/railway tickets.
    - **Sophisticated Users** include business analysts, engineers, scientists, and others who become intimately acquainted with the DBMS's features, so they may create custom apps that satisfy their intricate needs.

- **Stand-alone Users** employ pre-made program packages with user-friendly menu-based or graphics-based interfaces to manage personal datasets.
  - **Example:** Personal details for the tax purposes
- System Analysts and Application Programmers :
  - **System Analysts** identify end-user demands, particularly those of naive and parametric users, and create specifications for prefabricated transactions that address these needs.
  - **Application Programmers** develop, test, record, and maintain programs that meet the requirements mentioned earlier.

  Application programmers are categorized by the following:

  - **System Designers**: As a software package, develop and implement the DBMS modules and interfaces. A database management system (DBMS) is an extremely intricate software system made up of numerous parts or modules, such as those for handling data recovery and security, query language processing, interface processing, data access and buffering, concurrency control, and catalog implementation.
  - **System Developers:** Create and put into use the tools that help with database system architecture, database modeling, and enhanced performance.
  - **System Maintenance:** Operating and maintaining the database system's hardware and software environment.

DBMS Interfaces

DBMS provides the interfaces as follows:

- **Menu-Driven Interfaces**: These user interfaces guide the user through the process of formulating a request by presenting lists of possibilities, sometimes known as menus. The user does not have to commit query language syntax and individual commands to memory. One of the most often used techniques in web-based user interfaces is pull-down menus.
- **Forms-Based Interfaces:** Every user is presented with a form via a forms-based interface. To insert new data, users can either fill out every field on the form or only some of them, in which case the DBMS will pull up matching data for the remaining fields. Typically, forms are created and coded as interfaces to pre-made transactions for unsuspecting consumers.
- **Graphical User Interfaces:** A diagrammatic representation of a schema is usually shown to the user via a GUI. Then, by adjusting the diagram, the user can define a query. GUIs frequently make use of both forms and menus. A

pointing device, like a mouse, is typically used by GUIs to select certain areas of the displayed schema diagram.

- **Natural Language Interfaces:** These interfaces try to interpret requests written in several languages, including English. A dictionary of key terms and its schema, akin to the conceptual schema of a database, are typical features of a natural language interface. To interpret the request, the natural language interface utilizes both the vocabulary in its dictionary and the words in its schema. If the interpretation is successful, the interface creates a high-level query in response to the natural language request and sends it to the database management system (DBMS) for processing; if not, the user is contacted to clarify the request.
- **Speech-Based Interfaces:** Speech input and output are being used in applications with a small vocabulary, like phone directory inquiries, airplane arrival/departure questions, and credit card account inquiries, to help users obtain this information. The parameters that are submitted to the queries are set up by employing a library of prepared terms to recognize speech input. A similar conversion from text or numbers into speech occurs for output.
- **Parametric User Interfaces**: Bank tellers are examples of parametric users who frequently have a limited range of tasks to complete regularly. For instance, a teller can perform repetitive and normal tasks like checking balances or making deposits into accounts with a single function key. Typically, a limited collection of shortened commands is provided to reduce the keystrokes needed for every request.
- **DBA Interfaces:** The majority of database systems have privileged commands that are exclusive to DBA personnel. These comprise commands that create accounts, modify a schema, grant account authorization, alter system parameters, and rearrange a database's storage structures.

Conclusion

This chapter has broadly covered the basic concepts and principles that underlie modern data management. We began by discussing the definition and importance of databases in efficiently organizing and retrieving structured information. Then we went on into the relational model which explains how data is organized in tables with relationships that maintain data integrity while allowing complex queries to be performed.

Furthermore, database design principles were also introduced in this chapter, highlighting normalization as a key concept for avoiding redundancy and maintaining consistency in data. Types such as DBMSs will be discussed, such as relational, NoSQL, and NewSQL systems, each designed for specific applications or scalability demands.

In conclusion, these foundational ideas are vital for any person engaging in data-driven decision-making or software development. This knowledge obtained would serve as a stepping stone towards advanced areas of study on database systems which will enable us to design manage and utilize them effectively in different real-life applications. In the next chapter, we will discuss the entity-relationship model and the cardinalities among the relationships.

Questions

1. Differentiate between a File-Processing System and a DBMS.
2. Differentiate between physical and logical data independence with the help of an example.
3. Define and discuss the roles and responsibilities of database systems. How these responsibilities are achieved, explain.
4. List and explain the roles and responsibilities of a database administrator.
5. List six major steps you would take in setting up a database for a particular enterprise.
6. Discuss the data abstraction layers of DBMS.
7. What are the disadvantages of file processing systems?
8. State the advantages and disadvantages of the database management system.
9. What are the different types of database users?
10. What is a data dictionary and what are its contents?
11. What are the key responsibilities of a DBA?
12. What are the different database languages? Explain with an example.
13. Explain the three-layer architecture of DBMS.
14. Differentiate between physical data independence and logical data independence.
15. Explain the key responsibilities of a Database manager.
16. Explain metadata.

CHAPTER 2
Data Modeling and Design

Introduction

Data modeling serves as the fundamental framework upon which databases are built, giving the massive volumes of data managed within a database management system (DBMS) structure, order, and clarity. The fundamental ideas of data modeling are examined in this section, along with its definition, significance in database design, and intricate relationship with database management systems.

Structure

In this chapter, the following topics will be covered:

- Overview of Data Modeling
- Data Modeling Tools and Methodologies
- Database Schema Design
- Entity-Relationship (ER) Modeling
- Normalization and Denormalization

Overview of Data Modeling

What does "data modeling" mean? To have a thorough understanding of the data and its connections, data modeling is the process of developing abstract representations of real-world data objects, properties, and relationships. To accomplish this, physical, logical, and conceptual models that depict constraints, characteristics, and hierarchical structure of data must be built. Data modeling aims to promote stakeholder communication around data requirements.

Data modeling;

- Uses normalization techniques to guarantee consistency and integrity of the data
- Oversees the architecture and design of databases to ensure efficient data retrieval and storage
- Allows databases to expand and adapt to changing business requirements

Data Modeling's Significance

Effective database design, implementation, and maintenance depend on data modeling. Several significant considerations emphasize its relevance:

- **Database Accuracy:** Data modeling guarantees that the database faithfully captures the essence of the business processes it supports by correctly describing the entities, properties, and connections inside an organization's data domain. One needs to be accurate to base decisions on trustworthy information.
- **Database Effectiveness**: Robust data models enhance database efficiency and responsiveness by streamlining the data retrieval, manipulation, and storage processes. Data modeling helps to improve database performance by streamlining data access patterns through indexing algorithms and normalization techniques.
- **Database Maintainability:** A database's capacity to expand and sustain itself becomes more crucial as it changes over time to meet shifting business needs and technology breakthroughs. When incorporating new requirements, data modeling offers an organized foundation that makes it easier to comprehend and modify the database design while causing the least amount of disturbance to currently operational systems.
- **Relationship with DBMS**: Data modeling and database management systems (DBMS) are closely related as each complements and balances the strengths of the other. The following characteristics can be used to describe the relationship between DBMS and data modeling:
    - **Schema**: The schema is a formal description of the structure and organization of a database. It serves as a blueprint for the Database Management System (DBMS); it specifies the database objects (tables, views, indexes), their attributes (columns), data types, and the relationships between them. The schema is derived from the data modeling process, which defines the conceptual design of the database based on the application requirement. It is crucial for the proper functioning of the DBMS, as it provides the necessary information for creating, maintaining, and accessing data within the database.

- **Data Integrity:** To guarantee the correctness, consistency, and reliability of the data kept in the database, data modeling applies integrity requirements and validation standards. The DBMS imposes these limitations to preserve the data's quality and integrity over time.
- **Query Optimization:** The processes of creating indexes, views, and other database structures that enable effective data access and retrieval are influenced by data modeling. These DBMS enhancements increase query performance and reduce response times, which boosts system efficiency overall.

  Database management systems (DBMS) and data modeling are complementary partners in database design and management, collaborating to deliver durable, effective, and readily maintained data systems that satisfy the demands of contemporary businesses.

Data Model Types

- **Conceptual Data Model**: Designates high-level relationships and entities irrespective of implementation details.
- **Logical Data Model**: Converts conceptual models into a complete framework that comprises relationships, entities, and characteristics.
- **Physical Data Model**: Defines the tables, columns, indexes, and storage configurations utilized to store data in a database.

Conceptual Data Modeling

The first step in the data modeling process is conceptual data modeling, which focuses on the high-level business-level representation of the organization's data domain. This section discusses entity-relationship diagrams (ERDs) as the main modeling tool, how to locate entities, attributes, and relationships, and the importance of cardinality and participation constraints. It also defines and explains the purposes of conceptual data modeling.

Objectives and Goals: The basic objective of conceptual data modeling is to get stakeholders, such as domain experts, database designers, and business analysts, on board with the business domain and its associated data requirements. Among the objectives of conceptual data modeling are the following:

- **Explicating Data Requirements:** Conceptual data modeling aids in the clarification of the data requirements required to support business operations and decision-making by eliciting and documenting the crucial entities, properties, and relationships inside the organization's data domain.
- **Improving Communication:** A visual aid to improve stakeholder

communication is conceptual data models. They facilitate mutual comprehension of one other's perspectives on data semantics, structural linkages, and the business domain.

- **Providing a Foundation for Logical Design:** Logical data models, developed from conceptual data models, refine business requirements into a structured representation suitable for database design. They serve as a crucial foundation for creating physical data models, which detail the technical implementation of the database schema.

Converting Conceptual Data Modeling to Logical Data Modeling

The transition from conceptual to logical data modeling is one of the most crucial phases in translating business requirements into a structured database architecture. It consists of:

- **Gaining Knowledge of the Conceptual Model:** Clearly states that the objective of the conceptual model is to capture high-level business relationships, entities, and attributes.
- **Entity Refinement and Identification:** Determine the key entities and their relationships using the conceptual model as a guide. Then, make the required corrections to guarantee accuracy and completeness.
- **Describe Characteristics:** For each entity, list the associations between properties, data types, and limitations, for example, consider a customer relationship management system, to reveal how entities, such as customers, orders, and products, are transformed into a logical data model.

Transforming Logical Data Models into Physical Data Models

Logical structures must be translated into actual database items to go from logical to physical data models. Crucial actions consist of:

- **Entity-to-Table Mapping**: Provides constraints, data types, and table properties when mapping entities from the logical model to tables in the physical model.
- **Relationship Implementation**: Ensures data consistency using foreign key constraints and integrity requirements while implementing relationships.
- **Data Normalization**: Reduces redundancy and maximizes data storage by using normalization techniques.

Physical Storage and Access Considerations

Database performance and scalability are contingent upon efficient physical storage and access, which encompasses the subsequent elements:

- **Storage Allocation**: Discusses how different storage allocation strategies, like tablespaces and filegroups, affect data management and organization.
- **Data Partitioning**: Uses data partitioning techniques to divide large datasets into manageable portions to speed up and improve maintenance.
- **Access Control**: Takes care of access control mechanisms (roles, permissions, and so on) to ensure data security and compliance with privacy laws.

Data Modeling Tools and Methodologies

Various data modeling tools and methodologies are used in the database systems:

Data Modeling Tools

The following are different tools used for data modeling:

- **ERwin Data Modeler**: This tool connects with multiple database management systems, allows forward and reverse engineering that enables a graphical interface, and updates data models.
- **Oracle SQL Developer Data Modeler**: Supporting both Oracle and other databases, it offers a graphical user interface for creating, describing, and implementing database structures.
- **Microsoft Visio**: This program provides templates for data modeling that may be used to create conceptual, logical, and physical data models. It is best suited for smaller tasks.
- **Lucid Chart**: A cloud-based platform for collaborative data modeling that includes features for version control, team collaboration, and tool integration.

Data Modeling Techniques

The following are the data modeling techniques used in database systems:

- **Entity-Relationship (ER) Modeling**: Represents entities as tables, attributes as columns, and connections as links between entities using cardinality rules (for example, one-to-one and one-to-many).
- **Normalization**: Data is organized into many tables to reduce redundancy and dependency using normalization forms (for example, 1NF, 2NF, and 3NF) to preserve data integrity.

- **Dimensional Modeling**: This approach focuses on using star or snowflake schemas for fact tables, dimension tables, and analytical queries for building data warehouses.
- **Agile Data Modeling**: By focusing on collaborative and iterative modeling processes, this methodology connects data modeling activities with agile software development methodologies.
- **Data Vault Modeling**: Structures data for data warehousing and business intelligence while facilitating data lineage and historical tracking using hubs, connections, and satellites.

Best Practices for Data Modeling:

- Before beginning the modeling process, ascertain the demands of stakeholders and business requirements.
- Ensure that all aspects of data models–entities, properties, relationships, and constraints–are clearly documented.
- Examine and update data models regularly to account for modifications to business procedures or data needs.
- Work together to guarantee alignment between database implementation and application development with stakeholders, database administrators, and developers.

Challenges in Data Modeling:

- Finding a balance between denormalization for speed optimization and normalization for data integrity are two challenges in data modeling. Managing intricate connections and structures throughout extensive databases.
- Ensuring consistency and quality of data across various integration points and data sources.

Future Trends in Data Modeling:

- Automation of data modeling and predictive analytics through using AI and ML.
- Development of tools for data modeling to support distributed and cloud-based databases.
- Using graph databases and NoSQL data modeling to manage linked and unstructured data.

Real-World Case Studies Explaining Data Modeling Ideas:

- **Online retail store:**
  - **Concept**: Creating a data model with entities, such as orders, suppliers, products, and customers for an online retail store.

   - **Data Modeling Concepts**: Highlight normalization strategies and referential integrity restrictions while demonstrating how entities, properties, and relationships are represented in the logical model.
- **Hospital Management System:**
   - **Concept**: Developing a data model incorporating entities, such as Medical Records, Patients, Doctors, and Appointments for a hospital management system.
   - **Concepts of Data Modeling**: Show how to handle complicated data structures and hierarchical linkages, and show the shift from conceptual to logical data modeling.
   - **Implementation**: Demonstrate how the data model enables features, such as billing, patient record management, and appointment scheduling.

Case Studies Highlighting Effective Data Modeling Initiative

Find the following case studies used for data modeling:

- **E-commerce Platform Optimization**: Improving an established e-commerce platform's scalability and performance is the current task at hand.
   - **Method**: Apply denormalization techniques, optimize indexing, partition data, and enhance access and management.
   - **Results**: Show enhanced performance, reduced query processing times, and higher user satisfaction.
- **Financial Analytics System:**
   - **Task**: Building a data model for a financial analytics system that can manage enormous volumes of transactional data.
   - **Method**: Using big data modeling techniques, ensuring data accuracy and consistency, and applying machine learning algorithms for predictive analytics.
   - **Outcomes**: Highlight the information gained, the decisions made based on solid evidence, and the return on investment via data-driven tactics.

Managing Changes and Updates to the Data Model

- **Change Management Process**: To supervise updates, revisions, and modifications to the data model that establish a systematic change management procedure.
   - Clearly identifies the persons responsible for submitting, reviewing, approving, and executing modification requests.

- **Version Control and Documentation**: Track data model versions, modifications, and history by implementing version control mechanisms.
    - o Keep thorough records of all documentation, such as change logs, data dictionaries, entity-relationship diagrams, and schema definitions.
- **Impact Analysis:** Examine the potential effects of suggested alterations to the data model on the current implementations of database architectures, software, and business procedures.
    - o Before implementing any changes, consider the risks, dependencies, and mitigation techniques.

Database Schema Design

Interpretation and Goals of a Database Schema: A database schema is a layout that describes the tables, columns, data types, constraints, and relationships of a database. It provides a logical viewpoint on how data should be organized and stored in database management systems (DBMS).

Database Schema Elements

- **Tables**: Collection of similar types of data entities, such as Employee, Account, and Customers.
- **Columns**: States the characteristics of the entities, such as Employee ID, Name, and Joining date.
- **Keys**: Ensures that each table's data is distinct. Some instances are as follows:
- **Primary Key**: This is an attribute in a table that uniquely identifies every record in a database.
- **Foreign Key**: Through the primary key of another table as a point of reference, relationships between tables are created.
- **Constraints**: Constraints that uphold the relationships and data integrity, like:
    - o **Unique Constraint**: Guarantees that values inside a column or group of columns remain distinct throughout rows.
    - o **Check Constraint**: Verifies data according to predetermined guidelines, such as an adult's age greater than 18.

Database Schema Design Steps

Here are the steps to design a database schema:

1. **Requirement analysis**: Compile and examine relationships, business rules, and data needs.

2. **Conceptual Design**: Identify entities, properties, and relationships by creating a high-level schema with entity-relationship diagrams (ERDs).
3. **Logical Design**: Using normalization techniques (for example, 1NF, 2NF, 3NF), translate the ERD into tables, columns, keys, and relationships.
4. **Physical Design**: Establish indexing, optimization techniques, and storage architectures for effective data storage and retrieval.

Normalization and Denormalization in Schema Design:

- **Normalization**: Splits data into several tables to remove dependencies and redundancies, guaranteeing data integrity. A university database's student and course tables serve as an example.
- **Denormalization**: This technique combines normalized tables to enhance query efficiency and streamline the retrieval of data, for example, combining the tables for students and courses to create a single table for reporting needs.

Database Schema Types:

- **Physical Schema**: Explains how data is stored on disk, including file systems, indexing, and access techniques.
- **Conceptual/Logical Schema**: Regardless of physical storage, this diagram illustrates the database's conceptual structure, which includes tables, columns, keys, and relationships.
- **External/View Schema**: Focuses on business needs and user viewpoints, offering a high-level view of data elements, properties, and relationships.

Best Practices for Database Schema Design:

- Give tables, columns, keys, and constraints meaningful and consistent names.
- Adhere to normalization guidelines to minimize duplication and guarantee data accuracy.
- For maintenance and clarity, document the schema using data dictionaries, ERDs, and schema diagrams.
- Use query optimization, partitioning, and indexing strategies to maximize performance.

Database Schema Example

Examine the following basic e-commerce database schema:

- **Tables**: `OrderDetails`, `Product`, `Customer`, and `Order` `Order` (`OrderID`, `CustomerID`, `OrderDate`), `Product` (`ProductID`, `Name`, `Price`), `Customer` (`CustomerID`, `Name`, `Email`, `Phone`), and `OrderDetails` (`OrderID`, `ProductID`, `Quantity`)

- **Keys**: Primary Key in the Customer table, Foreign Key in the Order table, Primary Key in the Product table, and Primary Key in the `OrderDetails`
- **Table Restrictions**: Check constraint on Quantity > 0 in `OrderDetails` table, unique constraint on Email in Customer table.

This schema shows how relationships and constraints are used to structure the data entities (orders, products, and customers) to preserve data integrity.

Challenges and Future Developments in Schema Design:

- **Difficulties:** Managing complicated interactions, flexibility vs. performance trade-offs, and scalability.
- **Future Trends:** Graph databases for intricate relationships, NoSQL for schema flexibility, and automated schema management solutions for dynamic database systems.
- **Scalability:** Building reliable, scalable databases that satisfy business needs and guarantee data integrity and performance requires effective database schema design.

Entity-Relationship (ER) Modeling

An entity-relationship model is known as an ER model. This data model is at a high level.

- Peter Chen first suggested the Entity Relationship model in 1976.
- An enterprise data model is a logical depiction of the data. The logical structure of a database is represented diagrammatically by the ER model. The ER model describes the link between entities and attributes.
- **Relationship between Entities**: The most effective means of communication throughout the system are diagrams. These diagrams show how data and information flow graphically. Business companies use these graphics most frequently to facilitate data transfer. Using this conceptual database model to communicate with people at all levels is a successful strategy.

The key elements and their corresponding symbols in ER Diagrams are as follows:

- **Rectangles**: Entity types are represented by this Entity Relationship Diagram symbol.
- **Diamonds**: This symbol specifically denotes the type of relationship (for example, one-to-one, one-to-many, many-to-many).
- **Lines:** It connects entity types, relationship types, and attributes, showing the associations between them.
  Features are underlined in the primary key. Multiple-valued characteristics are represented by double ellipses.

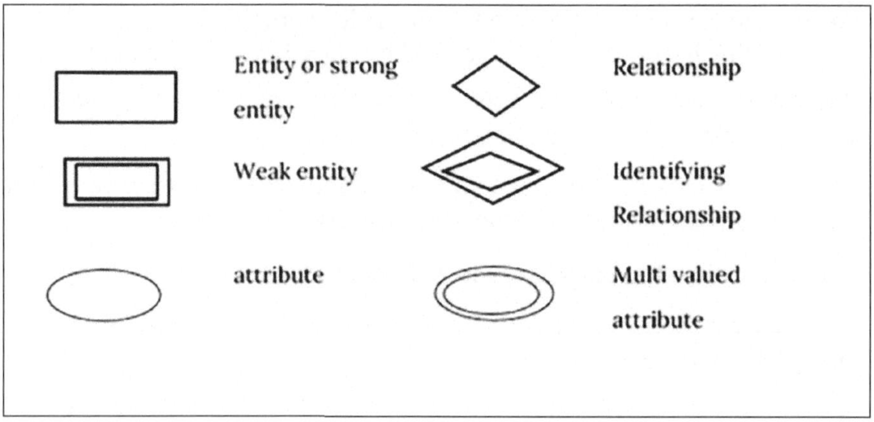

Figure 2.1: *Symbols used in the ER Model*

An Entity and Entity Set

Data can be stored in a database by an item, person, location, or event that can be termed as an entity. An entity is shown as a rectangle in the ER diagram, such as staff members, supervisors, students, and so on.

Entity Set is a grouping of similar-type entities with shared attributes. An entity set of students would be, for instance, a college student body.

Entity sets are classified into two categories:

- Strong entity set
- Weak entity set

Strong entity set: The entity sets having enough attributes to form the primary key are referred to as strong entity sets. It is depicted through a single-line border rectangle in the ER model.

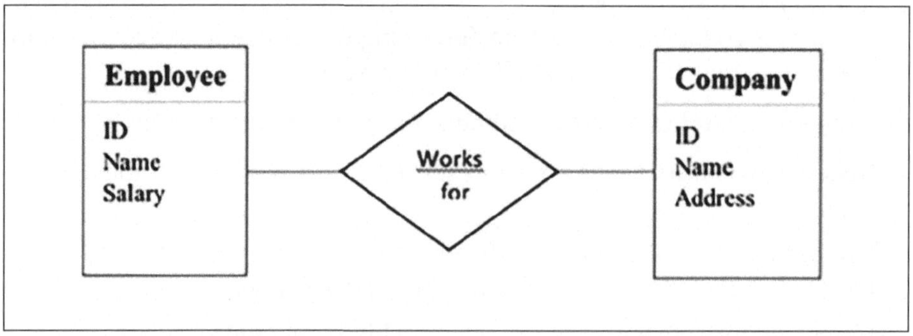

Figure 2.2: *ER Diagram for Employee Relation*

Weak entity set: An entity set that does not have sufficient attributes to form a primary key is called a weak entity set. This set can be converted into a strong entity set through identifying relationships. It is denoted through a double-bordered rectangle.

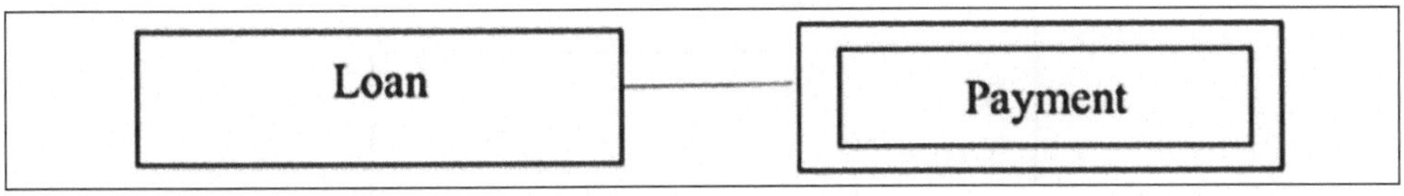

Figure 2.3: *Weak Entity Set Model*

Types of the Attributes:

- **Simple** and **Composite**

  Composite attributes may be partitioned further into sub-parts.

  - **Single-valued** and **multivalued attributes**

    Single-valued attributes will hold a single value and multivalued attributes may hold more than one value.

    Example: `Mobile_numbers`, `dependants _names`

- **Derived attributes**: Derived attributes are computed from other already existing attribute values.

  Example: age of a person from his/her `date_of_birth`, employment length from the given date of joining.

Domain: The set of permitted values for each attribute is called as domain or value set of that attribute.

Composite Attributes are shown as follows:

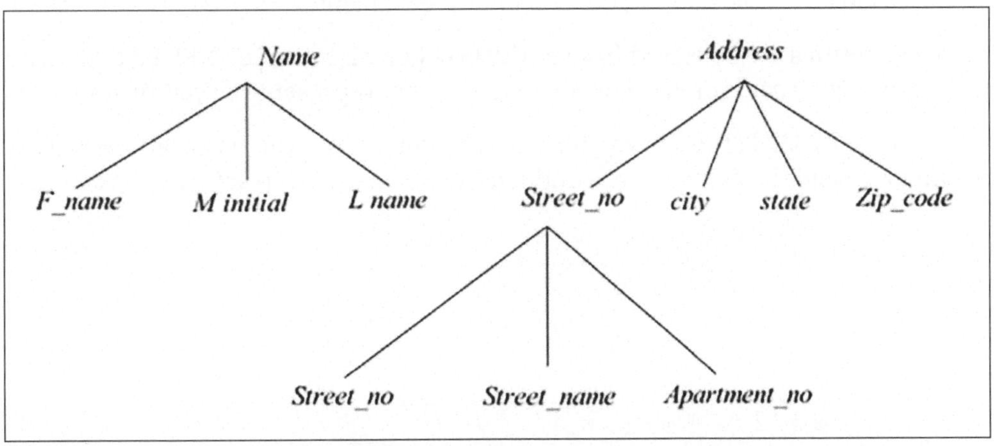

Figure 2.4: Composite attributes

Complex Attributes representation in ER Diagram:

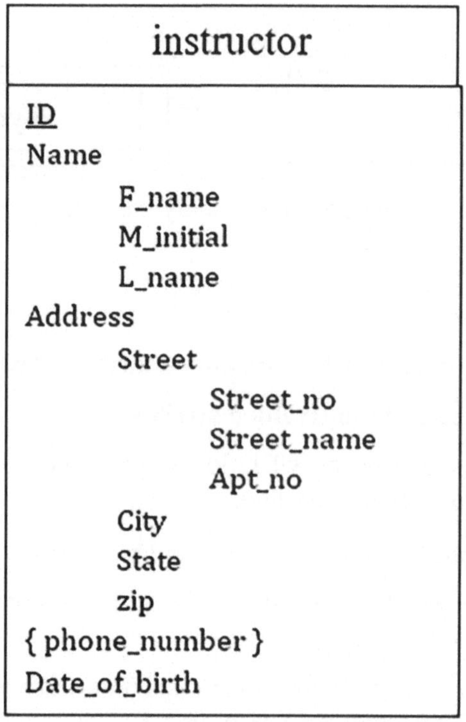

Figure 2.5: *ER Diagram*

Relationships and Relationship Sets

A relationship is an association between multiple elements.

When n≥2 entities are collected from entity sets {(e1, e2,..., en) | e1 ∈ E1, e2 ∈ E2,..., en ∈ En}, a relationship set is created, where (e1, e2,..., en) represents a relationship.

For instance, (12323,123) ∈ **`works_for`**. As an illustration, the associations between the employee and the company are defined by the relationship set **`works_for`**.

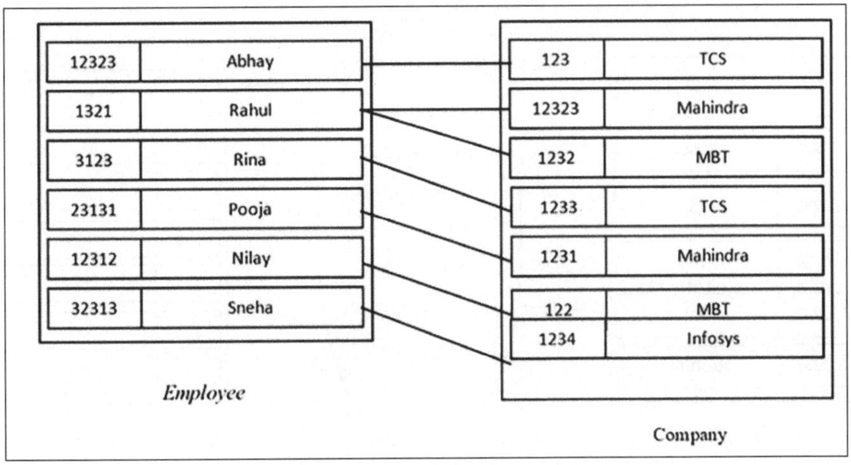

Figure 2.6: *Relationship Set*

ER Diagram Representation of Relationship

Diamond shapes denote relationship sets in the ER diagram.

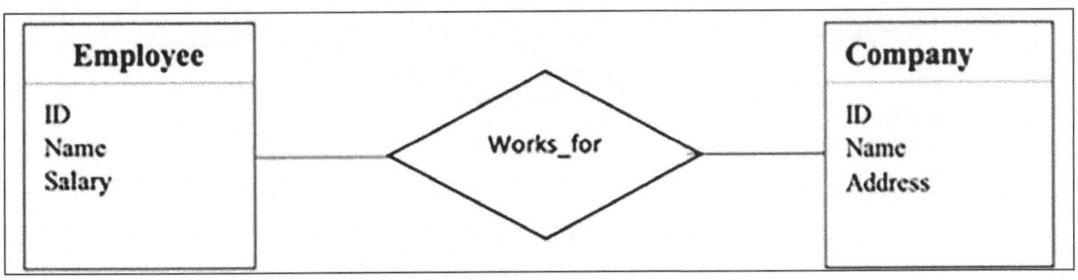

Figure 2.7: *ER Model with Relationship*

A relationship set may also be associated with an attribute.

For example, the attribute data that records the employee's affiliation with the company may be present in the `works_for` relationship set between the entity sets Employee and Company.

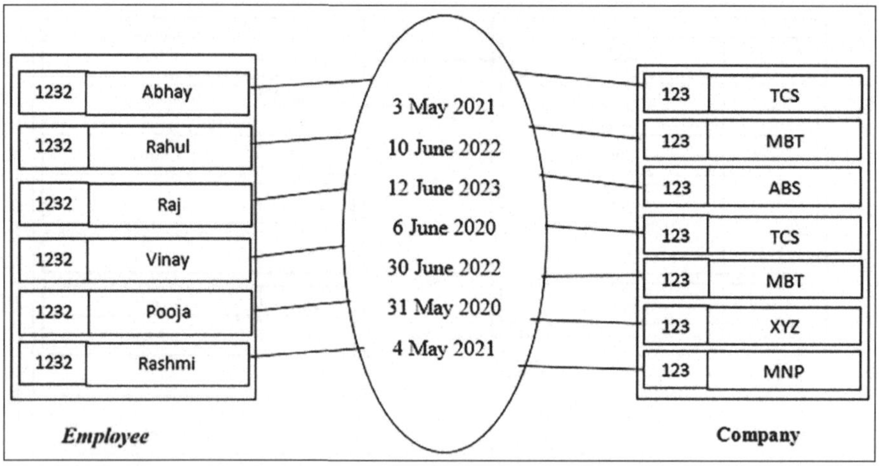

***Figure* 2.8:** *Relationship between entity sets*

Relationship Set having Attribute:

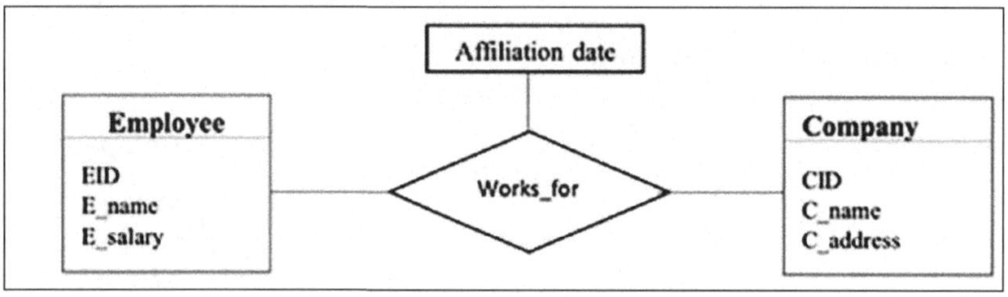

***Figure* 2.9**: *Relationship with attributes*

Roles

Every instance of an entity set has a "role" in the connection.

Roles are labeled as "**`course_id`**" and "**`prereq_id`**", as shown in *Figure* 2.10.

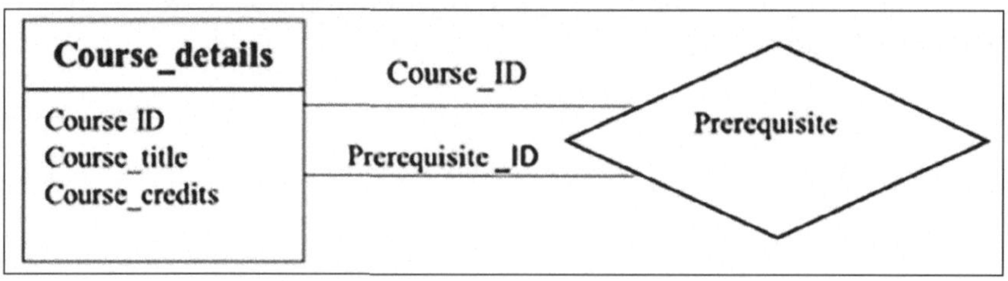

***Figure* 2.10:** *Relationship with roles*

Degree of a Relationship

Degree of Relationship: A degree of relationship is a relationship in which several distinct entities are involved. It falls under the following categories:

- **Unary Relationship**: When both participating entity types are the same, there is a unary relationship. When a relationship of this kind exists, it is said to have a degree of 1. Assume, for instance, that there are numerous kids in a classroom who are leaders of different clubs, such as the dancing club, basketball club, and so on. Thus, a specific student body is overseen by the leader of their individual club. Students both organize the group and select the club leaders in this instance. This means that the only party involved in this is the "`Student`." The unary relationship can be shown pictorially as follows:

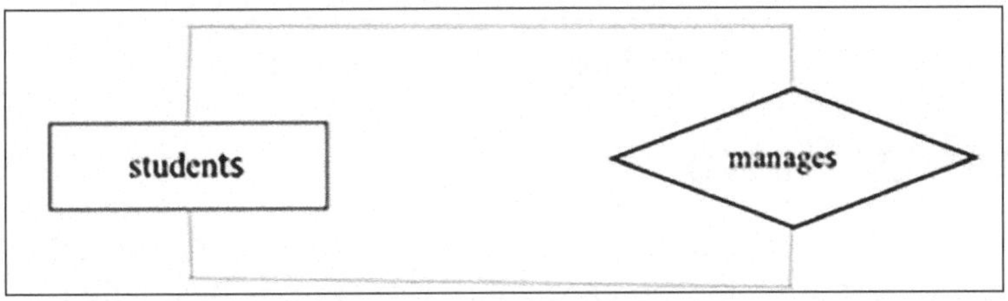

***Figure 2.11**: Unary or self-relationship*

- **Binary Relationship**: When precisely two different entity types interact, a binary relationship is formed. In cases where this kind of relationship exists, the degree is 2. The most typical relationship degree is this one. Such relationships are simple to manage since they are readily transformed into relational tables.

  As an illustration, we have two entity types: "`Customer`" and "`Account`," where each "`Customer`" has an "`Account`" that houses the information about their account. We refer to this relationship as binary since it involves two different entity kinds. Furthermore, a single "`Customer`" may have several "`Accounts`," but each "`Account`" should only belong to one "`Customer`." It can be characterized as a binary relationship of one-to-many.

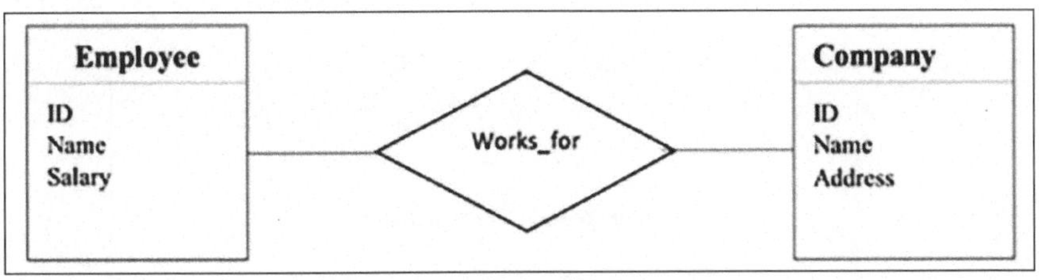

***Figure 2.12:** Binary Relationship*

- **Ternary Relationship:** A ternary relationship is when precisely three entity sets participate in the relationship. The degree of relationship is said to be 3.

  For example, we have three entity types '`teacher`', '`student_details`', and '`projects`'. The relationship between these entities is defined as a student working on a project guided by an instructor. Hence the degree of the relationship is a ternary relationship.

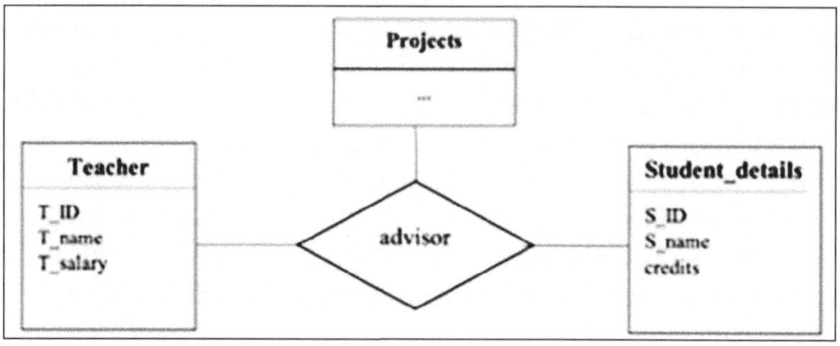

Figure 2.13: *Ternary Relationship*

Cardinality Ratio

The number of entities to which another entity can be associated through a relationship set is precisely determined by the cardinality ratio and is best suited for describing binary relationship sets.

In a binary relationship, the mapping cardinality needs to be one of the following:

- One-to-one
- One-to-many
- Many-to-one
- Many-to-many

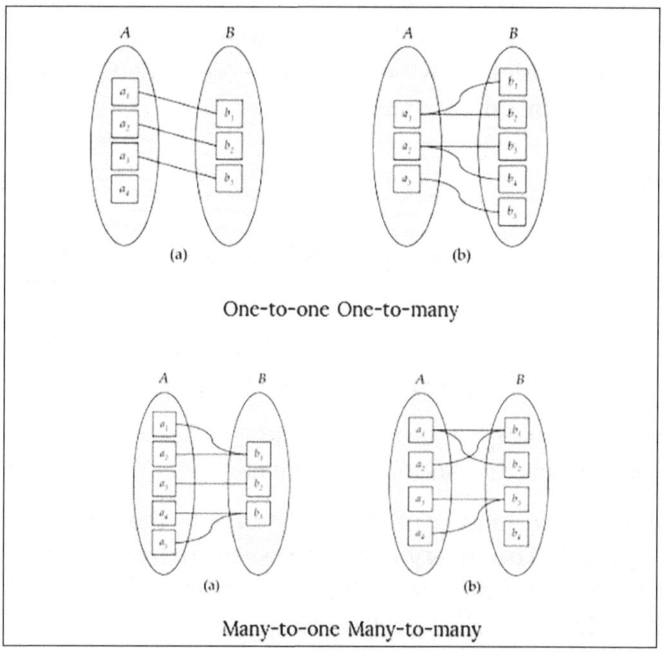

Figure 2.14: *Relationship Cardinality*

Representing Cardinality Constraints in ER Diagram

Drawing an undirected line (–), denoting "many," or a directed line (→), denoting "one," between the relationship set and the entity set is how we express cardinality constraints.

One-on-one relationship between a course and a student:

A student has a relationship with a maximum of one course via **`enrolled_for`**

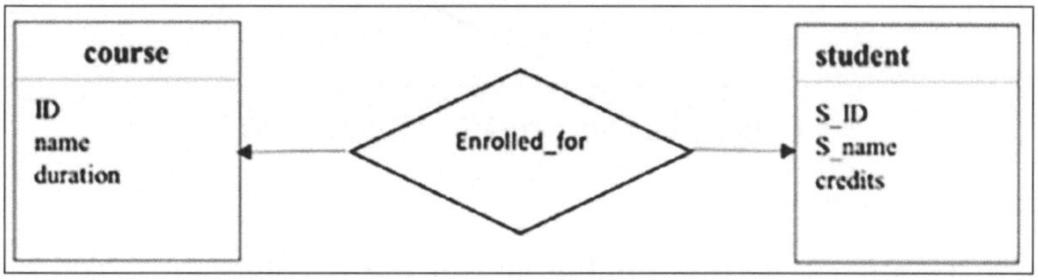

Figure 2.15: *One-to-one Relationship*

One-to-Many Relationship

One-to-many relationship between a course and a student:

Through **`enrolled_for`**, a student is connected to multiple courses, including zero.

Through **`enrolled_for`**, a student is connected to a maximum of one course.

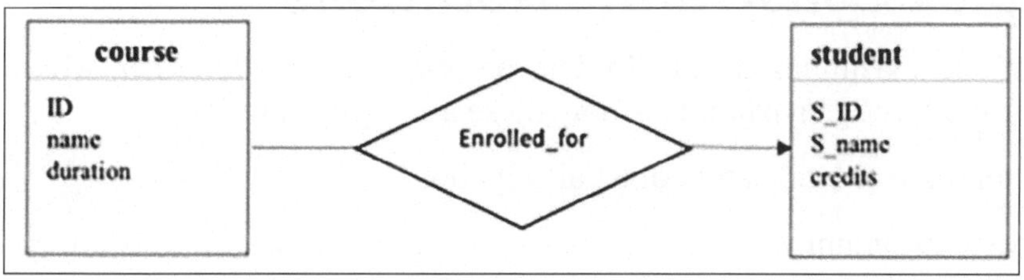

Figure 2.16: *One-to-Many Relationship*

Many-to-One Relationship

A course and a student have a many-to-one connection in which the course is connected to a maximum of one student through the **`enrolled_for`** and the student is connected to several courses through the **`enrolled_for`**.

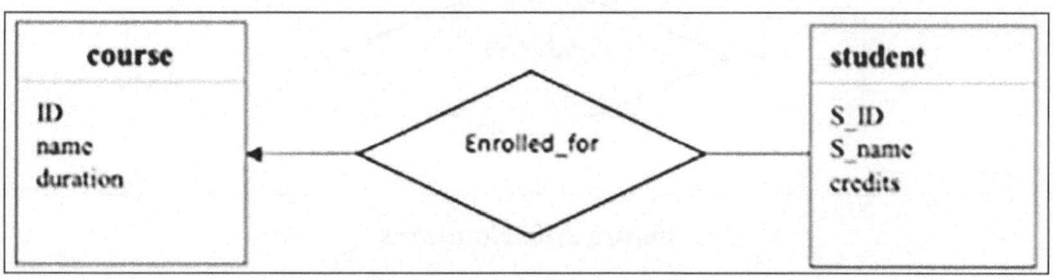

Figure 2.17: *Many-to-one Relationship*

Many-to-Many Relationship

In this type of relationship, many entities of all the participating entity sets are logically connected to each other.

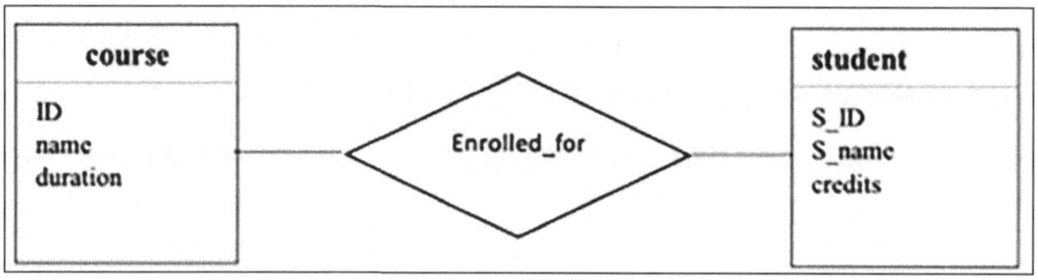

Figure 2.18: *Many-to-Many Relationship*

Participation constraints

Total participation (specified by double line in the ER diagram): Each entity in the entity set takes part in at least one relationship within the relationship set.

Partial participation: Some of the entities may not take part in any relationship within the relationship set.

Example: Participation of course entity set in enrolled_for relationship is partial

Complex Constraints Notations

Minimum and maximum cardinality can be assigned to a line. l..h, where l is the minimum and h is the maximum, is how these are represented.

A minimum value of 1 indicates total participation.

If an entity's maximum value is 1 and *, which indicates that there is no limit, then it can only be a part of one connection.

An instructor can counsel zero or more students. A student can only have one advisor; they cannot have more than one.

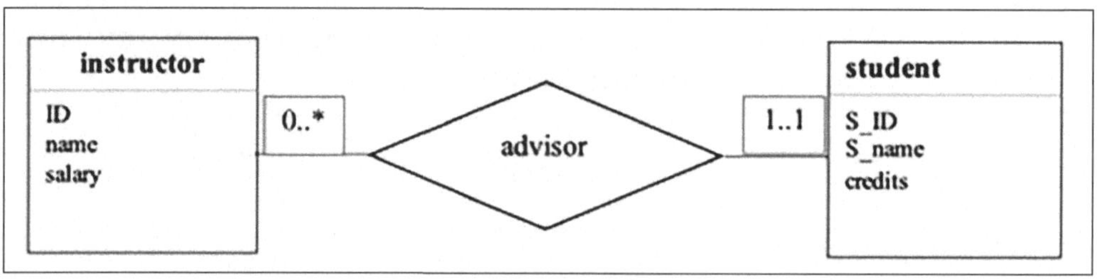

Figure 2.19: Notations

ER Diagram for a University Database can be shown as follows:

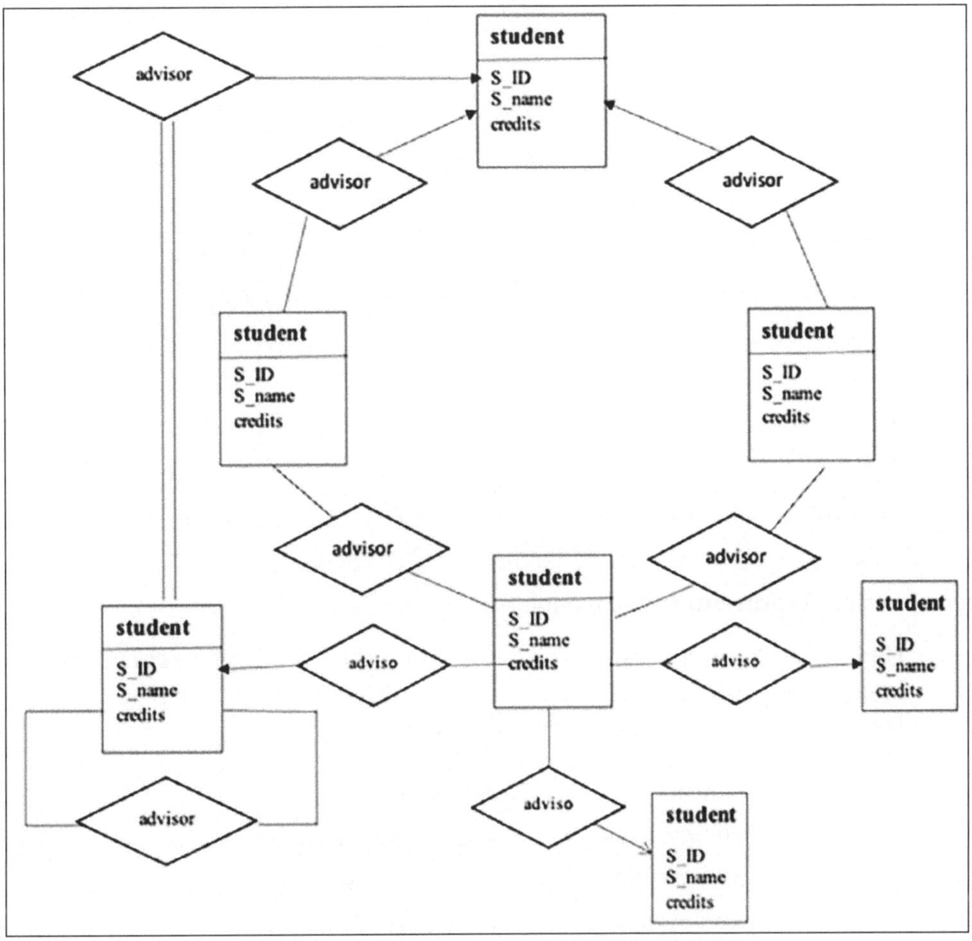

Figure 2.20: *ER Diagram for University System*

Extension in the ER Features

Specialization:

Top-down design process; we designate sub-groupings within an entity set that are distinctive from other entities in the set.

These sub-groupings become lower-level entity sets that have attributes or participate in relationships that do not apply to the higher-level entity set. Depicted by a *triangle* component labeled ISA (for example, *instructor* "is a" person).

Attribute inheritance: A lower-level entity set inherits all the attributes and relationships participation of the higher-level entity set to which it is linked.

Specialization Example:

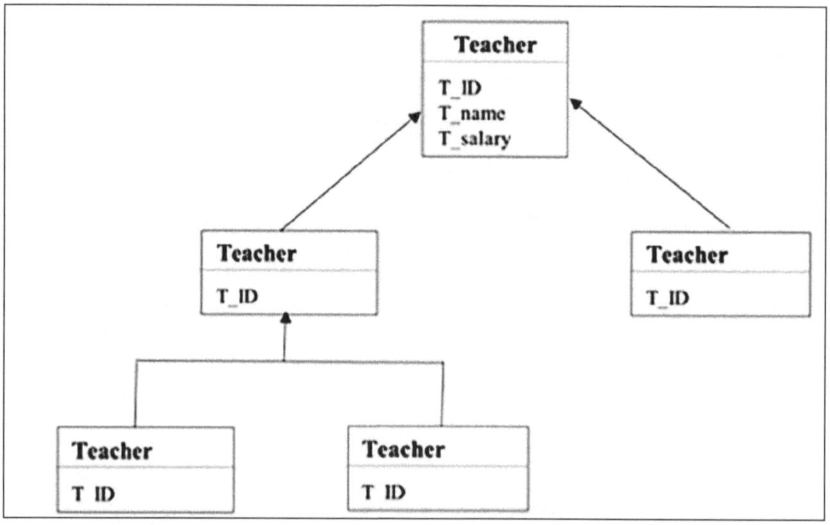

***Figure 2.21**: Specialization*

Specialization Representation through Schemas:

1. Higher-level entity schema formation is created first, then schema for every lower-level entity set, which includes the primary key of a higher-level entity set with attributes of the current entity set.

Schema	Attributes
Person_details	P_id, p_name, address
Student_details	P_id, credits
Employee_details	P_id, salary

***Table 2.1**: Schema 1 details*

Drawback: To obtain details on an employee, you need to access two relations: the low-level schema's corresponding relation and the high-level schema's corresponding relation.

2. Schema formation for every entity set is done comprising all the local and inherited attributes.

Schema	Attributes
Person_details	P_id, p_name, address
Student_deatils	P_id, p_name, address, credits
Employee_details	P_id, p_name, address, salary

***Table 2.2**: Schema 2 details*

Drawback: For individuals who are both employees and students, name, street, and city may be saved twice.

Generalization:

A higher-level entity set is created by combining many entity sets that have similar qualities using a bottom-up design approach. Generalization and specialization are not simply inversions of each other. They are related but distinct concepts with different starting points and purposes; an ER diagram illustrates this. Specialization and generalization are concepts that are used synonymously.

Constraint on completeness:

The completeness constraint outlines the requirement that an entity in a generalization's higher-level entity set be a member of at least one of its lower-level entity sets.

- Total: An entity needs to be a part of a lower-level entity set.
- Partial: An entity does not necessarily have to be a part of a lower-level entity set, partial generalization is the default.

Aggregation:

Consider the ternary relationship ***proj_guide***, *for example*, evaluations of a student by a guide for a project needed to be recorded then:

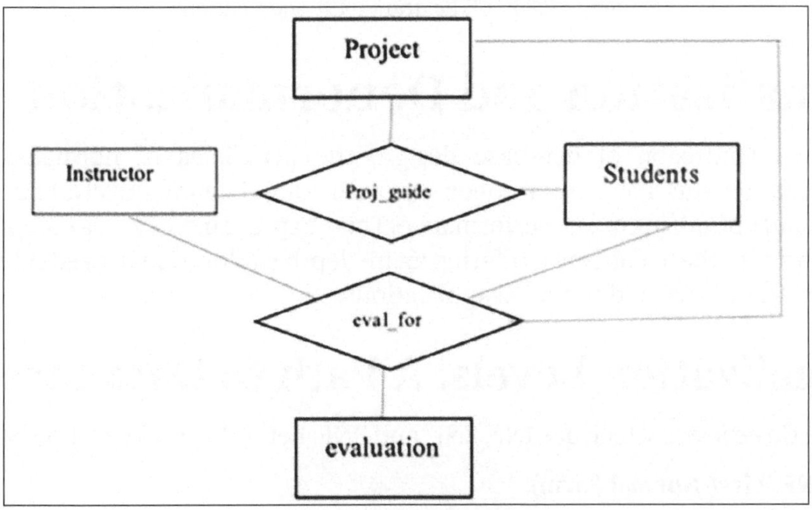

***Figure 2.22**: Aggregation*

Relationship settings **proj_guide** and **eval_for** show information that is overlapping.

There is a **proj_guide** relationship for every **eval_for** relationship. Nevertheless, there are **proj_guide** relationships that may not have any **eval_for** relationships, in which case the **proj_guide** relationship cannot be eliminated.

This redundancy can be removed through aggregation. Connections between connections are allowed through aggregation, and relationships themselves are recognized as entities in this process. As illustrated in the following diagram a specific instructor mentors a student on a specific project.

There might be an evaluation linked to a student, teacher, and project combination.

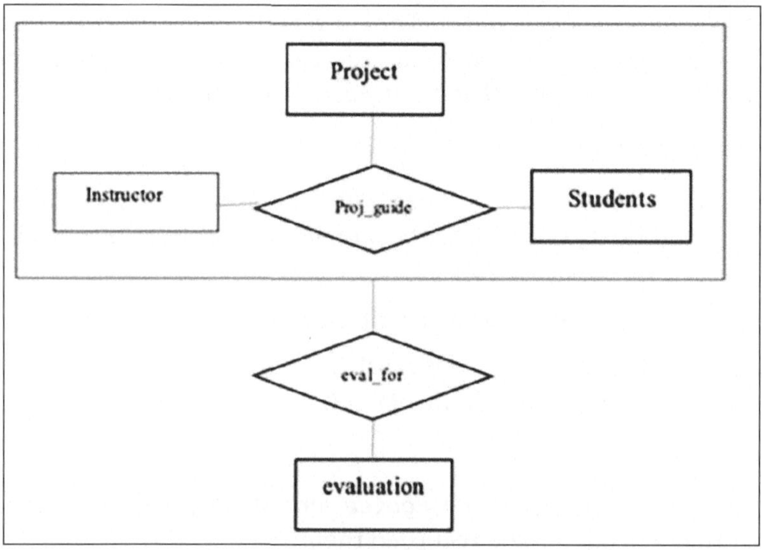

***Figure* 2.23**: *ER Relation with Aggregation*

Normalization and Denormalization

In the vast landscape of database design, the principles of normalization and denormalization stand as cornerstones for organizing data effectively, ensuring data integrity, and optimizing query performance. This chapter embarks on a comprehensive journey through these concepts, offering an in-depth exploration backed by examples, strategies, trade-offs, and practical applications.

Normalization Levels: A Path to Data Integrity

There are three levels which are 1NF, 2NF, and 3NF. Let us have a look at them in detail:

- **1NF (First Normal Form):**

  1NF mandates that each attribute in a table must hold a single value, avoiding repeating groups. Example: As an illustration, consider a product table that first merges supplier and product details. In accordance with 1NF guidelines, this should be normalized into distinct tables for Product Details, Categories, and Suppliers to minimize data redundancy.

- **2NF (Second Normal Form):**

  For 2NF to work, it must first satisfy the requirements of 1NF (First Normal Form), that is, it has no repeating groups. Additionally, all non-key attributes must be functionally dependent on the entire primary key.

- **3NF (Third Normal Form):**

  By removing transitive dependencies from tables, 3NF improves data consistency and lowers anomalies. To comply with 3NF requirements, normalizing an Employee table into distinct entities for Employee, Department, and Department Location eliminates any indirect dependencies.

The Normalization Process: A Structured Approach

1. **Determine Dependencies**: To determine functional dependencies and relationships within the data, perform a thorough examination. To reach the necessary normalization levels, create different tables based on the dependencies that have been established.
2. **Define Primary Keys**: To maintain data integrity and promote relationships, give each table a unique identity.
3. **Create Linkages**: To create strong linkages between tables and preserve data consistency, use foreign keys.
4. **Remove Redundancy**: To minimize data anomalies and maximize storage efficiency, apply normalization techniques to eliminate redundant data.

Conditions in which Denormalization is Necessary

Denormalization is useful even if it contradicts the normalization principles. In situations where denormalization is suitable, consider the following:

- **Performance Optimization**: When complex queries or frequent joins affect query performance, denormalization helps speed up data retrieval.
- **Reporting and Analytics**: Denormalized data structures are helpful for reporting and analytical applications because they speed up access to aggregated data.
- **Data Warehousing**: In data warehousing environments, denormalization improves query efficiency for decision support systems and streamlines data mart structures.

Normalization and Denormalization Trade-offs

The trade-offs and contributing elements of normalization and denormalization include:

- **Redundancy in the Data**: Normalization reduces redundancy in the data, but it may also lead to more joint operations, which may impact performance.
- **Query Efficiency**: Denormalization may result in update anomalies and data redundancy, but it may also improve query efficiency.
- **Maintenance Overhead**: Normalized structures are easier to update and maintain than denormalized structures, which require strict management to prevent data inconsistencies.
- **Comparison Table**: Provides a table that compares the benefits and drawbacks of normalization versus denormalization so that readers may make informed design decisions.

Best Practices for Denormalization

The recommended practices for successful denormalization include:

- **Finding Performance Bottlenecks**: Evaluate system performance to identify areas where denormalization can provide appreciable benefits.
- **Strategic Denormalization**: By carefully choosing which tables or data subsets to denormalize, you can strike a balance between data integrity issues and performance gains.
- **Indexing and Optimization**: Using the appropriate indexing and query optimization techniques to lessen the likelihood of denormalization-related performance issues.
- **Monitoring and Maintenance**: Set up monitoring systems and regular maintenance programs to address data consistency issues and update anomalies in denormalized structures.

Denormalization Strategies: Balancing Efficiency and Performance

Denormalization strategies intend to enhance the query performance by bringing back some redundancy:

- **Duplication of Data**: To improve query efficiency and streamline queries, combine relevant data into a single denormalized table.
- **Aggregate Data**: To reduce processing costs during searches and speed up response times, precompute and save aggregated data.

- **Materialized Views**: To further improve query performance and cut down on processing time, create materialized views that store pre-computed results of difficult queries.

Trade-offs: Navigating the Balance

- **Data Integrity vs. Performance**: Normalization prioritizes data integrity by minimizing redundancy, but this can sometimes lead to more complex queries and potentially impact performance. Denormalization sacrifices some data integrity by introducing redundancy, but it can significantly improve query performance, especially for read-heavy workloads.
- **Efficient Storage**: Normalization reduces storage needs by removing redundant data, but denormalization could result in more storage being needed because of duplicate data.
- **Query Performance**: Denormalization can simplify queries and improve read performance, also it can introduce additional overhead for write operations due to the need to maintain consistency across redundant data, whereas in normalized databases, complex queries may require joins, but careful design and indexing can mitigate potential performance issues.

Practical Examples:

- **Online Retail**: Normalize data for Customers, Orders, and Products to maintain data integrity. Implement denormalization for faster order retrieval and reporting, enhancing user experience.
- **Social Media Platforms**: Normalize data for Users, Posts, Comments, and Likes to ensure data consistency. Utilize denormalization for generating trending posts or user activity reports, improving platform performance.

Conclusion

Data modeling and design are the primary mechanisms of creating and running databases. They create a framework, bring about simplicity, ensure correctness, and enhance performance through optimization; hence playing an important role in the efficiency of data handling within firms. Continuous evaluation and refinement of data models should enable them to remain in tandem with business objectives as well as technological changes. In the next chapter, we are going to discuss one of the widely used data models called relational database management systems.

Questions

1. Define and discuss the Critical Relationship Types found in a Data Model.
2. What is the difference between Conceptual, Logical, and Physical data models?

3. Explain the ER (Entity-Relationship) diagram with the help of a real-life example.
4. Discuss the various types of normal forms with the help of an example.
5. What is normalization and explain the process of denormalization?
6. Explain the advantages of NoSQL databases over relational databases.
7. Analyze one-to-many and many-to-many relationships in NoSQL data modeling.
8. Explain the possible cardinalities of a relationship in the entity-relationship (ER) model.
9. Explain the process of self or recursive relation in the ER model with the help of an example.
10. Draw an ER diagram for the University Management system and reduce the ER model in the relational model.

Chapter 3
Relational Database Management Systems

Introduction

Relational Database Management System is referred to as RDBMS. Records, fields, and database tables make up the structure of RDBMS data. Database table rows make up each RDBMS table. One or more database table fields make up each entry in the database table. RDBMSs store the data in sets of tables that may be connected by shared fields (columns in database tables). Relational operators are another feature that RDBMS offers for modifying data that is stored in database tables. SQL is the database query language used by most RDBMS. The most widely used RDBMSs are MySQL, Oracle, and DB2.

Structure

In this chapter, the following topics will be covered:

- Relational Model Principles
- Structured Query Language (SQL) Basics
- Database Schema Creation and Manipulation using SQL
- Data Integrity Constraints (Primary Keys, Foreign Keys)
- Views, Stored Procedures, Cursors, Indexes, and Triggers in SQL

Relational Model Principles

An unsatisfactory or bad database design is the reason for the challenges encountered during system implementation. Systems frequently need to be regularly updated in several ways according to the changes required by the users. It is imperative that careful planning be undertaken. In a relational database, a relation is built upon a relational schema, which is made up of several properties. Many relations and matching relational database structures make up a relational database. A relational database design aims to produce a set of relation schema that facilitates the easy retrieval of information and the redundant storage of data, a method for creating schemas in a suitable, standard form. The normal forms are utilized to ensure that different kinds of anomalies and inconsistencies are not added to the database.

Introduction to RDBMS

The relational model, which offers an organized framework for arranging, retrieving, and modifying data, is the cornerstone of contemporary database management systems (DBMS). In the DBMS framework, this chapter examines the fundamental ideas of the relational model, including tables, keys, normalization, data integrity, and operations. By grasping these concepts, database professionals may create and maintain scalable and effective databases that satisfy the needs of today's data-driven world.

Large volumes of data must be effectively organized and managed, and database management systems are essential for this. Edgar F. Codd's relational model, which offered an organized method for organizing and manipulating data, transformed database administration in the 1970s.

Understanding RDBMS

One type of record-based model is the relational model. The database is organized in fixed format records of various kinds, hence the name record-based models. Records of a specific sort are contained in each table. There are a set number of fields or characteristics, defined for each record type. The table's columns match the characteristics of the various record kinds. Most modern database systems are built on the relational data model, which is the most extensively used data model.

Dr. E.F. Codd, a mathematician and research scientist at IBM, created the relational model. Many contemporary DBMSs are still regarded as RDBMSs even though they do not meet Codd's criteria for what constitutes an RDBMS. Improving data integrity in database systems and reducing data redundancy were two of Dr. Codd's primary goals while creating the relational model.

Dr. Codd's work in 1970 A *Relational Model of Data for Large Shared Data Banks* served as the inspiration for the relational model. The following ideas were covered in this paper and they relate to relational database management systems. In the relational data model, the relation is the single data structure that is utilized to describe both entities and the relationships that exist between them. Columns are the characteristics of the connection, and rows are the tuples of the relation. Every column's attribute is taken from the domain, which is a collection of values. The range of values that an attribute can assume is included in its domain. The relational data model is very young when viewed historically. Either network or hierarchical models served as the foundation for the earliest database systems. For commercial data processing applications, the relational data model has become the *de facto* standard. Because of its success in this field, it is also used in settings other than data processing such as computer-aided design systems.

Differences Between DBMS and RDBMS

An RDBMS is a specific type of DBMS. While all RDBMSs are DBMSs, not all DBMSs are relational. Other models exist, for example, hierarchical, networks, and so on.

ACID properties are crucial for ensuring data integrity in any DBMS, not just RDBMS.

It's inaccurate to say that a general DBMS doesn't impose security or constraints. Many DBMSs have features, such as access controls, authorization, and data validation to ensure data security and integrity.

Structured Query Language (SQL)

The inception of Structured Query Language (SQL) dates back to the early 1970s when IBM researchers created a database query language known as SEQUEL (Structured English Query Language). SEQUEL developed into SQL over time, and the American National Standards Institute (ANSI) and the International Organization for Standardization (ISO) formally standardized SQL.

Introduction to SQL

SQL is not a direct combination of relational calculus and mathematics; it is influenced by relational algebra and calculus and is designed to be more practical for interacting with databases. It is a data sublanguage that the Relational Database Management System (RDBMS) uses to organize, manage, and retrieve data from relational databases. SQL is the programming language used by DBMS vendors, such as Oracle, IBM, DB2, Sybase, and Ingress for their databases. The System R project at IBM's San Jose Research Center in 1974 served as the inspiration for SQL. The first iteration of SQL was called SEQUEL, and it served as the system R Project's Application Program Interface (API).

The most recent version and standard is SQL-92. One of the two methods to use the SQL language is either interactively or by embedding it into another program. SQL is utilized interactively to handle a database directly and get the intended results. When the user types a SQL command, it is executed right away. Most databases come with a tool that lets you run SQL queries interactively. These consist of Microsoft's SQL Server 7 Query Analyzer, SQL Server Management Studio, Oracle's SQL Plus, and SQL Base's SQL Talk. SQL commands are integrated into applications written in other programming languages, allowing those applications to interact with the database.

Importance of SQL

SQL provides a standardized language for querying, updating, and maintaining relational databases. Hence it plays a vital role in DBMS. SQL is necessary for many data-related operations, such as data analysis, database structure modification, and information retrieval. For data workers, knowing SQL is essential since it allows them to work with databases efficiently and glean insightful information from the data.

Divisions of SQL

Based on their purpose, SQL is divided into three groups of commands, which are as follows:

- **Data Definition Language (DDL):**

  The SQL feature, known as Data Definition Language, is responsible for creating, updating, and deleting tables. It is also responsible for creating views and indexes. The DDL commands are as follows:

  `CREATE TABLE`, **`DROP TABLE`**, **`ALTER TABLE`**, **`CREATE VIEW`**, and **`CREATE INDEX`**

- **Data Manipulation Language (DML):**

  Data can be altered (inserted, deleted, updated, and retrieved) using data manipulation commands. The DML language has commands for doing data modifications and inquiries. The following commands are included in it:

  `SELECT`, **`UPDATE`**, **`DELETE`**, and **`INSERT`**

- **Data Control Language (DCL):**

  The commands that make up the data control language are concerned with maintaining database security by allocating privileges to users so that they can access particular database objects.

  The DCL commands are as follows:

  `GRANT`, **`REVOKE`**, **`COMMIT`**, and **`ROLLBACK`**

Data Definition Language

The SQL DDL offers commands to define relations, delete relations, create indices, and alter relations, such as **`CREATE VIEW`**, and **`CREATE SCHEMA`**.

Data Types in SQL:

The following Data Types are supported by the SQL- 92 standard:

- **Numeric data types**
  - Integer numbers of various sizes **`INT`** or **`INTEGER SMALLINT`**

- Real numbers of various precision **REAL**
- **DOUBLE PRECISION FLOAT** (n)
- Formatted numbers can be represented by using **DECIMAL** (p, q) or **DEC** (p, q) **NUMERIC** (p, q) or **NUMBER** (p, q)

where, p: the precision, represents the total number of digits, and q: the scale, represents the number of digits after the decimal point.

The default value of scale is zero and the default value of precision is defined in the implementation.

- **Character string data types**

  Character data types can be of varying length or fixed length.
  CHARACTER (n) or **CHAR** (n) represents a fixed-length character string with length n defined by the user.
  VARCHAR (n) represents a variable-length string of characters having a maximum length of n.

- **Date and Time data types:**

  There are new data types for date and time in SQL-92.

  - **DATE**: Represents a calendar date in the format as yyyy : mm : dd
  - **TIME**: Represents a time of day in the format as HH: MM: SS

Date, varying length character strings, and time were not supported in the SQL-89 standards.

DDL Commands

- **CREATE TABLE:**

  The **CREATE TABLE** STATEMENT/ COMMAND is used for creating a new table/ relation by giving it a name along with its attributes and constraints upon the table definition.

Syntax:

```
CREATE TABLE table_name
( Column_name 1 data type [NOT NULL],…..
Column_name n data_type [NOT NULL]);
```

where **table_name** is the name for the table/relation to be created and **column_name 1** to **column_name n** are the column names.

NOT NULL defines that the column is mandatory. **NOT NULL** feature permits to inhibit data from being entered into the table without the columns having any data in them. If **NOT NULL** is not stated, the column can have **NULL** values in the implementation.

Example:

```
Create Table Emp_details
(E_id varchar2(10) NOT NULL,
E_name varchar2 (20),
J_Date Date,
Salary Decimal(10, 12),
dept_name Varchar2 (30
);
```

Constraints:

CREATE TABLE command can impose various constraints on a table, such as primary key, foreign key, check constraints, and unique constraints.

The constraint clause can be imposed upon a single column or group of columns within a table.

There are two approaches for defining constraints:

- **A column constraint can** be imposed in the column definition
- **A table constraint** can be given at the end of the create table command

The Primary Key:

The primary key is defined as the set of columns that uniquely identifies every row/ record in the table.

It can be specified in the **CREATE TABLE** command as follows:

```
CREATE TABLE table_name
 ( Column_name 1 data_type [not null], ....,
Column_name n data type [NOT NULL],
[Constraint constraint_name]
[Primary key (Column_name X, Column_name Y... Column_name Z)]
);
```

where **table_name** is the name of the table.

column_name 1 through **column_name** n are the column names with their **data_type** constraint which is optional **constraint_name** identifies the primary key in the preceding relation **column_name X** through **column_name Z** are the table's columns that compose the primary key.

Example :

```
Create table Emp_details
(E_id varchar2(10),
E_name varchar2 (20) NOT NULL,
J_Date Date,
Salary Decimal(10, 12),
```

```
dept_name Varchar2 (30),
Constraint PK_ Emp_details Primary key (E_id));
```

We do not provide a **NOT NULL** constraint for the columns that make up the primary key because, by default, they are required columns. There are other limitations that apply to primary keys.

Foreign Key: A set of columns with values derived from the primary key values of another table constitutes a foreign key combination. Referential integrity constraints, sometimes referred to as foreign key constraints, state that the values of the foreign key must match the actual values of the primary key in another database. The foreign key is specified as follows in the **Create Table** command:

```
Create Table table_name
(Column_name 1 data type [NOT NULL],
:
:
Column_name N data type [NOT NULL], [constraintconstraint_name
Foreign key (column_name C1 … Column_name CN) references referenced-
table (column_name PK1, … column_name PKN)]);
```

where **table_name** is the name of the table.

Column_name 1 through **column_name N** are the columns in the table. **constraint_ name** defines the name of the foreign key.

referenced_table is the referenced table name referred to by the foreign key. **column_name C1** to **column_name CN** are the columns that compose the foreign key.

Column_name PK1 to **column_name PKN** are the columns that compose the primary key in the referenced table.

Example:

```
CREATE TABLE Dept (
Dept_id VARCHAR2(10),
Dept_name VARCHAR2(25),
CONSTRAINT PK_Dept PRIMARY KEY (Dept_id)
);

CREATE TABLE Course (
Course_id VARCHAR2(10),
Dept_id VARCHAR2(10),
Course_name VARCHAR2(20),
CONSTRAINT PK_course PRIMARY KEY (Course_id, Dept_id),
CONSTRAINT FK_course FOREIGN KEY (Dept_id) REFERENCES Dept (Dept_id)
);
```

Unique Constraint:

A set of values from one or more columns that together uniquely identify every row in the table is called a candidate key. The unique constraint is specified as follows via the Create Table command:

```
CREATE TABLE table_name
(column_name 1 data_type  [NOT NULL], …column_name ndata_type
[NOT NULL],
[constraint  constraint_name Unique (Column_name A,……… Column_
name Z)]);
```

Example:

```
CREATE TABLE student_details (
student_id VARCHAR2(20),
student_fname VARCHAR2(20) NOT NULL,
student_lname VARCHAR2(20),
B_Date DATE,
City VARCHAR2(20),
CONSTRAINT UK_student_details UNIQUE (student_fname, student_lname),
CONSTRAINT PK_student_details PRIMARY KEY (student_id)
);
```

Check Constraint:

SQL can specify the data validation for a column during table formation by using the **CHECK** constraint. A Boolean condition that can be either **TRUE** or **FALSE** is called a **CHECK** clause. The database will accept the column value if the condition evaluates to **TRUE**; if the condition evaluates to **FALSE**, the database will return an error code.

The check constraint is declared in the **CREATE TABLE** statement as follows:

```
Column_name datatype [constraint constraint_name] [CHECK (Condition)]
```

Examples:

```
CREATE TABLE worker (
Name VARCHAR2(25) NOT NULL,
Age NUMBER CHECK (Age BETWEEN 18 AND 65)
);

CREATE TABLE instructor (
Instructor_id VARCHAR2(20) NOT NULL,
Department_id VARCHAR2(20) NOT NULL,
Name VARCHAR2(25),
Position VARCHAR2(25) CONSTRAINT CK_instructor CHECK (Position IN
('ASSISTANT PROFESSOR', 'ASSOCIATE PROFESSOR', 'PROFESSOR')),
CONSTRAINT PK_instructor PRIMARY KEY (Instructor_id)
);
```

If the position of the instructor is not one of the three legal values, DBMS will return an error code indicating that a check constraint has been violated.

Setting a Default value for a column:

You can set a default value for a column using the **DEFAULT** clause while defining the column. When a row is inserted into the table without the column being specified in the **INSERT** statement, the column's default value is utilized.

Example:

```
CREATE TABLE student_details (
Student_id VARCHAR2(20) PRIMARY KEY,
L_name VARCHAR2(20) NOT NULL,
F_name VARCHAR2(20) NOT NULL,
B_Date DATE,
State VARCHAR2(20),
City VARCHAR2(20) DEFAULT 'PUNE', -- Default value for City
CONSTRAINT PK_student_details PRIMARY KEY (Student_id)
);
```

- **ALTER TABLE Command:**

  With the **ALTER TABLE** command, you can change a table's definition. This expression modifies a table's structure but not its contents. The table can be modified by using the **ALTER TABLE** command as follows:

  - **Adding a new column to an existing table:**

  Syntax:

  ```
  ALTER TABLE table_name ADD (Column_name datatype….Column_name n
  datatype);
  ```

Example:

```
ALTER TABLE Dept
ADD (
University VARCHAR2(30),
No_of_students NUMBER(5)
);
```

  - **Modify an existing column in the existing table:**

  Syntax:

  ```
  ALTER TABLE table_name
  MODIFY column_name new_data_type [constraint];
  ```

  Example: Alter Table **ex_table** modify (**current_value** number **Null**);

    - Changing a column definition from **NULL** to **NOT NULL**:
      If a table is empty, then you can define a column to be **NOT NULL**.

However, if the table is not empty, you cannot change a column to **NOT NULL** unless every row in the table has a value for that column.

- Increasing and Decreasing a Column's Width:
  You can increase a character column's width and the number of digits in a number column at any time.

- **Adding a constraint to an existing table**:

  With the **ALTER TABLE** command, any constraint, a primary key, foreign key, unique key, or check constraint, can be added to an already-existing table.

Syntax: `ALTER TABLE table_name  ADD (constraint)`

Example:

```
Create Table example(Record_No   Number (38),
Description  Varchar2 (40), Current_value Number);

Alter Table example add (Constraint PK_ex_table primary key
(Record-No));
```

- **Dropping the constraints:**
  `ALTER TABLE table_name DROP Primary key`

Using this you can drop the primary key of the table.

`ALTER TABLE Table_name DROP constraint constraint_name`

Using this you can drop any constraint of the table.

Guidelines for adding or modifying a column:

The guidelines for adding a column to a table are as follows:

1. If **NOT NULL** is not stated, you are free to add a column at any point.
2. There are three easy steps to adding a **NOT NULL** column:
   a. Add a column without specifying that it is **NOT NULL**
   b. Insert data into each row of that column
   c. Change the column's designation to **BE NOT NULL**

The guidelines for editing a column are as follows:

1. The width of a character column can be expanded at any moment.
2. A **NUMBER** column's digit count can be increased at any moment.
3. The number of places in a **NUMBER** column can be changed at any moment.

If a column in the table has **NULL** values for each row, you can modify it as follows. You can:

a. Modify the data type

b. Reduce the width of a character column

c. Reduce the number of digits in a NUMBER column

- **DROP TABLE Command:**

  To drop a table is to remove its definition from the database. To drop the table, use the **DROP TABLE** command as follows:

  Syntax: `DROP TABLE table_name;`

  Example: `Drop table Emp;`

  The truncate command in ORACLE can delete only the rows or data within the table but not the table definition. It cannot be rolled back.

  Example:

  ```
  Truncate Emp;
  ```

DML Commands

The SQL DML contains commands for adding, removing, and altering tuples within databases. It has a query language built on tuple relational calculus and relational algebra. This section describes the various DML commands.

- **INSERT Command:**

  Syntax:

  ```
  INSERT INTO your_table_name
  VALUES (value1, value2, value3, ...);
  ```

where the table name is to be given in which the records or rows are to be inserted. Column Name is one of the table's columns. Column Value corresponds to the relevant column name and can be either an expression or a literal value. The number of literal values or expressions that follow the keyword values in parentheses must equal the number of columns in the list of column names.

Example:

```
INSERT INTO employees (emp_name, join__date, salary, address)
VALUES
('John', '2023-05-15', 55000.00, 10),
('Jane', '2024-02-01', 60000.00, 20);
```

An error is returned if the Insert statement's supplied column names exceed the number of values. Datatypes for columns and values must match. The column list is an optional element in accordance with the syntax of the **INSERT** statement. Therefore, DBMS uses all the columns by default if you do not provide the column names to be allocated values. The order in which the columns were defined at the time the table was formed is the column order that DBMS utilizes. It is risky to use the Insert statement without a column list, though.

- **DELETE Command:**

  Syntax: `DELETE FROM tablename [WHERE condition]`
  where **tablename** is the name of the table. condition contains a valid SQL condition/clause to be applied.
  DELETE command without **WHERE** clause will delete all the records from the table.

  Example:

  ```
  Delete from Employee Where Emp_id = 'E101';
  Delete from Employee Where Emp_id = 'E201' and  fname='Atul';
  ```

- **UPDATE Command:**

  If you want to modify existing data in the database, the **UPDATE** command can be used to do that. With this statement, you can update zero or more rows in a table.

  Syntax:

  ```
  UPDATE table_name
  SET column1 = value1, column2 = value2, ...
  ```

  `WHERE` condition;
  where **table_name** has the name of the table to be updated and **column_name** specifies the table column being updated; expression specifies an SQL expression, and condition specifies a SQL condition.
  The **UPDATE** statement gives at least one column an expression and refers to a single table. The **WHERE** clause is optional; if one is not present in an UPDATE statement, the value assigned to a column will be applied to every row in the table.

  Example:

  ```
  Update Employee Set City = 'Mumbai', State = 'Maharashtra';
  ```

- **SELECT Command:**

  SQL **SELECT** command is used to retrieve the data from a table in the database. The output results are also treated as a table and the result tables are titled result-sets.

  Syntax: `SELECT column1, column2, columnN FROM Tablename;`

  ```
  Options:   [WHERE condition(s)]
  [GROUPBY column-list]
  ```

```
[HAVING condition(s)]
[ORDER BY column-name(s)];
```

Here, column1, column2...are the columns/fields in a table whose values we want to retrieve. If we want to retrieve all the columns in the table, we can use the following command:

```
Select * from tablename;
```

Example: Consider the following employee table having the following records:

```
Select * from employee;
```

Output:

E_ID	E_name	E_dname	E_DOJ	E_salary
E101	ABHAY	RESEARCH	12-JAN-2020	70000
E102	NITA	FINANCE	08-FEB-2021	60000
E103	SOHAM	MARKETING	01-MAR-2022	50000
E104	POOJA	RESEARCH	08-MAR-2022	75000

If we want to retrieve **E_ID** and **E_name** from the employee table, we need to write the query as:

```
Select E_ID, E_name from employee;
```

Output:

E_ID	E_name
E101	ABHAY
E102	NITA
E103	SOHAM
E104	POOJA

- **DISTINCT clause:**

  To remove all duplicate records and retrieve only the unique records, the **SELECT** command is used with the **SQL DISTINCT** keyword.

  Some tables may contain several duplicate records; in this situation, it is required to retrieve only the unique records rather than retrieving duplicate records.

  Syntax: Syntax of **DISTINCT** keyword to retrieve unique records :

  ```
  Select distinct column1,column2….columnN  from tablename where condition;
  ```

  Example: Consider the following employee table:

E_ID	E_name	E_dname	E_DOJ	E_salary
E101	ABHAY	RESEARCH	12-JAN-2020	70000
E102	NITA	FINANCE	08-FEB-2021	60000

E103	SOHAM	MARKETING	01-MAR-2022	50000
E104	POOJA	RESEARCH	08-MAR-2022	75000

The query `Select distinct E_dname from the employee;`

will return the department name from the employee table having a unique name without any duplicate entry.

- **WHERE clause:**
    - The SQL **WHERE** clause is specified with the select command for giving a condition to retrieve the data from a table or from multiple tables after joining.
    - This query will filter and retrieve only those records from the table, upon which the condition given in the where clause is satisfied or holds true.
    - The **WHERE** clause can be used with the **UPDATE** and **DELETE** commands also.

  Syntax:

```
Select columnname1,columnname2,…..,columnnameN from tablename
where condition;
```

  Conditions may comprise logical or comparison operators such as **NOT**, **LIKE**, **>**, **<**, **=**, and so on.

  Examples:

  1. `select  E_ID from employee where salary>60000;`
  2. `select * from employee where E_dname='MARKETING';`

  Note:

  All the string values must be given within single quotes and numeric values without quotes.

  - *The SQL **AND** and **OR** operators are used to combine multiple conditions to narrow data in an SQL statement. These two operators are called **conjunctive operators.***
  - *These operators provide a means to make multiple comparisons with different operators in the same SQL statement.*

- **The AND operator**

  Multiple conditions can be combined in the where clause by using the **AND** operator.

  Syntax:

```
Select columnname1,columnname2,…..,columnnameN from tablename
where condition1  AND condition2 AND condition3;
```

- N number of conditions can be combined through the **AND** operator. All the conditions specified using this construct must hold **TRUE** while retrieving the results.

- Example: To retrieve the employee details from the employee table working in the research department and having a **salary >70000**, the query will be:

```
Select * from employee where salary>70000 AND E_dname='RESEARCH';
```

- **The OR Operator:**

  Many conditions can be combined using the **OR** operator with the **WHERE** clause in the **SELECT** query.

  Syntax:

```
Select columnname1, columnname2,…..,columnnameN from tablename
where condition1 OR condition2 OR condition3 ;
```

  N number of conditions can be combined using the **OR** operator with the **WHERE** clause.

  Any one of the conditions separated by OR specified using this construct must hold **TRUE** while retrieving the results.

- **Example:** To retrieve the employee details from the employee table working in the research department or having a **salary <75000**, the query will be:

```
SELECT * FROM employee WHERE salary < 75000 OR E_dname = 'RE-
SEARCH';
```

- **ORDER BY CLAUSE**

  The data can be retrieved in ascending or descending order based on single or multiple columns with the help of **ORDER BY** clause.

  Syntax:

```
SELECT column1, column2, ...
FROM table_name
WHERE condition
ORDER BY column_name [ASC | DESC], ...;
```

  More than one column from the column list in the table can be given with the ORDER BY clause.

- **Example:** To retrieve the employee details from the employee table order by their names having a salary >60000, the query will be:

```
SELECT * From employee where salary>60000 ORDER BY E_name;
```

Simple Calculations With SELECT Command

SQL allows you to perform simple arithmetic calculations directly within a **SELECT** statement. For instance, you can write queries such as **SELECT 20/5**; or **SELECT 100 - 20**.

In some database systems (such as, Oracle), if your calculation does not reference columns from a table, you need to include a dummy table in the FROM clause.

A common dummy table is **DUAL**, which contains a single row and a single column. You can use it like this:

```
SELECT 20/5 FROM DUAL;
```

Also, note that many database systems (such as, MySQL or PostgreSQL) do not require a dummy table in these cases. The previous calculations would work without a FROM clause.

Example:

- **Arithmetic calculation**:
  ```
  Select 10* 8 from dual;
  ```
- **Retrieving system date using dual**:
  ```
  Select sysdate from dual;
  ```

LIKE operator to find rows

In SQL, patterns are specified with the like operator. Pattern matching using the operator like is the most often used operation on strings. Two special characters are used to describe patterns.

- **Percent (%)**: Any substring is matched by the `%` character.
- The character matches any character with an underscore of (_).

For example, consider the following instances:

- Any string starting with `'aus'` is matched by "**aus%**".
- Any string that has "**dni**" as a substring is matched by **"%dni%"**.
- Any three characters can match "- - -".
- A string of at least three characters is matched by "- - - %".

Example:

To find the names of employees with names including "**ada**"

```
select emp_name from employee where e_name like "%ada";
```

SQL Functions:

- SQL built-in functions are used for data manipulation and retrieval of results.
- SQL functions can be classified as:
  - **Group Functions**
  - **Scalar Functions**

Group Functions:

- Group Functions work upon a group or set of values.
- A group functions input is the entire column of data as its arguments and an output is a single value summarizing that column.
- Some of the SQL group functions are:

Function	Description
`AVG`	Returns the average value of „N", ignoring NULL values
`COUNT(expr)`	Returns the number of rows where „expr" is not NULL
`COUNT(*)`	Returns the number of rows in the table including duplicates and those with NULL values
`MIN`	Returns the minimum value of „expr"
`MAX`	Returns the maximum value of „expr"
`SUM`	Returns sum of values „N"

Table 3.1: *SQL Group Functions*

Scalar Functions:

- Functions that act on only one value at a time are called scalar functions.
- We can further classify the functions using the type of data with which they are designed to work.

Function	Description
Numeric Functions	Work with numbers. Examples: **ABS**, **POWER**, **ROUND**, **SQRT**
String Functions	Work with character-based data. Examples: **LOWER**, **INITCAP**, **UPPER**, **SUBSTR**, **LENGTH**, **LTRIM**, **RTRIM**
Date Functions	Work with Date data types. Example: **ADD_MONTHS**, **LAST_DAY**, **MONTHS_BETWEEN**, **NEXT_DAY**
Conversion Functions	These functions are used to convert one type of data to another. Example: **TO_NUMBER**, **TO_CHAR**, **TO_DATE**

Table 3.2: *Classification of Functions*

`COUNT ( )` Function:

The number of values in a column can be counted using **`COUNT`** FUNCTION.

`COUNT (*)` returns the count of the number of rows in the table including duplicates and those with **`NULL`** values.

Example:

```
SELECT COUNT (*) FROM Employee;
```

This query will return the total no of rows in the employee table.

AVG ( ) Function:

The average of the numeric values in a column can be calculated using the **AVG** Function.

Example:

```
SELECT AVG (salary) FROM EMPLOYEE;
```

SUM ( ) Function:

The summation of the numeric values in a column can be calculated using the **SUM** Function.

Example:

```
SELECT SUM (salary) FROM EMPLOYEE;
```

MAX ( ) Function:

MAX( ) function returns the maximum value within the column from a table.

Example:

```
SELECT MAX (salary) FROM EMPLOYEE;
```

MIN ( ) Function:

MIN ( ) function returns the minimum value within the column from a table.

```
SELECT MIN (salary) FROM EMPLOYEE;
```

GROUP BY clause:

The Group By clause is used with the **SELECT** command for grouping similar or identical data in the form of groups.

Syntax:

```
Select columnname1, columnname2 from tablename where condition/conditions group by columnname1, columnname2 order by columnname1, columnname2;
```

Example: To find the number of employees in each department.

```
SELECT emp_ID, COUNT (emp_ID) FROM employee group by d_name;
```

HAVING CLAUSE

The **Having** clause is used with the **SELECT** command for giving condition. The difference between a Having clause and a Where clause is, a **Having** clause is used to give a condition upon a group of rows, and a Where clause is used to give a condition upon a single row. The difference lies in the processing of the query as, in having clause, first, the group formation is done and then the search condition is processed upon the group. However, in a where clause, the search condition on the row is implemented prior to the rows being grouped.

Syntax:

```
select columnname from tablename [where condition1…… conditionN] [group-
by columname1, columname 2, …… columnameN] [Having condition];
```

Example:

```
Select * from employee Group By department Having department = 'Finance';
```

Data Control Language

The instructions in the data control language have dealt with database security. They carry out the responsibilities of granting privileges and enabling users to access particular database items. This section focuses on DCL commands.

GRANT Command:

Other users cannot access an object produced by another user unless the owner of the item gives permission to do so. These permissions can be granted using the **GRANT** statement. A user can grant permission to another user if he is the owner of the object or if he is authorized to grant access to other users. The grant statement offers multiple ways to grant access to database objects including tables, views, and sequences.

Syntax:

```
GRANT privilege_name
ON object_name
TO {user_name |PUBLIC |role_name}
[WITH GRANT OPTION];
```

Object privileges:

The list of privileges that can be granted to a user is as follows:

- ***Alter***: Enables the grantee to change the table definition using the **ALTER TABLE** command.
- ***Delete***: Enables the grantee to remove the records from the table using the **DELETE** command.
- ***Index***: Enables the grantee to create or drop indexes on a table using the **CREATE INDEX** or **DROP INDEX** commands.

- ***Insert***: Enables the grantee to add records to the table using the **INSERT** command.
- ***Select***: Enables the grantee to query the tables using the **SELECT** command.
- ***Update***: Enables the grantee to modify the records in tables using the **UPDATE** command.
- ***With grant option***: Allows the grantee to grant object privileges to additional users.

Examples:

1. Grant all privileges on the Department table to user Rohan

   ```
   GRANT ALL ON Department to Rohan;
   ```

2. Grant select and update privileges on the Department table to Nita

   ```
   GRANT SELECT, UPDATE ON Department to Nita;
   ```

3. Grant all privileges on the Department table to user Rashmi with the grant option.

   ```
   GRANT ALL ON Department to Rashmi WITH GRANT OPTION;
   ```

REVOKE Command:

The **REVOKE** command is used to withdraw the grant given on an object.

Syntax:

```
REVOKE {object privileges} ON object name FROM user name;
```

The list of object privileges:

- ***Alter***: Permits the grantee to use the **ALTER TABLE** command to modify the table definition.
- ***Delete***: Permits the grantee to use the **DELETE** command to remove the records from the table.
- ***Index***: Permits the grantee to use the construct **INDEX** command to construct an index on a table.
- ***Insert***: Permits the grantee to use the **INSERT** command to add records to the table.
- ***Select***: Permits the grantee to use the **SELECT** command to query the tables.
- ***Update***: Permits the grantee to use the **UPDATE** command to change the records in tables.
- **REVOKE** command cannot be used in the following cases:
  1. To revoke the privileges that have not been granted by you.
  2. To Revoke the privileges granted through the operating system.

Example: Revoke Delete privilege on the Employee table from Pooja.

```
REVOKE DELETE ON employee from Pooja;
```

Revoke all the privileges on Employee that were granted to Pooja.

```
Revoke ALL ON Employee FROM Pooja.
```

`COMMIT` Command:

All changes made by the user to the database after the last commit command was issued, or since the start of the database session, are permanently recorded using the commit command.

Syntax:

```
COMMIT;
```

Implicit `COMMIT`:

Also, the list of commands provided is accurate for some database systems, especially Oracle, but it can vary slightly depending on the specific database system you are using. The general list of commands that typically cause implicit commits is as follows:

- **Data Definition Language (DDL) commands**: **`CREATE`**, **`ALTER`**, **`DROP`** (for tables, views, indexes, and so on.)
- **Data Control Language (DCL) commands**: **`GRANT`**, **`REVOKE`**
- **Transaction control commands**: **`COMMIT`**, **`ROLLBACK`**
- **Session control commands**: **`CONNECT`**, **`DISCONNECT`**

`ROLLBACK` command:

`COMMIT`: This command permanently saves the changes made within a transaction. Once you commit, you cannot undo those changes easily; you might need to restore from a backup).

`ROLLBACK`: This command undo all the changes made within a transaction. It reverts the database to the state it was in before the transaction started.

Syntax:

```
BEGIN TRANSACTION;
INSERT INTO employees VALUES (101, 'Alice');
SAVEPOINT before_insert_bob;
INSERT INTO employees VALUES (102, 'Bob');
ROLLBACK TO SAVEPOINT before_insert_bob; -- Undo only the insertion of Bob
COMMIT; -- Commits the insertion of Alice
```

where **`WORK`**: is optional and is provided for ANSI compatibility

`SAVEPOINT`: Savepoints are markers within a transaction that allow you to partially roll back a transaction to a specific point instead of undoing everything.

Rollback without savepoint clause can be used as:

- Completes the transaction
- Reverses every alteration made to the ongoing transaction
- Ends the transaction's savepoints
- Releases the locks on the transactions

Rollback with savepoint clause can be used as:

- Reverses only a part of the transaction
- Loses any savepoints produced after the designated savepoint but keeps the savepoint that was rolled back to
- Releases all row and table locks that have been obtained after the savepoint was made

Example:

To rollback entire transaction: `ROLLBACK`

To rollback to savepoint lp: `ROLLBACK TO SAVEPOINT lp`

Savepoint:

Savepoint identifies and records the current stage of a transaction's processing. Partially reverse a transaction using savepoint in conjunction with the **`ROLLBACK`** statement. The savepoint that has been specified since the most recent commit or rollback is active.

Syntax: `SAVEPOINT savepoint1:`

SET Operations in SQL

Two or more SQL select commands can be combined using SET operations in SQL.

The following types of SET operations are permissible in SQL:

- Union
- UnionAll
- Intersect
- Minus

- **Union**
    - The results retrieved using two or more select commands can be combined using the **`UNION`** operation.

- For the **UNION** operation to be applied upon, the number of columns and their data types from both the tables must be the same.
- The resultant table of **UNION** operation does not have any duplicate rows.

Syntax

```
SELECT columnname FROM tablename1 UNION SELECT columnname FROM
tablename2;
```

Example:

```
SELECT * from Employee UNION SELECT * from Department;
```

- **Union All**

Union all works in the same pattern as union operation. The resultant table/set returns all the rows containing duplicate rows as well.

Syntax:

```
SELECT columnname from tablename1   UNION ALL SELECT columnname
FROM tablename2;
```

Example: `SELECT * from Employee UNION ALL SELECT * from Department;`

- **Intersect**
  - The intersect operation returns the common rows present in both the tables upon which it is applied.
  - For the **INTERSECT** operation to be applied upon, the number of columns and their data types from both the tables must be the same.
  - The resulting table does not contain any duplicate rows. The data may be arranged in ascending order by default, but the specific ordering behavior can depend on the database system an explicit ORDER BY clause can be used to ensure a specific sorting order.

Syntax

```
SELECT columnname FROM tablename1 INTERSECT SELECT columnname
FROM tablename2;
```

Example:

```
SELECT * from Employee INTERSECT SELECT * from Department;
```

- **Minus**
  - The results of two select queries are combined using Minus operator. Minus operation returns the rows present in the first query but not in the second query.
  - This operation returns the results excluding the duplicate rows.

Syntax:

```
SELECT columnname FROM tablename1 MINUS SELECT columnname FROM tablename2;
```

Example:

```
SELECT * FROM Employee MINUS SELECT * FROM Department;
```

Views in SQL

Views are virtual tables in SQL. Views are created by selecting the fields from one or more than one table within the database. Views can also be created by selecting only selected rows within a table filtered based on some condition.

Syntax:

```
CREATE VIEW viewname AS  SELECT columname1, columname2..... FROM tablename
WHERE condition;
```

Creation of a View from a single table

```
CREATE VIEW EmpDetails AS SELECT Emp_name, Emp_address FROM Employee WHERE   emp_department= "finance";
```

Creation of a View from multiple tables

Views can be created by selecting the rows from multiple tables using the select query.

Example:

```
CREATE VIEW empDetails AS
SELECT
Employee.Emp_name,
Employee.Emp_address,
Department.Dname
FROM Employee
JOIN Department ON Employee.dept_id = Department.Dept_id;
```

We can retrieve the records from view using the command:

```
SELECT * FROM empDetails;
```

Deleting a View:

The drop view query can be used to delete the view.

Syntax

```
DROP VIEW viewname;
```

Example:

```
DROP VIEW empDetails;
```

Updating a View

Create or replace view query can be used for updating any view.

Syntax

```
CREATE OR REPLACE VIEW viewname AS SELECT columnname1, columnname2, ...
FROM tablename WHERE condition;
```

The following conditions must be satisfied for updating in any view using this create or replace view query.

- The **SELECT** statement which is used to create the view should not include a **GROUP BY** clause or **ORDER BY** clause.
- The **SELECT** statement should not have the **DISTINCT** keyword.
- The View should have all **NOT NULL** values.
- The view should not be created using nested queries or complex queries.
- The view should be created from a single table. If the view is created using multiple tables, then we will not be allowed to update the view.

Insertion of a row in a view:

Insert into statement is used to insert any row in a view.

Syntax:

```
INSERT INTO viewname (columnname1, columnname2, columnname3,..) VALUES
(value1, value2, value3..);
```

Example:

```
INSERT INTO EmpDetails (Emp_name, Emp_address) VALUES('Abhay','Mumbai');
```

Check Option with the Views

The **WITH CHECK OPTION** clause in SQL is a useful clause for views. It applies to an updatable view. If the view is not updatable, then there is no meaning in including this clause in the **CREATE VIEW** statement.

- The **WITH CHECK OPTION** clause is used to prevent the insertion of rows in the view where the condition in the **WHERE** clause in the **CREATE VIEW** statement is not satisfied.
- If we have used the **WITH CHECK OPTION** clause in the **CREATE VIEW** statement, and if the **UPDATE** or **INSERT** clause does not satisfy the conditions, then they will return an error.

Example:

```
CREATE VIEW EmpDetails AS SELECT Emp_ID, Emp_Name FROM Employee WHERE
Emp_Name IS NOT NULL WITH CHECK OPTION;
```

In this View, if we now try to insert a new row with a null value in the `NAME` column, then it will give an error because the View is created with the condition for `Emp_Name` column as `NOT NULL`.

For example, although the View is updatable then also the following query for this View is not valid:

```
INSERT INTO EmpDetails (Emp_ID) VALUES(E101);
```

Uses of a View:

Following are some of the valid reasons for the creation of views in the database:

- Restricting Data Access:

  Views provide an additional level of table security by restricting access to a predetermined set of rows and columns of a table.

- Hiding Data Complexity:

  A view can hide the complexity that exists in a multiple table join.

- Simplify Commands for the User:

  Views allow the user to select information from multiple tables without requiring the users to know how to perform a join.

- Store Complex Queries:

  Views can be used to store complex queries.

- Rename Columns:

  Views can also be used to rename the columns without affecting the base tables provided the number of columns in view must match the number of columns specified in the select statement. Thus, renaming helps to hide the names of the columns of the base tables.

- Multiple View Facility:

  Different views can be created on the same table for different users.

Stored Procedures in SQL

Stored Procedures are created to perform one or more DML operations on the Database. It is nothing but the group of SQL statements that accepts user input in the form of parameters, performs tasks, and may or may not return a value.

Syntax:

Creating a Procedure

```
CREATE or REPLACE PROCEDURE name(parameters) IS
variables;
BEGIN
//statements;
END;
```

Parameters are used to pass values to the Procedure. There are three different types of parameters, they are as follows:

- **IN**:
  This is the Default Parameter for the procedure. It always receives the values from the calling program.
- **OUT**:
  This parameter always sends the values to the calling program.
- **IN OUT**:
  This parameter performs both operations. It receives value from as well as sends the values to the calling program.

Example:

Consider a table named with employees present in the Database.

A Procedure is created to update the salary of employee with 2000.

```
CREATE or REPLACE PROCEDURE SAL_INC (empno IN NUMBER, sal_up OUT NUMBER)
IS BEGIN
UPDATE employee SET salary = salary+2000 WHERE empno = eno;
COMMIT;
SELECT salary INTO sal_up FROM employee WHERE empno = eno;
END;
```

Steps to execute the Procedure:

1. Declare a Variable to Store the value coming out from Procedure
   `VARIABLE n NUMBER;`
2. Execution of the Procedure:
   `EXECUTE SAL_INC (2002, :n);`
3. To check the updated salary, use **`SELECT`** statement:
   `SELECT * FROM employee WHERE empno = 2002;`
4. or Use print statement:
   `PRINT:n`

Stored Procedure with One Parameter: The following SQL statement creates a stored Procedure that selects employees from a city from the "**employee**" table:

Example

```
CREATE PROCEDURE SelectAllEmployees @City varchar2(20) AS
SELECT * FROM employee WHERE City = @City GO;
Execute the preceding stored procedure as follows:
Example

EXEC SelectAllEmployees @City = 'Nagpur';
```

Stored Procedure with Multiple Parameters:

To create a stored Procedure with multiple parameters, each parameter and the data type separated by a comma is listed as follows:

Example:

The following SQL statement creates a stored Procedure that selects employees from a city with a specific Postal Code from the "employees" table:

Example:

```
CREATE PROCEDURE SelectAllEmployees @City nvarchar(20), @PostalCode
nvarchar(15)
AS
SELECT * FROM employee WHERE City = @City AND PostalCode = @PostalCode
GO;
```

Example:

```
EXEC SelectAllEmployees @City = 'Nagpur', @PostalCode = 'N440002';
```

Cursors in SQL

A cursor is a database object that allows you to iterate through the result set of a query one row at a time. It acts as a pointer to the current row in the result set, enabling you to fetch and process data row by row.

Cursors are not temporary memory or workstations; they are managed by the database system to control access to the result set.

Cursors are not used to store database tables; they are used to retrieve and process data from tables.

Types of Cursor:

- **Implicit Cursor:**

  Implicit Cursor is also known as Default Cursors of SQL SERVER. These Cursors are allocated by SQL SERVER when the user performs DML operations.

- **Explicit Cursor:**

  Explicit Cursor is Created by Users whenever the user requires them. Explicit Cursors are used for Fetching data from Table in Row-By-Row Manner.

Creation of Explicit Cursor:

1. Declare Cursor Object.

   Syntax:

   ```
   DECLARE cursorname CURSOR FOR SELECT * FROM  tablename;
   ```

   Example:

   ```
   DECLARE c1 CURSOR FOR SELECT * FROM Employee;
   ```

2. **Open Cursor Connection.**

   Syntax: `OPEN cursor_connection   example: OPEN c1;`

3. **Fetch Data from the cursor**

   There are six methods to access data from the cursor.

   a. **`FIRST`** is used to fetch only the first row from the cursor table.

   b. **`LAST`** is used to fetch only the last row from the cursor table.

   c. **`NEXT`** is used to fetch data in the forward direction from the cursor table.

   d. **`PRIOR`** is used to fetch data in a backward direction from the cursor table.

   e. **`ABSOLUTE n`** is used to fetch the exact *n*th row from the cursor table.

   f. **`RELATIVE n`** is used to fetch the data in an incremental way as well as a decremental way.

   Syntax:

   ```
   FETCH NEXT/FIRST/LAST/PRIOR/ABSOLUTE n/RELATIVE n FROM cursorname;

   FETCH FIRST FROM c1; FETCH LAST FROM  c1; FETCH NEXT FROM  c1;
   FETCH PRIOR FROM c1;
   FETCH ABSOLUTE 6 FROM c1; FETCH RELATIVE -3 FROM c1;
   ```

4. **Close cursor connection.**

   Syntax: `CLOSE cursorname;`

   ```
   CLOSE c1;
   ```

5. **Deallocate cursor memory.**

   Syntax: `DEALLOCATE cursorname`

   ```
   DEALLOCATE c1;
   ```

Index in SQL

An index in SQL is a database object that increases the data retrieval operations speed on a table at the cost of additional writes and storage space. Indexes are created on columns that are frequently searched or used in query conditions, resulting in efficient data retrieval.

Types of Indexes:

- **Primary Index:**
    - Automatically created when a primary key is defined
    - Ensures uniqueness of the key
    - Efficiently retrieves rows based on the primary key
- **Unique Index:**
    - Ensures that all values in the indexed column(s) are unique
    - Can be created on any column, not just primary keys
- **Non-Unique Index:**
    - Speeds up data retrieval for columns with non-unique values
    - Does not enforce the uniqueness of the values
- **Clustered Index:**
    - Alters the physical order of the table and organizes data rows in the index order
    - Only one clustered index per table
    - Often created on the primary key
- **Non-Clustered Index:**
    - Creates a separate structure from the data rows
    - Can be multiple non-clustered indexes per table
    - Contains pointers to the data rows
- **Composite Index:**
    - Created on multiple columns
    - Useful for queries that filter based on multiple columns
- **Full-Text Index:**
    - Used for full-text searches
    - Suitable for text-heavy columns, like descriptions or large text fields

Creating Indexes:

- **Syntax:**
  ```
  CREATE INDEX index-name ON table-name (columnname1, columnname2, ...);
  ```
- **Example:**
  ```
  CREATE INDEX employee_name_idx ON Employee (LName, FName);
  ```

Dropping Indexes

- **Syntax:**
  ```
  DROP INDEX index-name ON table-name;
  ```
- **Example:**
  ```
  DROP INDEX employee_name_idx ON Employee;
  ```

Best Practices for indexing in SQL:

- **Wise Selection of Columns:**
  Index columns frequently used in **`WHERE`**, **`JOIN`**, and **`ORDER BY`** clauses
- **Limitation on the Number of Indexes:**
  Excessive indexing can degrade performance for **`INSERT`**, **`UPDATE`**, and **`DELETE`** operations
- **Use of Composite Indexes When Essential:**
  Create composite indexes for queries that filter on multiple columns
- **Monitoring of Index Usage:**
  Use database tools to analyze and monitor index usage and performance.
- **Avoid Indexing Columns with High Cardinality:**
  Columns with many unique values may not benefit from indexing.

Viewing Index Information:

- **View Existing Indexes:**
  ```
  SELECT * FROM sys.indexes WHERE object_id = OBJECT_ID ('table-name');
  ```
- **View Index Usage Statistics:**
  ```
  SELECT
  OBJECT_NAME(IXS.OBJECT_ID) AS Table_Name,
  IXS.NAME AS Index_Name,
  USER_SEEKS,
  USER_SCANS,
  USER_LOOKUPS,
  USER_UPDATES
  FROM SYS.DM_DB_INDEX_USAGE_STATS AS IXS
  WHERE OBJECTPROPERTY(IXS.OBJECT_ID, 'IsUserTable') = 1;
  ```

Triggers in SQL

A trigger is a special stored procedure that automatically executes/fires when any event occurs in the database server. Triggers are used to impose data integrity and business rules and accomplish automatic actions.

Types of Triggers

- **Data Definition Language(DDL) Triggers:**
  - Fire in response to DDL events, such as **CREATE**, **ALTER**, and **DROP** statements.
- **Data Manipulation Language(DML) Triggers:**
  - **AFTER Triggers (FOR Triggers):** Execute after an insert, update, or delete operation on a table.
  - **INSTEAD OF Triggers:** Execute in place of an insert, update, or delete operation.
- **Logon Triggers:**
  - Fire in response to logon events is used to control logon activity and manage security.

Creating DML Triggers

- **AFTER INSERT Trigger:**
```
CREATE TRIGGER trig_1 ON table_name AFTER INSERT AS BEGIN --
Trigger logic here PRINT 'AFTER INSERT Trigger fired';
END;
```
- **AFTER UPDATE Trigger:**
```
CREATE TRIGGER trig_2 ON table_name AFTER UPDATE AS BEGIN --
Trigger logic here PRINT 'AFTER UPDATE Trigger fired';
END;
```
- **AFTER DELETE Trigger:**
```
CREATE TRIGGER trig_3 ON table_name AFTER DELETE AS BEGIN --
Trigger logic here PRINT 'AFTER DELETE Trigger fired';
END;
```
- **INSTEAD OF INSERT Trigger:**
```
CREATE TRIGGER trig_4  ON table_name INSTEAD OF INSERT AS BEGIN
-- Trigger logic here PRINT 'INSTEAD OF INSERT Trigger fired';
 END;
```
- **INSTEAD OF UPDATE Trigger:**
```
CREATE TRIGGER trig_5 ON table_name INSTEAD OF UPDATE AS BEGIN --
Trigger logic here PRINT 'INSTEAD OF UPDATE Trigger fired';
END;
```

- **`INSTEAD OF DELETE` Trigger:**
  ```
  CREATE TRIGGER trig_6 ON table_name INSTEAD OF DELETE AS BEGIN --
  Trigger logic here PRINT 'INSTEAD OF DELETE Trigger fired';
   END;
  ```

Creating DDL Triggers

Example:

```
CREATE TRIGGER trig_ddl1 ON DATABASE FOR CREATE_TABLE, ALTER_TABLE,
DROP_TABLE AS BEGIN -- Trigger logic here PRINT 'DDL Trigger fired'; END;
```

Creating Logon Triggers

- **Logon Trigger Example:**
  ```
  CREATE TRIGGER trig_logon ON ALL SERVER FOR LOGON AS BEGIN --
  Trigger logic here PRINT 'Logon Trigger fired'; END;
  ```

Modifying and Dropping Triggers

- **Modifying a Trigger:**
  ```
  ALTER TRIGGER trig_name ON table_name FOR INSERT, UPDATE, DELETE
  AS BEGIN -- Updated trigger logic here PRINT 'Trigger logic up-
  dated'; END;
  ```
- **Dropping a Trigger:**
  ```
  DROP TRIGGER trig-name;
  ```

Using the `INSERTED` and `DELETED` Tables

- Triggers use special tables called **`INSERTED`** and **`DELETED`** to track changes.
  - **`INSERTED` Table:** Holds the new data being inserted or updated
  - **`DELETED` Table:** Holds the old data being deleted or updated

Example:

1. ```
   CREATE TRIGGER trig_after_insert ON Employee AFTER INSERT AS BE-
   GIN DECLARE @EmpID INT, @EmpName NVARCHAR(50); SELECT @EmpID =
   EmpID, @EmpName = EmpName FROM INSERTED; PRINT 'New Employee ID:
   ' + CAST(@EmpID AS NVARCHAR) + ', Name: ' + @EmpName; END;
   ```
2. ```
   CREATE TRIGGER trg_after_delete_example ON Employees AFTER DELETE
   AS BEGIN DECLARE @EmpID INT, @EmpName NVARCHAR(50); SELECT @EmpID
   = EmpID, @EmpName = EmpName FROM DELETED; PRINT 'Deleted Employee
   ID: ' + CAST(@EmpID AS NVARCHAR) + ', Name: ' + @EmpName; END;
   ```

Conclusion

Many applications still consider RDBMS a basic and trusted selection due to its offering of structured data management, strong consistency, and transactional support. Their ability to manage complex queries and ensure data integrity makes them critical for mission-critical systems in many industries. Despite this, the rise in data volumes and changing needs could make companies more open to using other databases to deal with special scalability or flexibility issues while relying on the strong base given by RDBMS. The next chapter focuses on query optimization and query processing where we will discuss how to optimize and process the query in database systems.

Questions

1. Differentiate between Unique Keys and Primary Keys with an example.
2. Explain the purpose of Referential Integrity and discuss the Foreign Key with a suitable example.
3. Distinguish between **DELETE** and **TRUNCATE** Commands.
4. Elaborate Local and Global variables in the context of RDBMS.
5. Differentiate between Relational Algebra and Relational Calculus with an example.
6. Define and discuss the unary operations in Relational Algebra.
7. Describe any four of Codd's rules/laws of RDBMS.
8. Explain the Referential Integrity constraint and **On Delete** Cascade with a suitable example.
9. Consider the schema student (**r_no**, **name**, **course**, **dob**, **percentage**, **class**) solve the following queries.
    a. Display the name of the students having name starting with letter 'M'.
    b. Display the list of students having a percentage more than 80 and having a course as '**Software engineering**'.
    c. Change the course to '**DBMS**' of student '**Amit**'.
    d. Display the list of students having more than 60% in the '**AIML**' course.
10. Consider the following Schema **Employee** (**ENO**, **ENAME**, **Department**, **Designation**, **DOJ**, **Salary**, **Dept_Location**)

Solve the following query.

a. List the employees having Designation as "**Dy. Manager**" and **Dept_Location** as "**Dehradun**"

b. Set the salary as ₹ 90,000/- having Designation as "**Project Leader**"

c. List **ENO**, **ENAME**, and **Salary** of employees having Salary between ₹10,000/- to ₹20,000/-

d. List **Ename** of employees having the second alphabet in the name as "M".

11. Cursors are very critical to searching for an element in a database. Justify this statement with an example.
12. Differentiate between row-level and column-level triggers.

Chapter 4
Query Optimization

Introduction

The query optimization is a key component of database management systems (DBMS), which looks at several query execution methodologies to find the most effective way to run a particular query. In other words, query optimization is the process of deciding on an effective execution strategy for a query. Reducing the number of system resources needed to answer the query and speeding up the return of answers are the objectives.

Query optimization is a crucial component of query processing. It seeks to select the transformation that uses the least number of resources among several comparable versions of a given high-level query. Generally speaking, our goal is to minimize the query's overall execution time, which is the total of the query's operation execution time. But resource consumption can also be understood as query response time, in which case we focus on increasing the number of parallel operations. The approach taken is typically limited to locating a near-optimal solution because the problem is computationally difficult with a higher number of relations.

Structure

In this chapter, we will cover the following topics

- Query Processing and Optimization
- Query Optimizer
- Challenges in Query Optimization
- Query Optimizer in DBMS
- Methods of Query Optimization in DBMS
- Analogy for the Optimizer
- Adaptive Query Optimization
- Cost Estimation for the Relational Algebra
- Optimizing Database Design
- Tools for Optimizing MySQL Queries

Query Processing and Optimization

One of the main complaints that were frequently raised during the relational model's initial commercial release was its poor query performance. Since then, a great deal of research has gone into creating extremely effective query-processing algorithms. There are numerous ways to execute a complex query, and one goal of query processing is to identify the most economical one. The low-level procedural query language in first-generation networks and hierarchical database systems is typically embedded in a high-level programming language like COBOL, and it is the programmer's job to choose the best execution method. On the other hand, the user defines what data is needed rather than how it will be retrieved when using declarative languages like SQL. This makes the terminology more widely applicable and absolves the user of the burden of figuring out–or even knowing–what makes an effective execution plan. Giving the DBMS the task of choosing the optimal approach also gives the DBMS more control over system performance and keeps users from selecting known to be inefficient strategies. Although the two approaches are typically blended in practice, there are two primary methods for query optimization. The first method arranges a query's operations according to heuristic principles. The other method chooses the strategy that uses the fewest resources by comparing several approaches according to their respective costs. Disc access is typically the primary cost in query processing for a centralized DBMS because it is slower than memory access.

The database statistics are necessary for both query optimization techniques to accurately assess the various possibilities. The effectiveness of the chosen execution approach is strongly influenced by the precision and timeliness of these statistics. Information regarding relations, properties, and indexes is covered by the statistics. Statistics indicating the cardinality of relations, the number of distinct values for each characteristic, and the number of levels in a multilevel index, for instance, may be stored in the system catalog.

Maintaining the statistics can present challenges. Performance would be severely impacted during peak times if the DBMS updated the statistics each time a tuple was added, changed, or removed. A different, and usually better, strategy would be to update the statistics regularly, for instance, every night or anytime the machine is inactive. Certain systems also impose an obligation on users to specify when they want the data to be updated.

This SQL statement has three comparable relational algebra queries. They are,

1. σ(Branch='CSE')∧(city='Delhi')∧(Student1.RollNo=Student2.RollNo) (Student1*Student2)

2. σ(Branch='CSE')∧ (city ='Delhi')(Student1.RollNo=Student2.RollNo)

3. (σBranch='CSE'(Student1))Student1.RollNo=Student2.RollNo (σcity='Delhi'(Student2))

In this instance, we'll assume that Student1 has 1000 tuples, Student2 has 50 tuples, 50 students in a branch, and five distinct cities are home to the students. Based on the number of disc accesses needed, we contrast these three queries. We'll assume for the sake of simplicity that neither relation has any sort of keys or indexes, and that any intermediate operations' output is saved to disc. Since the final write costs the same in every instance, they are disregarded. We also assume that the main memory is large enough to handle full relations for each relational algebra operation and that tuples are accessed one at a time.

The first query builds a connection with (1000 * 50) tuples and computes the Cartesian product of Student1 and Student2. Reading the relations requires (1000 + 50) disc accesses. After that, at a cost of additional (1000 * 50) disc accesses, we must read each of these tuples once more to test them against the selection criteria. This results in a total cost of:

$$(1000 + 50) + 2*(1000 * 50) = 101\ 050$$

To link Students 1 and 2 on the RollNo, the second query necessitates (1000 + 50) disc accesses to read each relation. We are aware that there are 1000 tuples in the joining of the two relations, one for each student in Student1. Consequently, 1000 disc accesses are needed for the Selection operation to read the join result, resulting in a total cost of:

$$2*1000 + (1000 + 50) = 3050$$

To identify the CSE tuples—which involve 1000 disc accesses and result in a relation of 50 tuples—the final query first reads each Student1 tuple. To identify the Delhi cities, the second selection operation reads each Student2 tuple. This takes 50 disc accesses and generates a relation with 5 tuples. The joining of the decreased Student1 and Student2 relations is the last operation, and it costs a total of (50 + 5) disc accesses.

$$1000 + 2*50 + 5 + (50 + 5) = 1160$$

By a ratio of 87:1, the third choice is the best in this scenario. The improvement would be by a factor of about 870:1 if we increased the number of tuples in Student1 to 10,000 and the number in Student2 to 500. Given that, the third alternative drastically reduces the size of the relations being brought together and since the Cartesian product and Join procedures are far more expensive than the Selection operation, it may have seemed intuitive to anticipate this. As we'll see in a moment, completing the unary operations of selection and projection as soon as possible reduces the operands of any later binary operations and is one of the core methods in query processing.

One possibility is to do optimization and decomposition dynamically each time the query is executed. The benefit of dynamic query optimization is that all the data needed to choose the best course of action is current. The drawback is that the query's performance is impacted since it must first be processed, validated, and optimized before it can be run. It may also be necessary to reduce the number of execution strategies that must be looked at to achieve an acceptable overhead, which could result in the choice of a less-than-ideal method.

Static query optimization is an alternative that involves parsing, validating, and optimizing the query only once. This method is comparable to that used by a programming language compiler. Static optimization has the advantage of eliminating runtime overhead and potentially freeing up more time for evaluating a greater number of execution strategies, which increases the likelihood of identifying a more optimal solution. Finding a more optimal plan may take some extra effort, but it can be quite helpful for queries that are run frequently. The reason for the drawbacks is that the optimal execution technique selected during query compilation might not remain such during query execution. To get around this drawback, a hybrid strategy might be employed, in which the query is re-optimized if the system notices that there have been significant changes in the database statistics since the query was last generated.

As an alternative, the system might generate the query for each session's first execution and then cache the best plan for the duration of the session, distributing the cost over the course of the whole DBMS session. The initial step in query processing is called query decomposition. A high-level query is transformed into a relational algebra query using query decomposition, which also verifies the query's syntactic and semantic accuracy. Analysis, normalization, semantic analysis, simplification, and query rearrangement are the usual phases of query decomposition.

Analysis

Here, the question is examined syntactically and lexically through the use of programming language compiler techniques. Furthermore, this phase confirms that the properties and relations mentioned in the query are defined in the system catalog. Additionally, it confirms that any modifications made to database objects are suitable for the particular kind of item. For instance, think about the following question:

```
Student
(
RollNo Varchar(10),
Name Char(20),
Branch Char(20)
);
 SELECT RollNumber  FROM Student WHERE Branch= 10;
```

This query would be rejected on two grounds:

- In the select list, the attribute `RollNumber` is not defined for the `Student` relation (should be `RollNo`).
- The comparison in the WHERE clause '`>10`' is incompatible with the data type Branch, which is a variable character string.

The high-level query has been converted into an internal representation that is better suited for processing at this point. Usually, some sort of query tree is selected as the internal form, and it is built as follows:

- For every base relation in the query, a leaf node is constructed; for every intermediary relation generated by a relational algebra action, a non-leaf node is created.
- The query's outcome is represented by the tree's root.
- The operations are carried out in a leaf-to-root order.

Normalization

During the normalization phase of query processing, the query's predicate (the WHERE clause condition) is transformed into a simpler and more standardized form to facilitate subsequent optimization steps. This often involves converting the predicate into conjunctive normal form (CNF) or disjunctive normal form (DNF) or applying other transformations like constant folding and predicate pushdown.

- **Conjunctive Normal Form (CNF)**: A series of AND-connected clauses, where each clause is an OR-connected set of literals (atomic conditions).
- **Disjunctive Normal Form (DNF)**: A series of OR-connected clauses, where each clause is an AND-connected set of literals.

These normal forms, along with other transformations, help the query optimizer identify potential optimizations and select the most efficient execution plan.

Semantic Analysis

Semantic analysis aims to reject normalized questions that are inconsistent or poorly constructed. If some join specifications are missing and some components do not contribute to the creation of the result, then the query is wrongly formulated. If no tuple can satisfy the predicate of a query, then it is contradictory.

Correctness algorithms are available exclusively for the subset of queries free of negation and disjunction. We may use the following tests for these queries:

- Create a graph of relations between connections. The query is formulated wrongly if there is no connectivity in the graph. We make a node for the result and a node for each relation to build a relation connection graph. Next, we make edges between nodes that indicate a join and between nodes that indicate the projection operations' source.
- Create an attribute connection graph that is normalized.

The query is paradoxical if there is a cycle in the graph for which the valuation sum is negative. For every reference to an attribute, or constant 0, we establish a node to build a normalized attribute connection network. Next, a directed edge representing a join is created between nodes, and another representing a selection operation is created between an attribute node and a constant 0 node. Subsequently, we assign a value of c to the edges $a \rightarrow b$ in case they represent the inequality condition $(a < b + c)$, and a value of $-c$ to the edges $0 \rightarrow$ an in case they represent the inequality condition $(a \geq c)$.

Simplification

The goals of the simplification stage are identifying superfluous qualifications, getting rid of repetitive subexpressions, and changing the question into a semantically identical but easier-to-calculate form. At this point, view definitions, integrity requirements, and access limitations are typically taken into account; some of them may also cause redundancy. The query must be refused if the user lacks the necessary access to any of its components.

Query Restructuring

During the ultimate phase of decomposing a query, it is reorganized to yield a more effective implementation.

Query Optimizer

SQL is a structured query language that provides the database with "what" it wants but not "how" to get the desired results. The query optimizer, the "brain" of the database, decides this "how". A highly trained travel agent who arranges the most economical route for a vacation might be likened to a query optimizer. The travel agent does more than simply pick the easiest route on a map when you give them your intended locations. Rather, they take into account a variety of criteria, including the cost of the trip, the time it takes to get between locations, the accessibility of the transportation alternatives, and any potential delays like bad weather or traffic.

Similar to this, a query optimizer looks at different query plans and their associated costs to discover the most cost-effective way to execute a SQL query. To guarantee that the database operates at peak efficiency, it considers several choices before selecting the best execution plan. Similar to a travel agent, the query optimizer operates in the background to provide the user with the optimal outcome without requiring them to be concerned with the minute details of the procedure.

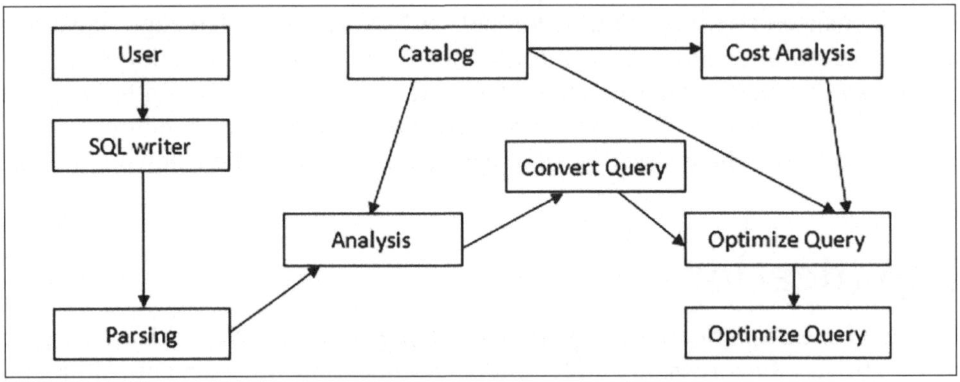

Figure 4.1: *Query Optimizer*

Optimization

The process of query optimizer is divided into three main categories

A database keeps records of customers and orders. We are interested in finding out which customers have placed orders.

- **Enumerate alternative execution plans:** Several execution plans can be generated by the optimizer for the desired query results. In this example, different possible plans would include:
    a. Get all rows from the orders table where the order date is within the last 30 days and then join with the customer's table.
    b. Quickly identify relevant orders using the index on the order date and join with the customer's table.
    c. First, filter the customer's table according to any available criteria and join the filtered customer data with the orders table. These plans are generated by considering factors, such as table structure, availability of indexes, and system resources.
- **Estimate the cost of each execution plan:** Each execution plan's cost is assessed by an optimizer based on statistical information as well as a cost model. Cost estimation in this case may involve:
    - **Time taken for execution**: Expected duration for each scheme
    - **CPU usage**: The level of processing power required for every solution
    - **I/O operations**: The number of disks needed for reading and writing for each plan
    - Data transfer between nodes in distributed systems

- **Choose the optimal execution plan:** To ensure the most efficient query execution feasible, the optimizer chooses the execution plan among the listed plans with the lowest estimated cost. In this case, if the cost estimates indicate that plan B—which employs an index based on the order date—is the most cost-effective alternative, it may select it.

Rule-Based Optimizer (RBO) and Cost-Based Optimizer (CBO)

An RBO is comparable to a conventional paper map for navigation, which uses a predetermined set of routes to lead to the destination without taking into account other circumstances or the state of the traffic. A CBO is comparable to a contemporary GPS navigation system that estimates the duration and cost of each route based on real-time traffic data, road conditions, and many route possibilities.

- **Rule-Based Optimizer (RBO):** The routes are precise and current, this approach may work well; however, it is less adaptable and might not take into consideration unforeseen events, such as construction, heavy traffic, or road closures, which occasionally results in less-than-ideal routes.
- **Cost-Based Optimizer (CBO):**

  The navigation system ensures faster and smoother travel by choosing the proper way. Similarly, this technique requires accurate traffic information and a reasonable estimation model to work effectively like CBO needs accurate statistics data and a suitable cost model to optimize query execution. RBO is a stricter optimizer than CBO. It may not generate the best plan when data changes. Instead, CBO relies on statistics and cost models to determine the best plan. The quality of statistics and the cost model impact the capability of CBO to select the best plan.

  Statistics calculate the cost while the cost model is the main algorithm. In addition, they work in unison for costing purposes. When there are no statistics, default values are used by the cost model which can be far different from actual values leading to an inefficient plan being chosen. Hence, accurate statistics are required for the CBO model to perform better. If we don't have correct statistical data, then it will be hard to optimize queries.

Challenges in Query Optimization

When it comes to relational database systems, the query optimizer forms the fundamental component that is primarily concerned with kernel development in databases. Moreover, it acts as a "peg" for gauging how mature the whole database system is. Despite existing for over forty years now, there is still this condition where core challenges remain unsolved regarding query optimization–how to get the best execution plan given limited system resources.

Challenge 1: Accurate statistical information and cost models help in calculating costs that are used by execution plans, particularly statistical info and cost models for query optimization. Obtaining accurate statistical information and creating sound cost models has always been difficult for database systems for the following reasons:

- **Statistical information**: From a database perspective, there are two major problems associated with collecting statistical information. Firstly, sampling error necessarily occurs when data is collected through sampling methods. Secondly, there is a certain delay in gathering statistical information. This means that the optimization of an SQL query often involves the use of statistical information from previous times.
- **Calculation for Selectivity and Estimation Using Intermediate Results**: Calculation of selectivity has always been a challenge in database systems. Techniques have been developed by both academia and industry to enhance the accuracy of selectivity calculation including dynamic sampling, and multi-column histograms among others. However, there are still some challenges that remain unresolved; to illustrate this, one can consider calculating the selectivity of JOIN predicates as an example.

Challenge 2: Complex Plan: The number of possible execution plans for complex queries is enormous. In fact, enumeration of all equivalent execution plans may not be possible even in most cases. Query optimizers have always experienced difficulties with effectively enumerating execution plans in such a large plan space.

Query Optimizer in DBMS

The optimizer attempts to generate the optimal SQL statement execution plan. The optimizer selects the plan with the lowest cost out of all the candidate plans that are assessed. Based on the information the optimizer calculates costs. For a particular query in a given environment, the cost computation for query execution depends on the factors, such as I/O, CPU, and communication.

Sr. No	Class	Name	Role
01	10	Shrey	CR
02	10	Tanvi	
03	10	Manoviraj	
04	10	Uttkarsh	

Table 4.1: *Student Details*

One question, for instance, asks for details about students who hold leadership positions, such as class representatives. The optimizer may determine that a full table search is the most effective if the statistics indicate that % of students hold leadership positions. It might be more effective to read an index first, then use row ID to access the database rather than doing a full table scan if the data indicate that just a small percentage of students hold leadership roles.

As the database has access to so much internal information and tools, the optimizer is often better able to determine how to execute a statement than the user. Thus, every SQL statement uses the optimizer.

Optimizer Components

The transformer, estimator, and plan generator are the three components that make up the optimizer. These are shown in the following figure:

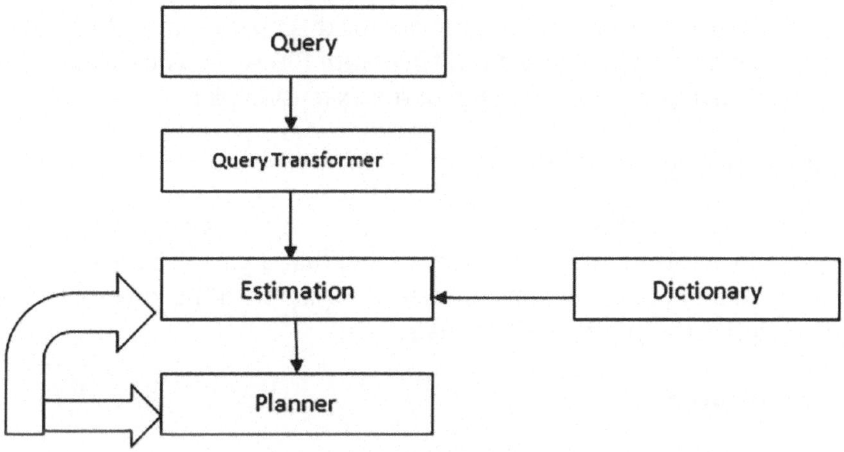

Figure 4.2: *Query Optimizer components*

Query Transformer

For certain statements, the query transformer decides whether it makes sense to rewrite the original SQL statement into a more affordable, semantically comparable version. The database selects the option with the lowest cost after comparing the expenses of each conceivable alternative.

Estimator

The optimizer component that determines the overall cost of a specific execution plan is called the estimator.

The estimator uses distinct techniques to calculate the cost:

- **Selectivity:** With 0 denoting no rows and 1 denoting every row in the row set, the query selects a proportion of the rows. A predicate becomes more selective as the selectivity value gets closer to zero, and less selective (or more unselective) as the value gets closer to one.

  The row set, for instance, could be the outcome of a join, a view, or a base table. A query predicate is connected to the selectivity, such as **`last_name = 'Patni'`**, or a combination of predicates, such as **`last_name = 'Patni' AND job_id = 'TCED'`**.

- **Cardinality**: The number of rows that each action returns is the cardinality of an execution plan. All cost functions share this input, which is crucial for choosing the optimal course of action. In DBMS, cardinality can be computed with the help of **`DBMS STATS`** table statistics or by considering the influence of predicates (filter, join, and more), **`DISTINCT`** or **`GROUP BY`** operations, and so on. An execution plan's estimated cardinality is shown in the Rows column. For instance, the cardinality estimate for this operation is 100 if the optimizer predicts that a full table scan will generate 100 rows. The cardinality estimate is displayed in the Rows column of the execution plan.

Cost Analysis

Cost analysis in query optimization involves estimating the amount of resources (such as disk I/O, CPU utilization, and memory usage) that a particular execution plan will consume. The query optimizer aims to select the plan with the lowest estimated cost, often a good indicator of better performance.

Plan Generator

The plan generator experiments with different join orders, join algorithms, and access paths to look into several possible plans for a query block.

Numerous designs are accessible due to the various combinations that the database can use to produce the same result. The optimizer selects the plan with the lowest cost.

Tuning Optimizer:

The optimization process carries out distinct tasks based on its mode of invocation.

The database provides the subsequent categories of optimization:

- **Typical optimization**: After parsing the SQL, the optimizer creates an execution plan. For most SQL statements, the standard mode provides a suitable plan. When running in normal mode, the optimizer has very strict time constraints–often a fraction of a second–that it must meet to find the best plan.

- **Optimizing SQL Tuning Advisor**: When one or more SQL statements are sent as input to the optimizer by SQL Tuning Advisor, it is referred to as the Automatic Tuning Optimizer. In this case, further analysis is carried out by the optimizer to enhance the plan produced in standard mode. To provide a much better plan, the optimizer generates a collection of tasks along with their justification and expected payoff.

Methods of Query Optimization in DBMS

The following are the approaches used for query optimization.

DBMS Cost-Based Query Optimization

The process of determining the most effective way to run a SQL statement is known as query optimization. The optimizer can combine, rearrange, and process data in any order as SQL is a nonprocedural language.

For a given query and environment, the optimizer assigns a numerical cost to each step of a feasible plan. It then aggregates these values to obtain a cost estimate for the plan or potential strategy. After comparing the costs of all workable designs, the optimizer seeks to identify the plan with the lowest estimated cost. It is because of this that the optimizer is occasionally referred to as the Cost-Based Optimizer.

Execution Plans

The ideal method for executing a SQL statement is specified in an execution plan. The plan outlines the actions that Oracle Database takes to carry out an SQL statement. For the user of the statement, each step physically retrieves or gets ready rows of data from the database.

An execution plan displays the cost of each operation in addition to the plan's total cost, which is indicated on line 0. To enable plan comparisons, a cost is an internal unit that only appears in the execution plan. Consequently, it is not possible to fine-tune or alter the cost value.

Query Blocks

An SQL statement's parsed form is fed into the optimizer. A query block serves as the internal representation for each SELECT block in the original SQL statement. A subquery, an unmerged view, or a top-level statement can all be found in a query block. Consider the following SQL statement, which consists of two query portions. The subquery included in parenthesis is the inner query block. The names of the employees in the departments whose IDs were provided by the subquery are obtained by the remaining outer query block of the SQL statement. The connections between query blocks are specified in the query form.

```
Select stu_name from student where dept_ID IN (Select dept_ID from
department where building_id=5);
```

Query Sub Plans

For each query block, the optimizer generates a query sub-plan.

The database optimizes query blocks independently from the bottom up. Consequently, the database generates a sub-plan for the innermost query block first, then optimizes it, and finally generates the outer query block, which is the whole query.

The number of items in the FROM clause corresponds to the number of query block plans. This number grows exponentially with the number of objects. For example, there are many more possibilities for a join of five tables than there are for a connection of just two tables.

Analogy for the Optimizer

One comparison for the optimizer would be an online travel advisor.

A cyclist wants to know which route from point A to point B is the most efficient. "I need the quickest route from point A to point B" or "I need the quickest route from point A to point B via point C" are comparable expressions to a query. The journey advisor uses an internal algorithm that considers variables, such as speed and difficulty to select the most effective route. By stating things like "I want to arrive as quickly as possible" or "I want the simplest route possible," the cyclist can influence the trip advisor's decision.

An execution plan in this case is a potential course that the travel advisor has created. The advisor may internally split the main route into several subroutes, or sub plans, and calculate the efficiency of each subroute independently. The trip advisor might predict, for instance, that a medium-difficulty subroute will take fifteen minutes, a low-difficulty subroute will take twenty-two minutes, and so on. The advisor determines the most efficient overall route based on the user-specified goals and easily accessible information about roads and traffic conditions. The numbers are more accurate when the guidance is better. For instance, the suggested route could not work well if the advisor is not kept informed about traffic jams, road closures, and unfavorable road conditions.

Adaptive Query Optimization

Using adaptive query optimization, the optimizer can modify execution plans at runtime and find fresh data that could produce better statistics. Adaptive optimization is useful in situations where the available data is insufficient to generate an optimal plan.

- **Adaptive Query Plans:** When deciding on a final plan for a statement using an adaptive plan, the optimizer can wait until execution time.
- **Purpose of Adaptive Query Plans:** Optimizer flexibility to modify a plan in response to execution-related information can greatly improve query performance.

  Adaptive plans are crucial because sometimes the optimizer selects a subpar default plan because of a cardinality misestimate. The ability to adjust the plan in real time based on execution statistics results in a final plan that is more optimal. After choosing the best plan, the optimizer uses it for subsequent executions, ensuring the bad plan is never utilized again.

Adaptive Query Plans

An optimizer statistics collector and multiple predetermined subplans comprise an adaptive plan.

A sub-plan is a portion of a plan that can be executed differently by the optimizer. For example, during execution, a nested loop join may become a hash join. A row source that is inserted at strategic junctures in a plan to gather run-time data is called an optimizer statistics collector. These numbers let the optimizer select a final option from a variety of subplans.

The statistics collector gathers execution data while the statement is being executed and buffers part of the rows that the sub-plan receives. The data that the collector gathers is used by the optimizer to choose a sub-plan. At this moment, rows are allowed to travel through and the collector ceases gathering statistics and buffering records. Until the plan ages out of the cache or is rendered incorrect by another optimizer feature (such as adaptive cursor sharing or statistics feedback), the optimizer uses the same plan on further executions of the child cursor.

Parallel Distribution Methods:

- Data redistribution is usually required for operations, such as parallel sorts, aggregations, and joins when using parallel processing. The Oracle Database offers a large selection of data distribution methods. The number of rows to be distributed and the number of concurrent server processes involved in the operation determine which strategy the database will use. Think about the possible situation that follows:
- Several server processes are running concurrently, distributing a few rows. The broadcast distribution mechanism is one that the database can choose to use. In this case, every row in the result set is received by every concurrent server process.

- A lot of rows are distributed by a small number of simultaneous server processes. The statement's performance can deteriorate if a data skew is discovered during the data redistribution process. To guarantee that every concurrent server process obtains an equivalent quantity of records, the database is likely to employ a hash distribution.

These techniques do not all have to be accurate. Additionally, the size of the table, the number of columns, the projection, the join sort, the constraints, the indexes, the statistics, and so on have a role.

Cost Estimation for the Relational Algebra

The relational algebra operations can be implemented in a DBMS in a variety of ways. The goal of query optimization is to select the most effective one. It accomplishes this by estimating the costs of multiple options using equations and choosing the option with the lowest cost. This section looks at the various ways to implement the primary operations in relational algebra. We include an estimated cost and a summary of the implementation for each. Since disc accesses are slower than memory accesses and typically account for most query processing costs, we have focused our calculations solely on disc access costs. With the exception of the expense of writing the result relation, each estimate indicates the necessary number of disc block accesses.

The cardinality of the relation serves as the foundation for many of the cost estimations. Consequently, we also present some typical estimates that can be derived for such cardinalities, as we also need to estimate the cardinality of intermediary links. To aid in cost assessment, we begin this section by looking at the kinds of statistics that the DBMS will keep in the system catalog.

Optimizing Database Design

Optimizing database design is crucial for handling large workloads and volumes of data efficiently, ensuring scalability and performance. Some key optimization strategies include:

- Normalized tables can aid in lowering unnecessary memory consumption.
- In SQL Shell, properly indexed tables can shorten the query loading time.
- An effective and simplified data management system is created by configuring the database according to RAM allocation, cache restrictions, and other database settings. This is also effective in managing large query workloads.

Understanding MySQL Queries

An SQL statement that directs the database to carry out particular actions is called a MySQL query. Data can be retrieved, added, updated, or deleted from a MySQL database using these queries.

Various parts make up a MySQL query's basic structure:

- `SELECT`: To retrieve the records as per the given condition.
- `FROM`: Specify the relational databases from which we want to retrieve records.
- `WHERE`: Specify the condition on which we want to retrieve the records, for example, find out the names of all the students whose city is Delhi.
- `JOIN`: To join the multiple relations and fetch the records.
- `GROUP BY`: To group the records based on a common value like finding the number of employees department-wise.
- `HAVING`: To be used with group by like where clause is used. For example, finding the average salary department-wise having an average salary greater than a specific amount.
- `ORDER BY`: Sorts the records based on the value of an attribute like we can sort the records in the increasing order of salary.
- `LIMIT`: It limits the number of records.
- **Data Retrieval:** For data retrieval, you usually utilize the **`SELECT`** command. It lets you use the **`WHERE`** clause to filter the data according to circumstances and to define the columns you wish to retrieve from the MySQL database. As an illustration:

  ```
  SELECT name, Roll_no  FROM student where Branch = 'CSE';
  ```
- **`INSERT INTO`** command is used for inserting the records

  ```
  INSERT INTO student values (Roll_no, Name, City, Branch) Values
  (11, 'Mohit', 'Dehradun', 'CSE');
  ```
- We can also update the data within the relation by using the update command.

  ```
  Update student
  Set name='Rohit' where Roll_no=11;
  ```

  This command will change the name from Mohit to Rohit.
- The delete command is used for deleting the records from a relation.

  ```
  Delete from student where roll_no=11;
  ```

  In this case, the record having `roll_no` will be deleted.

MySQL is also used for more complex queries, such as join, trigger, cursor, and so on.

- **Joins:** It gives the records from multiple relations.
- **Aggregate Functions:** Result based on the aggregate function, such as calculating sum, average, and count.
- **Subqueries:** It is divided into two parts inner query and outer query; the result of the inner query will be the input for the outer query.

- **Indexing:** For quicker data retrieval, indexes should be created for columns that are used often.

Data engineers may efficiently interface with databases and perform operations to change data to the requirements of their applications by grasping these ideas. Common problems that affect MySQL query performance are as follows:

When implementing MySQL queries, data engineers encounter seven common problems:

- **Missing or Insufficient Indexes**: MySQL database performance can be greatly enhanced by indexing the columns used in WHERE, JOIN, and ORDER BY clauses. MySQL must do full table scans in the absence of suitable indexes, which slows down queries.
- **Ineffective Query Design**: Slow queries can be caused by poorly written queries that include intricate joins, subqueries, or pointless calculations. Performance can be increased by streamlining and optimizing the query format.
- **Big Result Sets**: MySQL speed may suffer and memory usage may be high if a lot of rows are retrieved from the database. To obtain only the information they require, LIMIT clauses or pagination can be employed.
- **Inadequate Hardware Resources**: Database performance may suffer if the MySQL server is operating on hardware with constrained capabilities, such as CPU, RAM, and disc I/O.
- **Locking and Contention**: Problems with locking and contention might arise from concurrent access to the same data.
- **Improper Database Schema Design**: Complicated queries and poorer performance might arise from ill-conceived database schemas with redundant or excessive normalization.
- **Inadequate Network Connectivity**: Performance is hampered by sluggish connections between the client and the MySQL server, particularly for queries with big result sets.

Importance of MySQL Query Optimization

MySQL query optimization has a direct impact on the success and overall performance of the application by improving the speed and efficiency of data retrieval. Among the main advantages of improving MySQL performance are:

- **Enhanced Performance**: Quicker query execution results in shorter application response times. Higher customer satisfaction and a more seamless user experience are the results of this improved performance.
- **Scalability**: Optimized queries guarantee that the database can effectively

manage the additional load without compromising speed as your application expands and manages greater data volumes.

- **Resource Utilization**: Less CPU and memory usage by efficient searches results in cheaper infrastructure expenses.
- **Less Downtime**: Optimizing queries reduces the possibility of crashes and performance bottlenecks, which improves system stability and cuts down on downtime.
- **Quicker Development**: Developers may concentrate on creating new features and functions rather than spending time debugging slow queries, which results in shorter development cycles.
- **Better User Experience**: More responsive applications are able to retain users' attention and lower bounce rates. This is achieved through faster data retrieval and processing times.
- **Database Maintenance**: Managing and keeping an eye on the MySQL database is made simpler by well-designed queries.
- **Cost Savings**: As they minimize the need for additional hardware, maximize server utilization, and enhance system performance, efficient inquiries can result in cost savings.
- **Competitive Advantage**: Faster application performance might give your company an advantage over rivals in a highly competitive market, drawing and keeping clients.
- **Managing Significant Traffic**: Optimization guarantees that the system can manage a large number of concurrent queries without sacrificing speed for web applications that experience significant user traffic.
- **Future-Proofing**: Well-designed queries can adapt to shifting workloads and data patterns, preserving the responsiveness and dependability of your application throughout time.

Optimization Techniques

You can use `LIMIT` to limit the number of rows returned. Usually, SQL editors such as dbeaver provide a feature that restricts the amount of data that can be returned to 100 or 200. You won't inadvertently retrieve thousands of rows of data when you only want to look at a few, thanks to its built-in functionality. These functions come in handy when looking at the results of a transformation you've been working on or while creating validation queries. They are useful for trying things out and finding out more about how your code works. But in automated data models, where you want to return all of the data, these kinds of functions are not recommended.

```
Select student_name from student order by roll_no DESC LIMIT 100;
```

Even if you have more than 100 students, this will only return 100 rows. If you wish to skip certain rows in the first 100 but not return the first 100, you may also use an OFFSET clause in your LIMIT methods. To choose the next 100 clients after skipping the first 20 rows, you would write:

```
Select student_name from student order by roll_no DESC LIMIT 100 OFFSET
20;
```

Although these inquiries aid in data limitation, cloud data platforms also lessen the effect of repetitive requests by utilizing caching. Additionally, you can keep frequently asked queries in temporary tables on cloud platforms. Ensure that they are removed after using them.

Utilize Stored Procedures

SQL code is included in database objects called stored procedures. They can streamline logic and expedite development times by being automated and reused. Consider them as "functions" that can be saved and used in your programming environment, similar to those found in Python and Javascript.

As stored procedures compile and cache code, they enable faster execution of frequently used queries, which enhances performance in your cloud database. They also help engineers by streamlining numerous tasks as they are reusable pieces of code. The repetitive writing of the same code is not a concern for developers. Alternatively, they can use pre-existing SQL routines in the form of stored procedures.

Partitioning and Sharding

There are two methods you may employ to distribute data around the cloud: partitioning and sharding.

One big table can be partitioned into several smaller tables, each with its unique partition key. Usually, partition keys are determined by the timestamps of the rows' creation or even by the integer values contained in them. The server will automatically direct you to the partitioned table suitable for your query when you run a query on this table. The performance is improved because it is only searching a portion of the table and not the complete one.

The main difference between sharding and splitting a large table into smaller tables is that sharding splits a large database into smaller databases. A sharding key is used in place of a partition key to reroute queries to the relevant database. Sharding is recognized for its ability to boost processing speeds by distributing the load among multiple servers, each of which operates concurrently. As they are independent of one another, it also increases the availability and dependability of databases. The other databases remain unaffected if one goes down. Remember that this is something that contemporary cloud data platforms perform automatically when you specify the distribution type and partition key during load. Additionally, Aurora, a relational database product from AWS, automates sharding and partitioning.

Normalize Database Tables

It ensures that the values in your database tables are simple to find and the query is the foundation of normalization. To make it easier to query the values later on, normalization should be done at the layer that is closest to your raw data.

Monitor Query Performance

When trying to optimize SQL queries, monitoring query performance is essential. You'll never be able to tell which queries are taking the longest if you never check their run-time! This is essential for figuring out which ones will save the most money on cloud databases and which ones require optimization.

Query profiling is one tool for speed optimization. This makes it possible to identify the cause of performance problems by examining metrics like runtime and returned rows. Query execution plans, which provide information about the code being executed in what sequence before execution, are another component of query profiling. The server, any external apps connected to the cloud database, and database logs can all be examined to improve query efficiency.

`UNION ALL` instead of `UNION`

The operator **`UNION`** is used to combine the results of two SQL searches. When you need to merge two datasets with identical column names, it comes in helpful. You must be aware of the distinctions between **`UNION`** and **`UNION ALL`**, the two types of **`UNION`** operators. **`UNION`** combines the result sets of two or more **`SELECT`** statements and removes duplicate rows.

`UNION ALL` combines the result sets of two or more **`SELECT`** statements and keeps all rows, including duplicates.

Optimize Subquery Performance

Subqueries can be useful and quick for conducting a quick and dirty analysis, but they are not advised when attempting to maximize performance. It is preferable to utilize an **`EXISTS`** statement rather than an **`IN`** statement when you need to conduct tasks like verifying whether data are present in a different table or SQL subquery.

To swiftly compare data and move on to the next when a value is absent, **`EXISTS`** returns a boolean value. Because **`IN`** returns the value directly, it compares each value, which lengthens the query's processing time. Nonetheless, using IN is more effective than using an **`OR`** expression, which searches a table for several distinct conditions.

Instead of this,

```
SELECT roll_no FROM student where city='Mumbai' or city='Delhi' or city=
'Bengaluru';
Will do
SELECT roll_no FROM student where city IN (Delhi, Mumbai, Bengaluru);
```

Using the `IN` clause instead of the `OR` is far more efficient in this situation. However, when two different tables are being compared in the preceding example, it makes more sense to use an `EXISTS` rather than an `OR`.

Leverage Cloud Database-Specific Features

The features that are unique to cloud databases are just one of its many advantages. For instance, Snowflake contains numerous SQL functions that are unique to Snowflake and facilitate the creation of transforms. These comprise functions for handling various data types and processing JSON values. Check with them to find out if your cloud provider recommends any particular optimizations.

Tools for Optimizing MySQL Queries

Data engineers can use many tools and platforms for MySQL performance tuning. Some popular tools include:

MySQL Performance Schema

One tool that is already included for gathering comprehensive real-time data from the MySQL server is the MySQL Performance Schema. It offers insightful information for monitoring server activity overall, resource usage, and query execution. Monitor and troubleshoot performance problems and create a sluggish query log by turning on this option, which will assist you in locating bottlenecks and optimizing requests accordingly.

MySQL Workbench

The official graphical tool from MySQL for database design, management, and optimization is called MySQL Workbench. It has a visual EXPLAIN function that makes query execution plans easier to understand visually. MySQL Workbench is easy to use and is a good choice for database administrators and developers who want a graphical user interface.

Percona Toolkit

A popular MySQL consulting business called Percona created the Percona Toolkit, a collection of command-line utilities. This toolkit includes some useful tools for query analysis and optimization, such as pt-query-digest and pt-query-advisor. While pt-query-advisor provides suggestions for optimizing sluggish queries, pt-query-digest analyses MySQL query logs and summarizes the performance of database queries.

Best Practices for MySQL Query Optimization

For the best MySQL performance, data engineers should concentrate on three factors: routine, observation, and improvement.

Incorporate routine query performance monitoring as part of your database maintenance schedule. To find and fix sluggish queries and bottlenecks, use tools like Query Profiler, EXPLAIN, and MySQL Performance Schema. To keep up with evolving query trends and data volumes, database indexes should also be regularly reviewed and updated. The performance of the MySQL server is another topic to check. Adapt setup parameters to hardware capabilities and workload.

Instruction in optimization strategies for the database administrators, developers, and data engineers on how to evaluate `EXPLAIN` outputs, optimize MySQL performance, and implement indexing algorithms.

Encourage cooperation and a culture of awareness among the development team members to optimize queries during code reviews and database design talks. For efficient data retrieval and normalization, we will optimize the database from the beginning of the application.

During the application design process, carefully consider and optimize important and frequently used queries.

When creating the database structure and query logic, take into account the expected volume of data and the need for scalability.

Advancements in MySQL databases and related technologies might change queries and performance tuning in specific ways:

- **Better Query Optimizer:** MySQL's query optimizer is always being improved to select the optimal query execution strategy with greater intelligence. We may anticipate that as MySQL develops, the optimizer will become more adept at processing complicated queries and more efficient overall.
- **Indexing Innovations:** New indexing strategies could be introduced as database technologies advance to speed up data retrieval and lower index maintenance costs. In MySQL, performance tuning, adaptive, partial, or hybrid indexing techniques may become more common.
- **Auto-tuning and query rewriting:** In the future, MySQL versions may have the ability to automatically optimize poorly written queries through query rewriting. Furthermore, depending on workload and query patterns, auto-tuning systems may dynamically modify server setup and indexing strategies.

- **Parallel Query Execution:** To handle complex queries more quickly, MySQL may make use of its parallel query execution capabilities. To enhance MySQL performance, distributed computing, and multi-core CPUs could be used more effectively.
- **Sophisticated Caching methods:** To lessen database load and speed up response times, future versions of MySQL may incorporate more complex caching methods such as intelligent caching based on query access patterns.
- **Hardware-Software Integration:** Better hardware integration with MySQL could optimize specific query operations and boost overall performance. Examples of these advancements in hardware technology include GPUs.

Machine learning and AI developments can also impact queries and MySQL performance in the future. Some potential scenarios include:

- **Query Plan Prediction:** By examining past query execution data, machine learning algorithms can forecast the best query plans for particular query kinds. This can result in more efficient query execution without depending entirely on the conventional rule-based query optimizer.
- **Auto-Tuning:** Based on workload observations, machine learning models can be used to automatically adjust different MySQL configuration parameters. This guarantees that the database is set up optimally for a given set of application requirements.
- **Anomaly Detection:** By identifying anomalies in query performance, machine learning approaches can assist in the early detection of performance problems and possible optimizations.
- **Index Recommendation:** By examining past query patterns and access frequency, AI-powered systems can recommend relevant indexes for commonly used queries.
- **Query Rewrite Suggestions:** Using past data and patterns learned, AI can help suggest query rewrites or alternative formulations to enhance query performance. Even if AI and machine learning offer a lot of potential for optimization, conventional optimization techniques still apply. MySQL performance optimization may be made even more effective and efficient by combining the advantages of both strategies.

Conclusion

Query Optimization in DBMS is the process of selecting the most efficient way to execute a SQL statement. Because SQL is a nonprocedural language, the optimizer can merge, restructure, and process data in any sequence. Query Optimization in DBMS has a significant application in database designing.

There are two types of query optimization in DBMS: Cost-Based Optimization and Adaptive Query Optimization. The purpose of Query Optimization in DBMS and techniques in database designing is it reduce the system resources required to fulfill a query and ultimately provide the user with the correct result set faster and cost-efficiently. In the next chapter, we will discuss normalization and concurrency control that is needed to make the database system more effective and efficient.

Questions

1. Consider the SQL query `select * from employee, department where employee.dept_id = department.dept_id`
   What evaluation plan would a query optimizer likely choose to get the optimal cost?
2. Suppose we have the following relations: **`employee (emp_id, salary, age, dept_id) department(dept_id, budget, status)`**
   Each employee record is 20 bytes long and each department record is 40 bytes long. There are 20,000 tuples in the employee table and 5000 tuples in the department table. The **`dept_id`** attribute in employee is a foreign key of the department relation. The file system supports a page size of 4000 bytes and there are 12 buffer pages available to the database. Assume we are using the number of page I/O's as the measure of a query's cost. The following indices exist:
   a. a clustering (primary) index on the **`dept_id`** attribute in an employee,
   b. a non-clustering (secondary) index on the age attribute in employees,
   c. a clustering index on the **`dept_id`** attribute in the department.
3. Consider the following SQL query on the schema branch (`branch_name`, `branch_city`, assets): select `t.branch_name` from branch t, branch s where t.assets > s.assets and s.branch_city = 'Mumbai';

   Write an efficient relational algebra expression that is equivalent to this query and **`JUSTIFY`** your choice with an explanation.
4. Consider these relations with the following properties:

   r(A, B, C), 25,000 tuples, 25 tuples fit on 1 block

   s(C, D, E) 50,000 tuples 30 tuples fit on 1 block

   a. Estimate the number of disk block accesses required for a natural join of r and s using a nested-loop join if r is used as the outer relation.
   b. Estimate the number of disk block accesses required for a natural join of r and s using a block nested-loop join if s is used as the outer relation. Assume

that there are more than 2000 memory buffers available to facilitate this operation, where each memory buffer can buffer one disk block.

5. Differentiate between query processing and query optimization.
6. Explain database optimization and why it is important.
7. Define and discuss indexes and how they help optimize database performance.
8. Elaborate on different types of joins in SQL and how they affect query performance.
9. Explain the concept of database partitioning and how it can improve performance.

Chapter 5
Database Normalization and Normal Forms

Introduction

A database can suffer from various kinds of anomalies and due to that, a relation can contain redundant values of the records. A good database means it should not suffer from anomalies. The three major database anomalies are delete, insert, and update. Normalization is a process where we can decompose an unsatisfactory or bad relation into further relations to remove the different types of anomalies, and while decomposition, we have to ensure that there should not be any loss of data while joining the relations; these properties are called as lossless join decomposition.

Structure

In this chapter, we will cover the following topics:

- Need of Normalization
- Functional Dependencies
- Introduction to Normalization
- Normal Forms

Need of Normalization

If we want to reduce redundancy and dependence, normalization is a vital step in database architecture that involves structuring table connections and fields. The key aim of normalization is to ensure that the organization of data is efficient, minimizes redundancy, and conserves the integrity of data. Database normalization becomes a critical part of constructing data management efficiently; as an organization, we rely on data for making decisions. Reducing redundancy and ensuring data integrity are key points for normalization, which is a basic aspect of database theory. Redundancy refers to the needless repetition of data, which only wastes storage capacity and also introduces possible data integrity issues. Inaccurate or inconsistent data can cause a gathering of problems in an organization, from incorrect business analytics to flawed customer interpretation.

For illustration, consider the initial development of databases in the 1960s when flat file systems were common. These systems had no mechanisms for data integrity, resulting in enormous redundancy and inefficiency. It was in response to these problems that the concept of relational databases and normalization arose, particularly through the work of Edgar F. Codd in 1970. Codd introduced the relational model, which forms the basis for normalization.

Use Case: Finance Sector

In the finance industry, where even the least inconsistency can lead to massive financial losses, database normalization ensures that critical customer information, transaction records, and audit traces are accurate. For example, in a banking database, details about a customer's personal information, transaction history, and account data should be stored separately to avoid duplication and ensure efficient updates. If a customer's address changes, this information needs to be updated in one place without risking inconsistencies across multiple records.

Example of Normalization:

Think about a basic table containing information regarding students, their courses, and their instructors:

S_ID	StudentName	CourseID	CourseName	InstructorName	InstructorPhone
1	Bharat	CS1001	DBMS Lab	Prof. Balaa	8234567332
2	Tarun	CS1002	Computer Networks Lab	Prof. Latika	9876343412
3	Ashwin	CS1001	DBMS Lab	Prof. Sudhanshu	9237456243
4	Sujal	CS1002	Computer Networks Lab	Prof. Monli	6789478928

Table 5.1: *Example of Normalization*

In this table, the following problems exist:

- **Redundant Data:** Some data has to be stored redundantly
- **Update Anomalies:** One copy of such redundant data is reorganized; an inconsistency is generated without all data copies being similarly updated
- **Insertion Anomalies:** To store data without storing the other data in the database may not be possible

- **Deletion Anomalies:** To delete some data without losing some other data may not be possible

To avoid these anomalies, the database needs to be normalized.

Functional Dependencies

Function dependency shows the dependency among the attributes in a relation. For example, in the student table **roll_no** and name are functionally dependent, and this can be shown by **roll_no name**. This means that the name is dependent on **roll_no** or the name is described by **roll_no**.

If a functional dependency XY exists, then it means,

T1[X]= T2[x] then T1[Y]= T2[Y]

Sr_No	Roll_No	Name
1	**12**	**Amit**
2	13	Sourabh
3	14	Rohan
4	**12**	**Amit**

Table 5.2: *Student*

In the preceding table, we can see that when the **roll_no** value repeats then the name will be automatically fetched. When the **roll_no** 12 is repeated the name will be automatically 'Amit'.

A relationship between two attributes, or more specifically, between a key and a non-key attribute inside a relation, is called a functional dependence. When attribute B is functionally dependent on attribute A (shown as A → B), then there is exactly one value of B for each value of A.

Consider the following table:

EmployeeID	EmployeeName	DepartmentID	DepartmentName
1	Joy	D1	HR
2	Rohan	D2	IT
3	Mona	D1	HR

Table 5.3: *Employee*

EmployeeID → EmployeeName: EmployeeName is dependent on **EmployeeID**, as each **EmployeeID** is associated with only one specific **EmployeeName**.

DepartmentID → DepartmentName: The DepartmentName is determined by the **DepartmentID** since each **DepartmentID** uniquely matches a specific **DepartmentName**

Functional dependencies play a crucial role in identifying a table's primary key and guiding the normalization process. They help ensure that the database follows normalization rules, which in turn helps preserve data integrity and minimize redundancy.

By comprehending and utilizing functional dependencies, we can create a database structure that efficiently and effectively manages relationships between data.

To achieve a good relation, a relation must be decomposed into multiple relations, and for the same, various normal forms are used. To achieve the process of normalization we should understand the concept of function dependency.

- **First Normal Form**: Ensures that each field holds only atomic values
- **Second Normal Form**: Eliminates every partial dependency
- **Third Normal Form**: Eliminates every transitive dependency
- **Boyce-Codd Normal Form (BCNF):** Slightly Stricter version of 3NF
- **Fourth Normal Form**: Eliminates every multivalued dependency.
- **Fifth Normal Form**: Takes off the join dependencies.

By normalizing the given table, we arrange the data into distinct tables:

```
Students Table: StudentID, StudentName
Courses Table: CourseID, CourseName
Instructors Table: InstructorName, InstructorPhone
Enrollment Table: StudentID, CourseID
CourseInstructor Table: CourseID, InstructorName
```

This reduces replication and ensures the integrity of the data.

Introduction to Normalization

Normalization is the process of organizing data in a database to condense data redundancy and advance data accuracy. This process entails dividing extensive tables into smaller, more controllable parts while ensuring that all essential information is retained. The main goal is to eliminate any issues that may arise while updating, inserting, or deleting data.

Importance and Benefits

Here are some key benefits of normalization:

- **Reduces Data Redundancy:**
    - By breaking down large tables into smaller ones, the occurrence of redundancy can be minimized.

    - Redundancy can lead to inconsistencies and unnecessary storage costs.
    - For case, if the same information (such as an instructor's phone number) is stored in multiple locations, in such cases it requires updating each instance, resulting in overhead.

- **Improves Data Integrity:**
    - Normalization plays a critical role in maintaining the accuracy and reliability of data.
    - It certifies that data dependencies are logical and properly imposed by the database constraints.
    - For instance, having a centralized location for updating a course name ensures that all records related to that course remain consistent.
- **Enhances Query Performance:**
    - Effective query performance is frequently attained by having tables that are arranged properly.
    - As there are fewer redundancies and more obvious relationships, running queries on normalized tables can result in faster execution.
    - This is especially helpful for big databases where productivity is essential.
- **Facilitates Maintenance:**
    - A normalized database is easier to maintain and update.
    - Changes to the database schema are simpler because there is a clear structure.
    - For example, adding new information about students or courses can be done without disrupting the entire database.

Normalization typically involves applying a series of normal forms to the database, each with specific rules and requirements:

- **First Normal Form:**
    - 1NF eliminates repeating groups within a single row
    - Each field contains only atomic (indivisible) values

  Example: In a student table, instead of storing multiple phone numbers in a single field, we store each phone number in a separate record.

Sr. No.	Roll_no	Name	Project_Loc
1	R11	Arnav	Delhi, Mumbai, Bengaluru
2	R12	Jatin	Singapore, Chennai
3.	R13	Priyanka	Texas, London

***Table 5.4**: Student Table 1*

The preceding relation is not in the first NF due to multivalued attributes, that is, **`Project_loc`** and as per the first normal form each attribute should have atomic values, so it will be in 1 NF when each record will have the atomic values.

Now we can perform the horizontal or vertical fragmentation to become the relation in 1NF.

Sr. No.	**Roll_no**	**Name**	**Project_Loc**
1	R11	Arnav	Delhi
1	R11	Arnav	Mumbai
1	R11	Arnav	Bengaluru
2	R12	Jatin	Singapore
2	R12	Jatin	Chennai
3.	R13	Priyanka	Texas
3.	R13	Priyanka	London

***Table* 5.5**: *Student Table 2*

Now the preceding relation has the atomic values, so it will be in 1NF.

- **Second Normal Form:**
  - Expands upon the first normal form by verifying that every non-key characteristic depends entirely on the main key
  - Removes partial dependencies when a feature depends on just a portion of the main key

  Example: In an enrollment table, the course name should not be stored with the student ID as the primary key; instead, it should be stored in a separate course table.

  For example, the preceding student table has the functional dependency Roll_No→ Name and the same functional dependency is not partial dependency, so we can say that the preceding relation is in 2NF.

- **Third Normal Form:**
  - Additionally, refines the table structure by checking that all non-key attributes are only reliant on the primary key and not on other non-key attributes
  - Eradicates transitive dependencies where a non-key attribute is dependent on another non-key attribute

  Example: If the instructor's phone number is stored in the courses table, it should be moved to an instructor's table to avoid dependency on non-key attributes.

- **Boyce-Codd Normal Form (BCNF):**
    - o Emphasizing its role in dealing with situations where 3NF is insufficient; a table is in BCNF if it is in 3NF and every determinant is a candidate key.
    - o Addresses more complex dependencies that are not handled by 3NF

    Example: A table where both InstructorID and CourseID serve as candidate keys. If we encounter a dependency between these candidate keys, we would need to further normalize the table to comply with BCNF, ensuring no anomalies occur.

For example, let's take a relation R(A, B, C) that has (A, B) as the super key for the relation and 1. A→B, 2. B→C, and 3. C→A is the set of functional dependencies.

So, it means A and B are part of the super key and C is a prime attribute.

As per the definition of 3NF if a functional dependency X→ A, then either X should be the super key or A should be a prime attribute. In BCNF only X should be the super key.

The preceding cited relation is in 3NF as the first two dependencies have X as the super key and the third dependency has A as the prime attribute but the relation is not in BCNF because the third function dependency does not satisfy the condition (C is not a super key).

- **Fourth Normal Form:**
    - o Ensures that the table has no multivalued dependencies other than a candidate key
    - o Eliminates multivalued dependencies, ensuring each attribute relies only on the primary key

    Example: In a table where a course can have multiple students and multiple instructors, separate tables should be created for students and instructors to eliminate multivalued dependencies.

- **Fifth Normal Form:**
    - o Ensures that the table has no join dependencies
    - o A table is decomposed into smaller tables that can be joined back without loss of information, eliminating join dependencies

    Example: In a table where projects can have multiple employees and tasks, separate tables for projects-employees, projects-tasks, and employees-tasks should be created to ensure no join dependencies.

Normal Forms

The following section will discuss in detail the various normal forms used in the database management system.

First Normal Form (1NF)

When a table is in First Normal Form, it means that all columns (attributes) contain only atomic (indivisible) values and there are no duplicated clusters of columns.

To clarify this further, let's dissect the definition:

- **Atomic Values:**
    - An atomic value cannot be broken down any further. For example, a phone number shouldn't include more than one digit in a field
    - A table's fields can only contain one value per row. For instance, a single course name rather than a list of names should be entered in the CourseName column
- **No Repeating Groups:**
    - Repeating groups occur when a table has multiple columns with similar data types stored in them. A recurring group is demonstrated, for example, by having columns labeled Course1, Course2, and Course3 to reflect the courses a student has taken
    - Every single data item must be positioned in its own row in the table to remove repetitive groups

Example:

There are no repeated groups in the first table; all columns contain atomic values. The table is therefore in first normal form, or 1NF. Let's examine the table once more to ensure this.

StudentID	StudentName	CourseID	CourseName	Instructor	InstructorPhone
1	Ambar	CS101	Database	Prof. Smriti	123-456-7890
2	Bharat	CS102	Networks	Prof. Jay	987-654-3210
1	Ambar	CS102	Networks	Prof. Jay	987-654-3210
3	Tarun	CS101	Database	Prof. Smriti	123-456-7890

Table 5.6: *Student course*

- Each cell contains a single value, ensuring atomicity
- The table does not contain any duplicate groups

Despite satisfying the conditions for the first normal form (1NF), the table still has issues with data redundancy. For instance, the phone number of the instructor is repeated for each course they teach. This redundancy could lead to problems if we forget to update an instructor's phone number across all entries, which could happen if their number changes.

Let's examine 1NF with more understanding and in more detail now and see how important it is to database design.

Importance of 1NF

Let's discuss the importance and advantages of 1NF.

- **Atomic Values:** Confirming the atomicity of each variable in the table is a crucial requirement for reaching 1NF. The following justifications make this principle essential.
- **Data Integrity**: Problems with data integrity may arise from non-atomic values. For example, it is hard to confirm that all the values in a cell are correct and up to date when the cell has numerous values.
- **Querying Easiness**: Possessing atomic values facilitates simpler database queries. For specimens, finding an exact value is easier when there is only one value stored in each cell.
- **Data Reliability**: Atomic values perform a crucial role in preserving database reliability. Since every cell has a single value, the contents of each cell are known for sure.

Let's look at an explanation in which atomic values are not sustained. Suppose we have a table with several phone numbers separated by commas in the PhoneNumbers column. This design has several drawbacks:

- **Update Anomalies**: If we need to update one of the phone numbers, we must analyze the string, make the change, and then update the cell. This procedure is accountable for mistakes and may result in inconsistencies.
- **Query Complexity**: Searching for a specific phone number becomes more multifaceted because we must search within strings.
- **Redundancy**: If the same phone number appears in multiple cells, any change to that number must be made in multiple places, leading to redundancy.

We can circumvent these problems and create a stronger database design by keeping atomic values within the table.

No Repeating Groups:

Repetitive group exclusion is a key component of the First Normal Form (1NF). Repeating groups can lead to several issues, including:

- **Update Anomalies**: If a table contains repeating groups, updating a value in one of the groups can lead to inconsistencies if the same value appears in multiple groups.
- **Anomalies Implementation**: The layout of the table makes it difficult to add new items, adding a new value may be difficult. For example, adding a fourth

course to a table that has columns called Course1, Course2, and Course3 requires changing the database's structure.

- **Anomalies Removal**: When a value is present in several categories, it may be difficult to remove. For illustration, eliminating Course2 would require us to ensure that every case of Course2 is gone, which might result in mistakes.

Ending these anomalies and providing a more flexible and manageable database architecture by getting rid of repeated groupings.

Role of 1NF in Database Design:

For numerous reasons, a table's adherence to the First Normal Form (1NF) is crucial:

- **Data Integrity:** By confirming that each cell has a single value and preventing duplicate groups, First Normal Form helps maintain data integrity.
- **Ease of Querying:** By guaranteeing that each cell has a single value, First Normal Form makes it easy to query the database.
- **Data Consistency:** By removing repeating groups and guaranteeing that each cell has a single value, First Normal Form helps maintain consistency throughout the database.
- **Foundation for higher normal forms:** Higher normal forms, such as 2NF, 3NF, and so on are built on the foundations provided by the First Normal Form. Verifying that the table is in 1NF provides a solid foundation for further normalization work.

Example Scenario Illustrating 1NF

Consider a database at a university that tracks student enrolment in courses. Initially, the database designer creates a table that looks like this:

StudentID	StudentName	Courses
1	Ambar	CS101, CS102
2	Bharat	CS102
3	Tarun	CS101

***Table 5.7**: Student Course 1*

The `Courses` column in this table defines First Normal Form (1NF) rules by containing non-atomic entries, such as lists of course IDs. To convert this table to 1NF, we need to ensure that each column contains atomic values and remove all repeating groups:

Converted Table:

StudentID	StudentName	CourseID
1	Ambar	CS101
1	Ambar	CS102
2	Bharat	CS102
3	Tarun	CS101

***Table 5.8**: Student Course 1 updated*

There are no instances of repeating groups in the updated dataset, and all values in the `CourseID` column are unique. This table is now in the first normal form.

In conclusion, the first normal form (1NF) is the key first stage of the normalization procedure. We create a database architecture that is more robust, easier to manage, and less prone to various anomalies by ensuring that every record in a table is atomic and that there are no repeating groups. This establishes the foundation for the next phases of normalization, such as achieving the Second Normal Form (2NF) and Third Normal Form (3NF), which improve the database structure even more to increase data integrity and reduce redundancy.

Second Normal Form(2NF)

If the data in a table is now in First Normal Form, then the table is said to be in Second Normal Form. Every non-key characteristic depends on the full main key to function. To put it another way, partial dependencies, which occur when a non-key property depends only partially on a composite main key, are eliminated by 2NF.

Understanding Partial Dependencies:

Partial dependencies may be understood by considering a composite primary key consisting of two or more columns. When a non-key property is affected by only a piece of the composite main key–rather than the complete key–this is known as a partial dependence. Potential problems and redundancies may result from this.

Example of 2NF:

Let's return to the initial sample table that we created to capture information on student enrolment:

StudentID	StudentName	CourseID	CourseName	Instructor	InstructorPhone
1	Ambar	CS101	Database	Prof. Smriti	123-456-7890
2	Bharat	CS102	Networks	Prof. Jay	987-654-3210
1	Ambar	CS102	Networks	Prof. Jay	987-654-3210
3	Tarun	CS101	Database	Prof. Smriti	123-456-7890

***Table 5.9**: Student Course 2*

We have a composite primary key in this database made up of the **StudentID** and **CourseID.**

Identifying Partial Dependencies:

- **StudentName** depends on **StudentID**.
- **CourseName**, **Instructor**, and **InstructorPhone** depend on **CourseID**.

These dependencies show that, because several characteristics depend only partially on the main key, our table does not fit the requirements for the Second Normal Form (2NF).

Transforming to 2NF:

We need to create separate tables for every object to remove the partial dependencies and convert the table to 2NF. Three tables–**Students**, **Courses**, and **Enrollments** will be made.

Student_ID	Student_Name
1	Ambar
2	Bharat
3	Tarun

***Table 5.10**: Student 2*

In this instance, **StudentID** serves as the main key, and **StudentName** is dependent upon it.

CourseID	CourseName	Instructor	InstructorPhone
CS101	Database	Prof. Smriti	123-456-7890
CS102	Networks	Prof. Jay	987-654-3210

***Table 5.11**: Course*

CourseID is the primary key in this table, and **CourseName**, **Instructor**, and **InstructorPhone** are all completely dependent on it.

StudentID	CourseID
1	CS101
2	CS102
1	CS102
3	CS101

***Table 5.12**: Enrolment*

There is a composite primary key in this database consisting of **StudentID** and **CourseID**; no attributes are absent from the key.

Advantages of 2NF:

Reaching the second normal form allows us to verify:

- **Elimination of Redundancy:** Each piece of information is stored only once, reducing data duplication.
- **Prevention of Update Anomalies:** Updating information, such as an instructor's phone number, is done in one place rather than multiple rows.
- **Simplified Data Maintenance:** It is easier to manage and maintain the database as each entity has a dedicated table.

Application of 2NF in Real-World Scenarios:

When creating relational databases for several applications, normalization to the second normal form is frequently used. For example, consider:

- **Student Management Systems:** Where student information, course details, and enrollment data are stored separately.
- **Inventory Systems:** Where product information, supplier details, and stock records are managed in distinct tables.
- **Customer Relationship Management (CRM) Systems:** Where customer information, interaction history, and sales data are organized in normalized tables.

By removing partial dependencies, the Second Normal Form (2NF) is essential to the normalizing of databases. It guarantees that each non-key characteristic depends entirely on the whole main key. With less redundancy, less chance of anomalies, and faster data management, this method creates a more reliable and effective database structure.

Third Normal Form(3NF)

If a table satisfies these two requirements, it is said to be in Third Normal Form (3NF): (1) It is already in Second Normal Form, and (2) Every non-key attribute depends only on the main key and not on any other non-key attribute (avoiding transitive dependencies).

To put it another way, transitive dependencies are eliminated by the third normal form when one non-key property indirectly depends on the primary key through another non-key attribute.

Understanding Transitive Dependencies:

When one non-key attribute depends on another, which in turn depends on the main key, a transitive dependency is created. This can lead to redundancy and raise the possibility of abnormalities.

For instance, consider the following example:

- If we have a table where **`CourseID`** is the primary key, and it includes **`CourseName`**, **`Instructor`**, and **`InstructorPhone`**.
- **`InstructorPhone`** is dependent on the **`Instructor`**, not directly on **`CourseID`**. Here, **`InstructorPhone`** has a transitive dependency on **`CourseID`** through Instructor.

Example:

Let's take another look at the tables we created in the second normal form.

Student_ID	Student_Name
1	Ambar
2	Bharat
3	Tarun

***Table 5.13**: Student 3*

CourseID	CourseName	Instructor	InstructorPhone
CS101	Database	Prof. Smriti	123-456-7890
CS102	Networks	Prof. Jay	987-654-3210

***Table 5.14**: Course 3*

StudentID	CourseID
1	CS101
2	CS102
1	CS102
3	CS101

***Table 5.15**: Enrollment 2*

Identifying Transitive Dependencies:

In the Courses table, the **`InstructorPhone`** is related to the Instructor instead of being solely linked to the **`CourseID`**. This signifies a transitive dependency.

Transforming to 3NF:

To achieve the third normal form, we must remove these transitive dependencies by establishing an independent table for instructors.

Instructor	InstructorPhone
Prof. Smriti	123-456-7890
Prof. Jay	987-654-3210

***Table 5.16:** Revised Instructors Table*

CourseID	CourseName	Instructor
CS101	Database	Prof. Smriti
CS102	Networks	Prof. Jay

Table 5.17: *Revised Courses Table*

StudentID	CourseID
1	CS101
2	CS102
1	CS102
3	CS101

Table 5.18: *Revised Enrollments Table*

In this new structure:

- The Courses table now contains only attributes that are directly associated with CourseID.
- The Instructors table maintains the relationship between Instructor and InstructorPhone, thereby removing any transitive dependencies.

Advantages of 3NF:

Advantages of reaching the third normal form:

- **Elimination of Transitive Dependencies:** Each non-key attribute relies only on the primary key, removing indirect dependencies.
- **Enhanced Data Integrity:** There is a much lower chance of anomalies, including update anomalies. There is only one place that has to be updated if an instructor's phone number changes.
- **Better Data Organization:** Each table corresponds to a singular entity, making the database easier to comprehend and manage.

Application of 3NF in Real-World Scenarios:

In many applications, normalization to the third normal form is essential, such as:

- **Library Management Systems:** These systems hold information about books, authors, and loan histories independently. This arrangement makes sure that an author's data is updated in a single place in its place of across several entries.
- **E-commerce Platforms:** Where product details, supplier information, and order records are organized in distinct tables. This helps in maintaining supplier contact information without redundancy.
- **Hospital Management Systems:** These systems standardize patient, physician, and appointment data to reduce duplication and ensure data integrity. You only need to change your doctor's contact details once, regardless of any changes.

In summary, achieving the third normal form (3NF) is a crucial step in the database normalization process. By removing intermediate dependencies, this step ensures that each non-key attribute has a direct association with the primary key. As a result, this approach optimizes data integrity, reduces redundancy, and strengthens the general structure of the database, leading to a more trusted and efficient database architecture.

Comprehensive Example with Advanced Normalization to 3NF

Take a closer look at a more complex example and steadily normalize it up to 3NF to gain more comprehensive and useful insights.

Initial Unnormalized Table:

Refer to the following table customer:

Order ID	Customer ID	Customer Name	Product ID	Product Name	Quantity	Price	Sales Person	SalesPerson Contact
1	1001	Ambar	P101	Laptop	1	1000	Bharat	555-1234
2	1002	Tarun	P102	Mouse	2	50	Ambar	555-5678
3	1001	Ambar	P103	Key board	1	75	Bharat	555-1234
4	1003	Bharat	P104	Monitor	1	200	Tarun	555-8765

Table 5.19: *Customer*

Step 1: First Normal Form:

Validate that all the values are atomic and remove any repeated groups to achieve the First Normal Form.

Order ID	Customer ID	Customer Name	Product ID	Product Name	Quantity	Price	Sales Person	SalesPerson Contact
1	1001	Ambar	P101	Laptop	1	1000	Bharat	555-1234
2	1002	Tarun	P102	Mouse	2	50	Ambar	555-5678
3	1001	Ambar	P103	Keyboard	1	75	Bharat	555-1234
4	1003	Bharat	P104	Monitor	1	200	Tarun	555-8765

Table 5.20: *Customer* (1NF)

Step 2: Second Normal Form:

Reject partial dependencies by making separate tables for customers and items to attain the Second Normal Form:

CustomerID	CustomerName
1001	Ambar
1002	Tarun
1003	Bharat

***Table 5.21**: Customer (2NF)*

ProductID	ProductName
P101	Laptop
P102	Mouse
P103	Keyboard
P104	Monitor

***Table 5.22**: Product*

Step 3: Third Normal Form:

Produce a discrete table for salespeople to remove transitive relationships in accordance with the Third Normal Form. Let's decompose the relationship in salesperson and customer (3NF).

SalesPerson	SalesPersonContact
Bharat	555-1234
Ambar	555-5678
Tarun	555-8765

***Table 5.23**: Salesperson*

OrderID	CustomerID	ProductID	Quantity	Price	SalesPerson
1	1001	P101	1	1000	Bharat
2	1002	P102	2	50	Ambar
3	1001	P103	1	75	Bharat
4	1003	P104	1	200	Tarun

***Table 5.24**: Customer(3NF)*

By adhering to the normalization procedure, the original unnormalized table has been converted into several tables that align with the Third Normal Form. This ensures data integrity, reduces redundancy, and organizes the data in a way that mirrors real-world entities and relationships. The normalized tables are easier to maintain, update, and query, providing a robust structure for the database.

Boyce-Codd Normal Form (BCNF)

A table can be said to be in **Boyce-Codd Normal Form (BCNF)** if:

- It is by now in **Third Normal Form (3NF)**
- For every functional dependency **X → Y**, **X** is a **superkey** of the table

More properly, a relational schema is in BCNF if, for every non-trivial functional dependency **X → Y**, **X** must be either a **candidate key** or a **superkey**.

BCNF is a stricter version of 3NF that handles specific anomalies not covered by 3NF, particularly those caused by overlapping candidate keys.

A **functional dependency** occurs when the value of one attribute (or a group of attributes) controls the value of another attribute in a table. For example, if **A → B** holds, then knowing the value of **A** allows you to uniquely regulate the value of **B**.

Conditions for BCNF:

- A relation is in **BCNF** if, for every functional dependency **X → Y**, **X** is a superkey.
- In easy terms, if a table is in BCNF, no attribute can depend on something other than a superkey (a unique identifier of a record).

Example:

Consider the following table with attributes `StudentID`, `CourseID`, and `InstructorID`, where:

- A student can enroll in multiple courses
- Each course is taught by a single instructor
- Each student can be taught by multiple instructors

StudentID	CourseID	InstructorID
1	CS101	Prof. Abbas
2	CS101	Prof. Abbas
1	CS101	Prof. Bhanu
2	CS102	Prof. Bhanu

Table 5.25: *Student* (BCNF)

Functional Dependencies:

1. `CourseID` → `InstructorID` (A course is taught by a unique instructor)
2. `StudentID`, `CourseID` → `InstructorID` (A specific student taking a course has an instructor)

Identifying the Problem:

In the preceding example, the combination of **`StudentID`** and **`CourseID`** is the primary key, but there is a functional dependency **`CourseID`** → **`InstructorID`**. Here, **`CourseID`** determines **`InstructorID`**, but **`CourseID`** is not a superkey. This disrupts BCNF.

Transforming to BCNF:

To satisfy BCNF, we need to split the table into two separate tables to remove the partial dependency.

- **`StudentCourses` Table**: This table contains information about students and their courses.

`StudentID`	`CourseID`
1	CS101
2	CS101
1	CS102
2	CS102

***Table 5.26**: Revised Student* (BCNF)

- **`CourseInstructors` Table**: This table contains information about courses and their instructors.

`CourseID`	`InstructorID`
CS101	Prof. Abbas
CS102	Prof. Bhanu

***Table 5.27**: Revised Course* (BCNF)

Now, the functional dependency **`CourseID`** → **`InstructorID`** exists in a separate table where **`CourseID`** is the superkey, and the **`StudentCourses`** table has a composite key of **`StudentID`**, and **`CourseID`**, satisfying BCNF.

Advantages of BCNF:

- **Eliminates Redundancy**: By ensuring that non-superkey attributes do not depend on anything other than a superkey, BCNF removes redundancy.
- **Avoids Anomalies**: BCNF prevents insertion, deletion, and update anomalies by removing partial dependencies that could lead to data inconsistency.
- **Ensures Data Integrity**: With stricter dependency rules, the chances of inconsistent data due to invalid dependencies are minimized.

BCNF vs. 3NF:

- **3NF** addresses transitive dependencies, where non-key attributes depend on other non-key attributes. However, it allows partial dependencies involving candidate keys.

- **BCNF** is a stricter form, ensuring that **all** dependencies involve only superkeys, further eliminating anomalies.

Example of 3NF Not in BCNF:

- Consider the following table with **`Course`**, **`Instructor`**, and **`Classroom`**:

`Course`	`Instructor`	`Classroom`
CS101	Prof. A	Room 1
CS102	Prof. B	Room 2

Table 5.28: *Course Instructor*

Functional dependencies:

1. **`Course`** → **`Instructor`** (Each course has a unique instructor).
2. **`Instructor`** → **`Classroom`** (Each instructor teaches in a unique classroom).

In this case, the table is in 3NF because:

- **`Course`** → **`Instructor`** is a valid functional dependency.
- There is no transitive dependency between **`Instructor`** and **`Classroom`** through **`Course`**.

However, it is **not in BCNF** because **`Instructor`** → **`Classroom`** interrupts the BCNF rule: **`Instructor`** is not a superkey but determines **`Classroom`**.

Real-World Applications of BCNF:

BCNF is applied to prevent complex anomalies in various systems:

- **University Databases**: To manage the relationships between courses, instructors, and classrooms
- **Inventory Systems**: In retail and manufacturing databases where different warehouses or suppliers handle multiple products
- **Financial Databases**: Managing the relationships between accounts, customers, and financial representatives

Key Points

- **BCNF** is a stricter form of 3NF, ensuring no anomalies in relational databases by handling more multifaceted functional dependencies.
- Tables that pass 3NF tests might still fail BCNF, making BCNF essential in situations where multiple candidate keys or overlapping functional dependencies exist.

- **Normalization** to BCNF ensures higher data consistency and integrity, especially in complex relational models.

Fourth Normal Form

A table is considered to be in 4NF if:

- It is already in Boyce Codd Normal Form.
- It contains no multi-valued dependencies apart from those involving a candidate key.
- To put it in simple terms, 4NF addresses multivalued dependencies, which arise when one attribute within a table uniquely influences another attribute without regard to any other attributes.

Understanding Multivalued Dependencies:

A multivalued dependency (MVD) exists when one attribute in a table uniquely determines another attribute, but there are multiple independent values of the second attribute for each value of the first attribute.

Example:

Consider a table where `CourseID` is the primary key, and it includes `StudentID` and `InstructorID`:

`CourseID`	`StudentID`	`InstructorID`
CS101	1	Abbas
CS101	2	Abbas
CS101	1	Bhanu
CS101	2	Bhanu

***Table* 5.29:** *Student Course*

In the preceding table:

`CourseID` determines `StudentID` (a course can have multiple students).

`CourseID` determines `InstructorID` (a course can have multiple instructors).

This table shows a multivalued dependency between `CourseID` and `StudentID` and between `CourseID` and `InstructorID`.

Transforming to 4NF

To convert the table into 4NF, we need to create separate tables to eliminate the multivalued dependencies:

`StudentsCourses` Table:

`CourseID`	`StudentID`
CS101	1
CS101	2

Table 5.30: *Course* (4NF)

`InstructorsCourses` Table:

`CourseID`	`InstructorID`
CS101	Abbas
CS101	Bhanu

Table 5.31: *Instructor* (4NF)

After decomposition, each table now represents a single entity and the multivalued dependencies are eliminated.

Advantages of 4NF:

By achieving 4NF, we ensure:

- Elimination of multivalued dependencies: Each attribute depends only on the primary key
- Improved data integrity: Reduces redundancy and potential anomalies
- Better data organization: Each table is more focused and easier to manage

Application of 4NF in Real-World Scenarios:

Normalization to 4NF is essential in various applications, such as:

- **Library Management Systems** where book genres and authors are maintained in separate tables.
- **E-commerce Platforms** where product features and suppliers are organized in distinct tables.
- **Hospital Management Systems** where patient treatments and doctors are normalized to prevent redundancy.

Fifth Normal Form or Project-Join Normal Form (PJNF)

A table achieves 5NF if:

- It is already in the Fourth Normal Form.
- It has no join dependencies (JD).

- In more straightforward language, the fifth normal form guarantees that a table is broken down into smaller tables that can be rejoined without any loss of data.

Understanding Join Dependencies:

A join dependency (JD) is present when a table can be separated into several tables, which can then be recombined to reconstruct the original table without losing any information.

Example:

Consider a table where **`ProjectID`**, **`EmployeeID`**, and **`TaskID`** are the primary keys:

`ProjectID`	`EmployeeID`	`TaskID`
P1	E1	T1
P1	E2	T2
P2	E1	T1
P2	E3	T3

***Table* 5.32:** *Employee Project*

In this table:

Each project can have multiple employees and tasks.

Each employee can work on multiple tasks for a project.

Transforming to 5NF:

To convert the table into 5NF, we need to create separate tables to eliminate the join dependencies:

`ProjectID`	`EmployeeID`
P1	E1
P1	E2
P2	E1
P2	E3

***Table* 5.33:** *ProjectsEmployees* (5NF)

ProjectID	**TaskID**
P1	T1
P1	T2
P2	T1
P2	T3

***Table* 5.34**: *ProjectsTasks* (5NF)

ProjectID	EmployeeID
E1	T1
E2	T2
E3	T3

Table 5.35: *EmployeesTasks* (5NF)

The tables can be reconnected to reconstruct the original table flawlessly, preserving all information. The join dependencies are eliminated.

Advantages of 5NF:

- **Elimination of Join Dependencies**: Each table can be joined back without loss of information.
- **Improved Data Integrity**: Reduces redundancy and potential anomalies.
- **Better Data Organization**: Each table is more focused and easier to manage.

Application of 5NF in Real-World Scenarios:

Normalization to 5NF is essential in various applications, such as:

- **Library Management Systems** where book categories, authors, and publishers are maintained in separate tables.
- **E-commerce Platforms** where product categories, suppliers, and customers are organized in distinct tables.
- **Hospital Management Systems** where patient records, treatments, and doctors are normalized to prevent redundancy.

Recent Advancements (Sixth Normal Form)

The Sixth Normal Form (6NF) is the final stage in the normalization process. Kith and kin are in 6NF if it is already in **Fifth Normal Form (5NF)** and cannot be decomposed any further while still preserving the constraints of the database. It deals with temporal data and confirms that no non-trivial join dependencies remain. In modest terms, 6NF is mainly used in **temporal databases**, which handle data that will change over time.

In 6NF, tables are split into the smallest possible parts while still maintaining full integrity and meaning in terms of dependencies. Each table represents a single atomic fact, and all redundancy is eliminated.

Understanding Temporal Data:

6NF is particularly useful when dealing with temporal databases where data changes over time. Temporal data captures information about the history of the data, such as when a value was true or valid. For instance, employee salary changes over time, and a database needs to store both current and historical salary information.

In temporal databases, a relation in 6NF ensures that for each time period, there is no redundancy in the stored data, even in cases where multiple time-dependent attributes are involved.

Example:

Consider a table that stores information about employees' salaries and job titles over time. Both the **`Salary`** and **`JobTitle`** can change independently over time:

`EmployeeID`	**`Salary`**	**`JobTitle`**	**`StartDate`**	**`EndDate`**
1	50,00	Dev	2021-01-01	2022-01-01
1	60,00	Dev	2022-01-01	2023-01-01
1	60,00	Manager	2023-01-01	NULL

Table 5.36: *Employee Job*

In this table, both **`Salary`** and **`JobTitle`** are time-dependent, meaning they can change independently for each **`EmployeeID`**.

Transforming to 6NF:

To achieve 6NF, the table must be decomposed so that each table contains data that depends only on a single attribute at a time (that is, either **`Salary`** or **`JobTitle`**, but not both together). This eliminates any dependency between the attributes, making the table atomic.

You would decompose the table as follows:

`EmployeeID`	**`Salary`**	**`StartDate`**	**`EndDate`**
1	50,00	2021-01-01	2022-01-01
1	60,00	2022-01-01	NULL

Table 5.37: *EmployeeSal(6NF)*

`EmployeeID`	**`JobTitle`**	**`StartDate`**	**`EndDate`**
1	Dev	2021-01-01	2023-01-01
1	Manager	2023-01-01	NULL

Table 5.38: *EmployeeJ_Title (6NF)*

Each table now represents a single, atomic fact about the employee, and there is no redundancy.

Advantages of 6NF

- **Effective Handling of Temporal Data**: 6NF is especially useful in databases that store historical data, confirming that no temporal redundancies exist and that changes over time are precisely captured.

- **Elimination of all Redundancies**: It ensures the complete elimination of any possible redundancy, providing better data integrity.
- **Minimal Storage Space**: By removing all unnecessary dependencies, data is stored in the densest form possible.
- **Improved Query Performance**: These databases allow more efficient querying of historical data.

Real-World Applications of 6NF:

- **Financial Systems**: Used to track the history of stock prices, currency rates, or loan interest rates over time.
- **Human Resource Systems**: When tracking employee job history, salary changes, or position changes, 6NF helps confirm that each piece of data is stored in a temporal form.
- **Inventory Systems**: 6NF can be used to track variations in product prices, stock levels, and supplier information over time.
- **Insurance Databases**: Where policy changes, coverage updates, or claim histories need to be achieved and stored competently across periods.

Conclusion

In this chapter, we discussed how the anomalies are to be taken care of, and for the same, we have introduced normal forms where we decomposed unsatisfactory and bad relations into multiple relations. Various normal forms are also discussed to understand the various perspectives of normalization. The functional dependency is one of the key areas to solve the problems of normal forms.

In the next chapter, we will discuss transactions and concurrency control that is required to manage the concurrent executions of the transactions.

Questions

1. Define and discuss ACID properties of transaction.
2. Explain the concept of database normalization and its role in optimization.
3. Given a relation R (A, B, C, D) and Functional Dependency set FD = { AB → CD, B → C }, determine whether the given R is in 2NF. If not, convert it into 2 NF.
4. Discuss the various types of normalization levels or normalization forms with a suitable example.
5. What are the problems caused by redundancy? Explain normalization and the need for normalization.

6. Explain the following: Multi-valued dependencies and fourth normal forms.
7. Differentiate between full functional and partial dependency with the help of an example.
8. BCNF is stronger than 3NF. Justify this statement with the help of an example.
9. Lossless join decomposition is the key factor while decomposing the unsatisfactory relation so explain the process of Lossless join decomposition with an example.
10. Given a relation R (A, B, C, D, E) and Functional Dependency set FD = { A → B, B → E, C → D}, determine whether the given R is in 3NF. If not, convert it into 3 NF.
11. Explain insertion, deletion, and modification anomalies. Why are they considered bad? Illustrate with example.
12. The following are two sets of FDs for a relation R(A, B, C, D, E). Are they equivalent? F={A->C,AC->D,E->AD,E->H} and G={A->CD,E->AH}.

CHAPTER 6
Transaction Management and Concurrency Control

Introduction

A transaction is a program that modifies or accesses data in a database. The two primary purposes of transactions are write (W) and read (R). The concept of a transaction has been extensively utilized by applications and database systems. Although transactions were first employed in financial applications, the idea is currently applied in real-time telecommunication applications and the administration of lengthy tasks like product design or administrative operations.

Managing and carrying out concurrent transactions or allowing users or several processes to manipulate data simultaneously without causing data loss, inconsistencies, or integrity issues is known as concurrency control. Controlling concurrency is essential in a multi-user database environment when multiple users are accessing, changing and executing, or manipulating the transitions.

Structure

In this chapter, we will cover the following topics:

- Transaction
- Concurrency Control
- ACID Properties of Transactions
- Transaction Isolation Levels
- Concurrency Control Methods (locks, timestamps)
- Transaction Rollback and Commit
- Logging and Recovery Techniques

Transactions

In a database management system (DBMS), a transaction is a group of actions (such as read or write) used to carry out a logical task. A transaction is a logical unit of work that requires completion of each phase. Transactions ensure the consistency and integrity of the database. Transactions are necessary to maintain the ACID (Atomicity, Consistency, Isolation, Durability) properties. These attributes guarantee that the database remains correct even in the face of concurrent access and failures.

Transaction States

A transaction has five major states:

- **Active**: This state shows that the transaction is currently active.
- **Partially Committed**: It shows that all the steps are completed but yet to be committed.
- **Committed**: This state means that the transaction is already completed, and all the changes are written permanently to the database.
- **Failed**: It means can't move further due to some failure or error transaction.
- **Aborted**: Due to some specific failure if the transaction fails then this has to roll back and undo the effects of the transaction.

Upon a customer's purchase from this business, several processes occur, updating multiple tables. One might think of the whole sequence of connected occurrences as an illustration of a transaction. From the perspective of the client, a single event occurred; a transaction occurred. From the perspective of the corporation, several things have to occur:

- The product inventory needed to be modified, which had an impact on the **`Product`** table; an invoice had to be issued, affecting the Invoice, Line, and Customer tables (where the balance is maintained).
- A new record for the customer's order was added to the **`Account_Transaction`** table.

A transaction consists of a sequence of database operations that are treated as a single unit of work. The number and type of operations within a transaction determine its complexity and execution path.

The **`COMMIT`** command is presented at the conclusion of that example. You shouldn't proceed unless you are certain that the necessary modifications have been made. It says that under that scenario, a DBMS that provides transaction management would roll back the completed transaction steps to restore the database to a consistent state. To indicate the start of a transaction sequence, you can alternatively use the command **`START TRANSACTION`**. **`BEGIN TRANSACTION`** is the phrase used by the MS SQL server.

Example of a transaction:

```
T1 (Transaction)
Read(A)
A=A-500
Write(A)
Read(B)
B=B+500
Write(B)
Commit;
```

In the preceding example, the transaction is performing a transfer of $500 from account A to account B. In this, first will read the value of A, perform the operation, and write the updated value of A. Now will read the value of B, perform the operation, and then write the final value of B. Finally, perform the commit operation to permanently save the values of A and B in the database.

The previous example was executed as a single transaction and the same can be executed in multiple transactions.

T1 (Transaction) Read(A) A=A-500 Write(A) Commit;	
	T2(transaction) Read(B) B=B+500 Write(B) Commit;

***Table 6.1:** Example of a Transaction*

Concurrency Control

In a database management system, concurrent execution refers to the process of carrying out several transactions concurrently. In an environment with numerous users, the same data is accessed by multiple users in the database; each carries out a separate action to access or edit the data. When transactions are executed concurrently, read or write operations are completed, and occasionally this leads to inconsistent states in the database.

However, controlling concurrent execution calls for careful consideration to ensure data integrity and avoid conflicts. Concurrent execution may be efficiently managed by utilizing suitable concurrency management in DBMS, maintaining data consistency, integrity, and isolation while maximizing system performance and concurrency.

Concurrency control gives users the ability to do concurrent operations in database management systems. For a transaction, there are primarily two sorts of operations: read (R) and write (W).

To prevent data inconsistency from becoming the outcome of transactions being carried out in database management systems (DBMS), concurrency control is mostly necessary. The idea of serializability is employed to accomplish this concurrency control objective.

While executing the transaction we face the following challenges:

- **Inconsistent Data**: Inconsistent data states might result from numerous users accessing and changing the same piece of information during a transaction. The final state of the data might only reflect one of the updates if, for instance, two transactions are making simultaneous modifications to the same record and there is insufficient concurrency control in place. This could lead to inconsistent outcomes.
- **Lost Updates**: This occurs when many transactions read the same piece of data and then update it with the correct value. Since no transaction may view the updates made by earlier transactions, the final value simply reflects the most recent update, "losing" the earlier updates.
- **Uncommitted Data**: Also referred to as dirty reads, uncommitted data concerns arise when a transaction accesses data that has been modified by another transaction but has not yet been committed. If the transaction that made the adjustments is rolled back, the data that was read by the first transaction is no longer valid. If a second transaction accesses a record that the previous transaction altered before it was committed, then it may be working with uncommitted data that could be rolled back.
- **Inconsistent Retrievals**: Also referred to as non-repeatable reads, inconsistent retrievals occur when a transaction reads the same data again and gets different results each time because another transaction changed the data in between the reads.

An inconsistent retrieval results, for instance, when one transaction reads a collection of data, another transaction alters that data, and then the first transaction reads the data again and notices different values.

A problem known as concurrency arises in transactions when several users attempt to carry out tasks such as reading or writing data or information. When a person accesses or edits data that is consistent but after performing certain activities, the data becomes inconsistent, this is known as concurrency.

Principles of Concurrency Control

The important principles of concurrency control are:

- Database changes are preserved as if a `COMMIT` command had been issued if a program that initiates a transaction terminates properly but does not call a `COMMIT` command.
- Should a transaction start program terminate unexpectedly before a **`COMMIT`** command is issued, the system ought to send a **`ROLLBACK`** command, eliminating any outstanding modifications from the examination.
- In some of the databases the automatic commit is anticipated at the end of a script, but you should always close a transaction with a **`COMMIT`** command that will be more appropriate.

Advantages of the Concurrency Method

One important technique for preventing data inconsistency in the concurrent execution of transactions is concurrency. However, there are a few things to take into account while utilizing concurrency control in DBMSs:

- **Data Inconsistency**: Concurrency control helps to prevent inconsistent data by averting conflicts between several transactions. The database may become inconsistent if transactions read and write data inconsistently. For correct concurrency control, utilize the concurrency control methods.
- **Avoid Dirty Reads**: A dirty read occurs when a transaction reads data that has been modified by an uncommitted transaction. In this case, if the modifying transaction is rolled back, the data that was read by the first transaction is no longer valid. Concurrency control aids in preventing dirty reads in transactions by ensuring that a transaction can only read data that has been committed.
- **Performance and Throughput**: By allowing many transactions to operate simultaneously, concurrency control improves a DBMS's performance and throughput. These transactions follow a stringent control mechanism and run concurrently. By limiting concurrent access to data, the DBMS may efficiently use system resources, reducing wait times and increasing total throughput.
- **Sharing of Data**: Concurrency control, which safeguards the consistency and integrity of the data, enables data sharing among several users and applications. In a multi-user setting, users need to be able to access and modify data concurrently without starting arguments.
- **Atomicity Protection**: Concurrency control guarantees that a transaction stays atomic throughout the state, treating it as a single unit. Concurrency control ensures that either every transaction is completed (successful) or aborted (failed) to maintain atomicity.

- **Conflict Avoidance**: Concurrency control guards against conflicts between transactions so that no data is overwritten while multiple users are altering a single piece of data.

Disadvantages of Concurrency

Here are some disadvantages of concurrency:

- The DBMS becomes much more complex when concurrency control is implemented. To ensure that transactions are completed in a way that maintains data consistency and integrity, the system needs sophisticated algorithms and procedures.
- Deadlocks can occur when many transactions are waiting on one another to release resources, which stops any further operations from happening. More complexity and money are needed for deadlock identification and resolution.
- Overall system performance can be improved by concurrency, but it can also be negatively impacted by resource disputes and contention. In highly contentious circumstances, the cost of maintaining concurrent access could exceed the benefits.
- Implementing concurrency control can be difficult, particularly in systems that are remote or have intricate transactional logic.

ACID Properties of Transactions

An effective method for retrieving, storing, manipulating, and analyzing data is offered by database management systems (DBMS). The major responsibility of DBMSs is to store data so that, even when authorized users make changes to the database, the data should always be consistent.

Four characteristics–referred to as ACID Properties in DBMS terminology maintain this consistency. These attributes are useful in the transactions that take place when the data is accessed. It's crucial to understand what a "transaction" is before studying the ACID properties of database management systems.

A transaction is a single work unit used for read-and-write operations to access and alter data in a database.

Stated differently, a transaction is a collection of logically connected actions carried out by a single user to change the data.

It is crucial to preserve data consistency and integrity at all times when a transaction is being processed. To do this, ACID properties in DBMS are therefore essential. The acronym for Atomicity, Consistency, Isolation, and Durability is "ACID," and these concepts are summarized as follows.

Atomicity

The idea behind atomicity is that the data should not change in the course of a transaction. It implies that the procedure ought to be carried out entirely or not at all. Let's use an example to better grasp this. Let's say your assignment is to complete the test. You have two options: either complete the entire assignment or not a single question. The assignment cannot be partially or half completed. This is how DBMS atomicity is defined. A transaction may proceed in one step or not at all. Another example is if user A wants to transfer money to user B but due to some error money was deducted from user A's account but not credited to user B's account, so in such cases, the transaction will be rollbacked and user A will get credited for what money was debited earlier. In DBMS, there is no such thing as a partial transaction.

Atomicity has two major operations in DBMS:

- **Abort**: In case of abort of a transaction no change will be marked in the database.
- **Commit**: If the transaction is used commit operation so all the changes will be permanently stored in the database.

Consistency

For the data to stay consistent, both before and after the transaction, the integrity constraints must be effectively upheld. In DBMS, the phrase "consistency of ACID properties" refers to the preservation of data both before and after the transaction process.

Let's user A have \$1000 as an account balance and transfer \$200 to user B that also has an account balance of \$1000, so once the transaction is successfully committed then user A should have an account balance of \$800 and user B should have \$1200 as account balance. In this scenario, we found that the sum of account balances in both accounts is the same (before transaction = after transaction). This means that the database is consistent, if any difference in the sum, then we call it an inconsistent database state.

Isolation

Multiple transactions can take place concurrently without influencing one another, thanks to isolation. Isolation, in simple terms, is the consistency of data between concurrent database transactions. It seeks to ensure that, when several transaction processes are underway, no data should impact another.

Let's say you and your friend make a simultaneous purchase. You can proceed with making an online payment as though it were a normal transaction. However, in reality, your friend's payment was completed simultaneously. As a result, isolation establishes the relationship between modifications made during one transaction and subsequent database transactions.

Durability

One of the key ACID Properties in DBMSs is durability, which guarantees that data will stay in the database permanently following successful transaction processes. This is significant since, if the system fails, then the data ought to be preserved and accessible.

Because of this, databases can endure system failures or crashes. Every time a modification is made to the data, it should be committed to the database to ensure durability. By doing this, the database's data will continue to be durable. In DBMSs, this is how the ACID Properties guarantee data integrity throughout the whole transaction process. These characteristics are necessary to understand DBMS transaction processing and concurrency control.

The applications of ACID characteristics in DBMSs are as follows:

- In database management systems (DBMS), the employment of ACID characteristics guarantees the secure, dependable, and consistent processing of transactions.
- The features of ACID ensure that data is accurate and consistent, concurrent transactions are segregated from one another, and transactions are performed atomically.
- These characteristics guarantee the preservation of data and the permanence of database modifications, even in the case of a system malfunction.

Transaction Isolation Levels

As is common knowledge, a database must adhere to ACID properties to preserve consistency. The way that transaction integrity is observable to other users and systems is determined by isolation, one of the four qualities consistency, atomicity, isolation, and durability). It indicates that a transaction needs to be executed in a database system so that it is the only one using the system's resources.

The degree to which a transaction needs to be isolated from the data modifications performed by any other transaction is determined by its isolation level.

Concurrency Control Problems

When transactions are being executed concurrently in an environment, many issues could come up. Data inconsistency in the database may result from improper concurrent control methods. Here are a few typical concurrency control issues:

- **Dirty Read Problem**

When a transaction tries to read the set of rows that meet a particular criterion, it frequently encounters this issue. However, before the first transaction finishes, another one takes place to make some changes to the rows that have an impact on the result set. As a result, when the first transaction runs the same query again, the results are different or inconsistent.

To put it another way, a dirty read issue arises when a transaction modifies a database entry and then fails for some reason. The modified database item was created by a different transaction and then changed back to its initial value.

Take schedule S, for instance, where transaction T2 rolls back following transaction T4's read (A) operation. The read values of the data item A that were never committed are now present in T3 and T4. They carry out the dirty read procedure. Transactions T3 and T4 read the value of a modified transaction T2, which is why this is the case. Transaction T2 receives the original value of A and cancels the modified value of A since it fails and rolls back. The updated value of A is processed by other transactions, such as T3 and T4, which leads to an inconsistent date in the database.

Schedule (S):

Lock X (A)
Read (A)
Lock S(B)
Read (B)
Write (A)
Unlock (A)
Lock X (A)
Read (A)
Write (A)
Unlock (A)
Lock S(A)
Read (A)

- **Lost Update Problem**

When two transactions that involve more than one data item perform differently, resulting in an inaccurate value for a database item, this is known as a lost update problem. When two or more transactions read the same piece of data and then update it with the actual value, this happens. The final value only reflects the most recent update because no transaction can see the updates performed by other transactions; thus, the earlier updates are essentially "lost."

One of the subtractions may be lost, for instance, if two transactions read the identical account balance and then deduct an amount without correctly locking. Let us examine an additional scenario in which the balance of a bank account is \$5000. First, transaction T1 reads the amount and returns \$5000. There are two transactions: T1 and T2. T2 now retrieves the account balance and finds that it is \$5000.

T1 now modifies the amount by deducting \$2000 from the account's starting balance. T2 adjusts the balance subsequent to deducting \$1000. Transaction T2 ignores the update made by Transaction T1 by reading the starting balance of \$5000 and updating it to \$4000. The final state is 5000 - 2000 - 1000 = \$2000. The update by T1 is lost.

Dirty Read:

A dirty read is a situation when a transaction reads the rows or data that is not yet committed. For example,

- Transaction 1 (T1) modifies a row and leaves the data uncommitted.
- Meanwhile, Transaction 2 (T2) reads some data including the row modified by T1.
- If T1 now rolls back the update, then T2 would have read data that is considered to have not existed.

Non-Repeatable Read:

It occurs when a transaction reads the same row twice and gets different data each time. For example,

- If Transaction 1 reads some data
- Now Transaction 2 modifies the same data and commits
- If T1 reads the same data again, now it will get a different value

Phantom Read:

This will execute the two same queries, but the results retrieved are different. Let's understand with the following example,

- If Transaction 1 reads a set of rows by the select command
- And Transaction 2 now adds a new row that is similar to the search of Transaction 1
- If T1 again executes the same query, will get different rows.

Isolation Levels

The following isolation levels are used in transaction management.

Read Uncommitted:

- As statements can read rows that have been altered by previous transactions but have not yet been committed, dirty reads are permitted at this level.
- Transactions with **READ UNCOMMITTED** level do not have shared locks to prevent other transactions from modifying data read by the current transaction.

A shared lock is also called a read lock, used for reading data items only. This will ensure that no records are going to be processed during the read-only process.

- This will ensure that no transactions can block the data item in the exclusive mode lock. This will also ensure that the transaction can access the data item in read-only mode.
- This is the lowest isolation level. No lock options are used for the execution of the transactions.

Read Committed:

- This level will ensure that no transaction can read the data item that is not committed. This will avoid the dirty-read problem.
- Non-repeatable reads or phantom data may emerge from other transactions changing the data between specific statements inside the current transaction. The default setting for SQL Server is this one.
- In this isolation level, the behavior depends on the setting of the **READ_COMMITTED_SNAPSHOT** database option:
    - If **READ_COMMITTED_SNAPSHOT** is set to OFF and the Database Engine uses shared locks, then the other transactions can't update the data item as the current transaction is reading the data item.
    - If **READ_COMMITTED_SNAPSHOT** Row versioning is used to provide each transaction with a consistent snapshot of the data as of the start of the transaction. This allows for greater concurrency because transactions don't block each other when reading data.

Repeatable Read:

- At this level of isolation, data that has been read by one transaction but not yet committed by another, cannot be read by statements, and until the current transaction is finished, no other transaction can alter the data that it has read.
- Until the transaction is finished, shared locks are applied to all the data that each statement in the transaction reads. Concurrency is lower than the **READ COMMITTED** isolation level by default because shared locks are maintained until the transaction is finished. Therefore, this level ought to be employed when needed.
- Nevertheless, if a query is run more than once with the same search parameters

(the same WHERE clause), each execution can provide a different set of rows. This could occur as a result of other transactions being permitted to add new rows that meet the search criteria or modify existing rows in a way that makes them meet the criteria once more, creating phantom reads.

Snapshot:

- In this case, the result is the same as if the committed data was captured at the beginning of the transaction and applied to the statements within it.
- It stipulates that the data read by any statement within a transaction shall be the data that was there at the beginning of the transaction and is consistent throughout transactions.

Serializable:

- This level of isolation ensures that data that has been changed but not yet committed by other transactions cannot be read by statements. Furthermore, until the current transaction is finished, no subsequent transaction can change the data that it has already read.
- Until the current transaction is finished, other transactions cannot insert new rows with key values that would fall inside the range of keys read by any statements in the current transaction (unlike repeating read isolation level).
- This is the highest level of isolation because it locks all key ranges and maintains the locks until the transaction is finished.
- Since this option has a lower concurrency, it is advised to utilize it sparingly.

Syntax for Set Transaction Isolation Level

```
Set Transaction Isolation Level {
      Read Uncommitted
      Read Committed
      Repeatable Read
      Snapshot
      Serializable
}
```

Choosing an Isolation Level

The locks that are obtained to guard against data alterations are unaffected by the transaction isolation level that is selected. Any data that a transaction updates is always subject to an exclusive lock. Regardless of the isolation level chosen for that transaction, it keeps that lock until the transaction is finished. Transaction isolation levels primarily specify how an operation is shielded from the consequences of other transactions when it comes to read operations.

Many users can access data simultaneously with a lower isolation level, but there are more concurrency effects (such as dirty reads or phantom reads) that users may experience.

The kinds of concurrent effects that consumers may experience are decreased with a higher isolation level. However, it raises the likelihood that one transaction may block another and calls for more system resources. The process of selecting a suitable isolation level involves weighing the application's data integrity needs against each isolation level's overhead.

To avoid missing changes that can happen when two transactions retrieve the same row simultaneously, transactions must be executed at an isolation level of at least a repeatable read.

Concurrency Control Protocols in DBMS

In DBMSs, concurrency control protocols are used to manage several concurrent operations without causing conflicts with one another. Concurrency control guarantees transaction speed, but it's also important to handle conflicts that may arise in multi-user systems and ensure that database transactions are carried out concurrently without compromising the data integrity of the corresponding databases.

Mostly two types of Concurrency control protocols are used. They are,

- Lock-Based Protocol
- Timestamp-Based Protocol

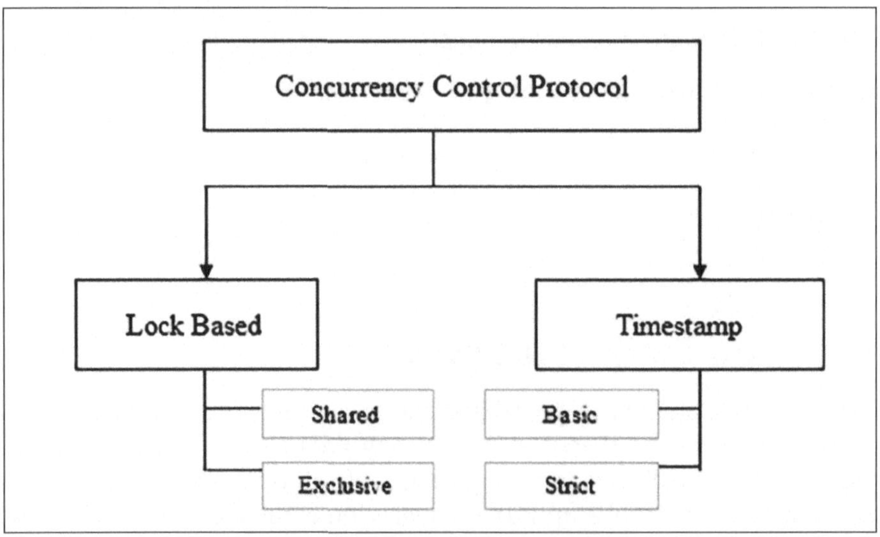

Figure 6.1: *Currency Control Protocol*

Lock-Based Protocol

Concurrency control, which regulates concurrent access to a data item, greatly benefits from the use of lock-based protocol mechanisms. These mechanisms ensure that one transaction cannot retrieve and update a record while another is writing to it.

Example

Similar to how only one transaction is completed at a time in a database transaction while other transactions are locked, only one transaction is carried out at a time.

- Lock the data item properly otherwise the database state will be inconsistent.
- It will ensure that only transactions can access the unique data item at a time.
- Two different modes of locks are:
  - Shared Lock(S)
  - Exclusive Lock(X)

Shared lock(S):

- In lock-based concurrency control protocols, a shared lock allows multiple transactions to read a data item concurrently.
- In lock-based protocol, it will be represented by S.
- It prevents any transaction from acquiring an exclusive lock (needed for writing) on the same data item, ensuring that the data remains consistent for the reading transactions.

Exclusive Lock(X):

- In this mode of locking, the transaction can perform both operations (read and write) with the data item.
- This will be represented by X.

Lock Compatibility Matrix:

It shows the compatibility between both modes of locking in the concurrency control.

Mode	**Shared**	**Exclusive**
Shared	Yes	No
Exclusive	No	No

Table 6.2: *Modes in Lock-based protocols*

- The matrix determines whether multiple transactions can obtain locks on the same resource at once.
- If a resource is already locked by another transaction, a new lock request can only be approved if its mode matches the lock currently in place.

- An object may be the subject of an unlimited number of shared lock transactions; but, if one transaction possesses an exclusive lock, no other transaction may hold a lock on the item.

Timestamp-based Protocols

Timestamp-based protocols give every transaction a distinct timestamp. A distinct timestamp is assigned to every transaction. Conflicting actions are carried out in timestamp order, thanks to the protocol. A transaction is rolled back and reopened with a new timestamp if it attempts to carry out an operation that is against the order. The attributes of the timestamp-based protocol are as follows.

- It has a unique identifier, with each transaction being assigned a timestamp when it is entered into the system.
- It is the most widely used concurrency protocol.
- It uses the system time or a logical counter as a timestamp, which begins working as soon as the transaction is created.
- It helps DBMS identify transactions and determines the serializability order.

Timestamp Ordering Protocol

The timestamp ordering protocol will ensure serializability among transactions in their conflicting read or write operations

- **TS(T)**: Transaction of timestamp (T)
- ***R-timestamp*(X)**: Read timestamp of Data item (X)
- ***W-timestamp*(X)**: Write timestamp of Data item (X)

Timestamp Ordering Algorithms:

The following are the types of timestamping algorithms:

- **Simple Timestamp ordering**
  - o It verifies that there is no violation of transaction execution by comparing T's timestamp with `Read_TS(X)` and `Write_TS(X)`.
  - o Transaction T is canceled and resubmitted to the system as a new transaction with a new timestamp when it discovers that the transaction execution sequence has been broken.
- **Strict Timestamp ordering**

  It ensures that the schedules are rigorous enough to allow conflict serializability and simple recoverability.

Validation Based Protocol

A validation-based protocol avoids transaction concurrency by operating under the presumption that interference won't arise if there are no concurrent transactions.

The different phases of validation-based protocol

1. **Read phase**: During this stage, a transaction stores the values of data items into temporary local variables by reading them from the database. The transaction then begins to run, but instead of updating the data items in the database, it uses temporary local variables for its activities.
2. **Validation phase**: During this stage, the temporary variables are checked for violations of the serializability requirements.
3. **Write phase**: This is the last stage in the validation-based protocol. In this stage, the transaction is committed, and the values of the temporary local variables are written to the database if the transaction validation is successful. The modifications are discarded, and the transaction is slowed down so that it can be reopened later if the validation in the second phase fails.

Timestamps of each phase of a transaction:

- **Start(Tn)**: This timestamp corresponds to the moment at which transaction Tn initiates execution.
- **Validation(Tn)**: This specifies the timestamp at which transaction Tn enters the validation phase after completing the read phase.
- **Finish(Tn)**: This timestamp indicates the point in time at which the transaction Tn completes all write operations.

Since this is the real phase of the transaction where all of the checks take place, this protocol utilizes Validation(Tn) as the timestamp of the transaction Tn. It follows that TS(Tn) = Validation(Tn) is safe to claim.

The validation will be successful if there are two transactions, T1 and T2, that are controlled by a validation-based protocol and if Finish(T1) < Start(T2). This is because serializability is preserved as T1 completed its execution well before T2 began the read phase.

Multi-Version Concurrency Control

The goal of the multi-version protocol is to shorten read operation delays. It keeps several copies of the data elements. To guarantee successful and conflict-free read operations, the protocol generates a fresh version of the transaction data whenever a write operation is carried out.

The following information is included in the recently produced version:

- **Content**: The data value for that version is contained in this field.
- **`Write_timestamp`**: The timestamp of the transaction that generated the new version is contained in this field.
- **`Read_timestamp`**: This column holds the transaction's timestamp, which will be used to read the newly produced value.

The multi-version protocol creates many copies of the data and ensures that read operations can access the right version of the data without any conflicts. Thus, the protocol minimizes read operation times and permits effective concurrency control.

Multiple Granularity

It's simply dividing the database into pieces that can be locked hierarchically. The Multiple Granularity protocol lowers lock overhead while improving concurrency. It keeps track of what needs to be locked, how to secure it, and when to lock or unlock a piece of data. A tree can be used as a graphic representation of this kind of hierarchy.

For example: Consider a tree that has four levels of nodes.

- The full database is displayed on the first level or higher level.
- An area node of type is represented by the second level.
- These are the exact regions that make up the upper-level database.
- Children nodes, sometimes referred to as files, make up the region.
- There cannot be more than one file in any one location.
- Lastly, records or child nodes are present in every file. The records in the file are precisely those that make up its child nodes. There are no records that appear in multiple files.

The various levels at multiple granularity will be represented as per the following:

1. Entire Database
2. Area
3. File
4. Record

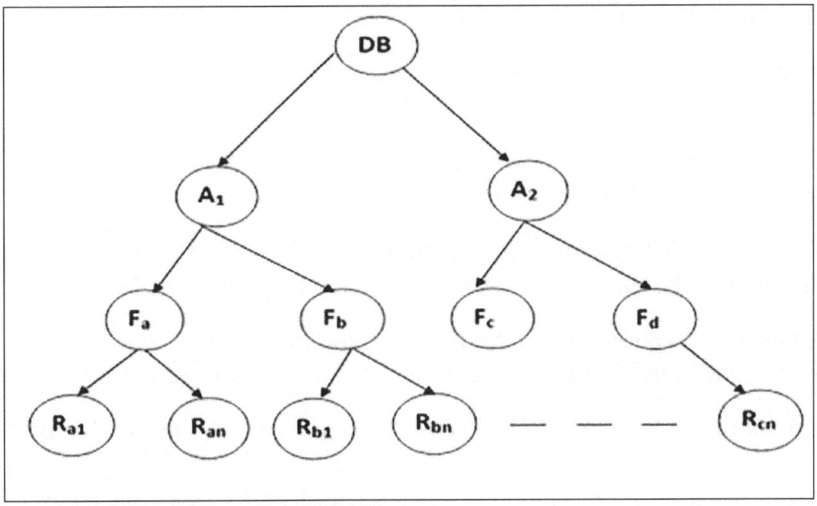

Figure 6.2: *Multiple Granularity*

The preceding figure shows an example of a database. In this figure, if we put the lock on the root then the entire database is locked. If we lock the root node, then all receding nodes will be implicitly locked.

Three types of locking are used in multiple granularity:

- **Intention-shared (IS):** In this type all the lower-level nodes will be locked in shared mode only.
- **Intention-Exclusive (IX):** In this mode the lower-level nodes will be locked in both modes but the intention is to acquire exclusive locks at lower levels.
- **Shared & Intention-Exclusive (SIX):** If the current node is locked in shared mode (S), and there's an intention to acquire exclusive locks (IX) at lower levels.

To guarantee serializability, it takes advantage of the intention lock modes. It mandates that a node adheres to these protocols for a transaction to attempt to lock it:

1. Transaction T1 needs to adhere to the compatibility matrix for locks.
2. Transaction T1 locks the tree's root initially. Any mode can be locked.
3. Transaction T1 will only lock a node in S or IS mode if the parent of the node is currently locked in either IX or IS mode.
4. Transaction T1 will lock a node in X, SIX, or IX mode if the parent of the node is currently locked in IX mode.
5. Transaction T1 can lock a node if it hasn't already unlocked any nodes.
6. Transaction T1 will unlock a node if it does not currently have any of the

offspring of the node locked only.

Keep in mind that with multiple granularity, locks must be released in a bottom-up sequence after being acquired in a top-down manner.

1. Transaction T1 must lock the database, region A1, and file Fa in IX mode if it reads record Ra9 in file Fa. Ra2 must then be locked in S mode.
2. Transaction T2 may update record Ra9 in file Fa only after locking region A1, file Fa, and the database in IX mode. Lastly, the Ra9 must be locked in X mode.
3. Transaction T3 must lock the database and place region A in IS mode if it reads every record in file Fa. It must finally lock Fa in S mode.
4. Transaction T4 must lock the database in S mode if it reads the full database.

Transaction Rollback and Commit

The statements for transaction control are **ROLLBACK** and **COMMIT**. A set of SQL statements performed all at once is called a transaction. The **COMMIT** statement is used to permanently store the changes to the database if every statement in a transaction is executed successfully. The **ROLLBACK** statement is used to reverse the changes made by the transaction in the event that any of its statements fail.

```
Start transaction
Write SQL statements
Successfully executed all the statements
   Perform COMMIT
        Exit
Else
    Perform ROLLBACK
     Exit
```

Example:

```
mysql> USE my_database;
mysql> START TRANSACTION;

mysql> UPDATE customers
    -> SET name = 'Jatin'
    -> WHERE customer_id = 1;

mysql> IF No ERROR  THEN
    ->  COMMIT;
    -> ELSE
    ->     ROLLBACK;
    -> END IF;
```

We can regulate how changes are made to the database, thanks to **COMMIT** and

ROLLBACK. This makes them crucial. For instance, we can preserve transaction modifications using **COMMIT** only if we are certain we want to make them permanent. If we make a mistake or something goes wrong, we can also use **ROLLBACK** to reverse the changes made during a transaction.

We only need to append **COMMIT** and **ROLLBACK** to the end of our SQL statements to use them. For instance, the employee table will be updated by the following SQL statement, which will then commit the modifications.

```
UPDATE employee
SET name = 'Jatin'
WHERE emp_id = 1;
COMMIT;
```

The employee table will likewise be updated by the subsequent SQL statement, but the changes won't be committed. Rather, it will hold off on making the modifications permanent until we specifically call the **COMMIT** statement.

```
UPDATE employee
SET name = 'Jatin'
WHERE emp_id = 1;
```

The **ROLLBACK** statement also allows us to reverse the modifications that a transaction has made. The employee table, for instance, will be updated by the SQL statement that follows, which will subsequently rollback the modifications:

```
UPDATE employee
SET name = 'Jatin'
WHERE emp_id = 1;
ROLLBACK;
```

When we are certain that we wish to permanently alter a transaction, we should utilize **COMMIT**. For instance, we should utilize **COMMIT** following the successful addition of a new record to a database table or the successful updating of an already-existing record.

Whenever we make a mistake, or a transaction goes awry, we should employ **ROLLBACK**. For instance, if we try to enter a duplicate record into a database table or update the incorrect record, we should use **ROLLBACK**.

Assume you are creating an application for a university. You wish to set up a transaction so that the marks of the students can be easily recorded.

Write a SQL statement for updating the marks, where first we deduct the two marks of a student whose roll_No is R1245 and subsequently two marks added to the student whose roll_No is R1246.

```
UPDATE student
SET marks = marks- 2
```

```
WHERE Roll_NO = R1245;
```

Now we will update the record for another student.

```
UPDATE student
SET marks = marks + 2
WHERE Roll_No = R1246;
```

Let's see the execution of the transaction.

```
BEGIN TRANSACTION;

UPDATE student
SET marks = marks- 2
WHERE Roll_NO = R1245;
UPDATE student
SET marks = marks + 2
WHERE Roll_No = R1246;

COMMIT;
```

This will guarantee that either the updates are successfully made to the database, or none at all.

Now consider a scenario in which the transaction fails due to an issue like a network connection issue or a power outage.

In this scenario, the transaction's modifications would all be reversed using the **ROLLBACK** command.

```
UPDATE student
SET marks = marks- 2
WHERE Roll_NO = R1245;

UPDATE student
SET marks = marks + 2
WHERE Roll_No = R1246;

ROLLBACK;
```

By doing this, you can ensure that the database is exactly where it was before the transaction began. You can ensure that your database transactions are always carried out securely and consistently by utilizing **COMMIT** and **ROLLBACK**.

Best practices for using COMMIT and ROLLBACK:

The following are some of the best practices used:

- Apply **COMMIT** often. Making modifications often is preferable to waiting until the end of a transaction to make all the changes at once. This is due to the fact that you may easily revert the changes to the most recent successful **COMMIT** if something goes wrong with a transaction.

- If something goes wrong, use **`ROLLBACK`** right away. Roll back the modifications right away if you make a mistake or if a transaction goes awry. By doing this, you can avoid unintentionally making the modifications permanent.
- To begin a transaction, use **`BEGIN TRANSACTION`**. Using the **`BEGIN TRANSACTION`** statement to begin a transaction is best practice. This will make it simple for you to undo all the modifications that the transaction performed if something goes wrong.

Logging and Recovery Techniques

The database logs enable recovery from failures and synchronization of primary and backup databases. Hence they are essential for your highly available database solution design. Every database has logs connected to it. Database modifications are documented in these logs. Logs are necessary to roll the data forward to the point of failure if a database needs to be restored to a point higher than the most recent complete offline backup.

Like any other computer system, database systems might malfunction, but the data they hold must always be accessible when needed. A database must have the means of recovering quickly in the event of a failure. Additionally, it must be atomic, meaning that transactions must either successfully finish and commit (recording the effect in the database permanently or not affect the database at all).

Recovery Techniques

Database management systems (DBMSs) employ database recovery strategies to bring a database back to a consistent state following a malfunction or error. Preventing data loss and ensuring data consistency and integrity are the two fundamental objectives of recovery procedures.

In DBMSs, three primary recovery strategies are employed.

- Rollback/Undo Recovery Technique
- Commit/Redo Recovery Technique
- CheckPoint Recovery Technique

Rollback/Undo Recovery Technique:

The idea behind the rollback/undo recovery strategy is to reverse the results of a transaction that was unsuccessfully completed because of a system error or malfunction. Using the log records kept in the transaction log, this procedure is carried out by reversing the modifications made by the transaction. Every transaction made on the database is documented in the transaction log. The unsuccessful transaction's modifications are reversed by the system using the log records, returning the database to its initial state.

Commit/Redo Recovery Technique:

The commit/redo recovery method is based on applying changes made by a successful transaction to the database again. This approach is about reapplying the changes made by committed transactions to ensure durability in case of mistake or failure by using the log records stored in the transaction log. The system uses the log records to reapply the changes made during the transaction, returning the database to its most recent consistent state.

Checkpoint Recovery Technique:

A technique called checkpoint recovery is utilized, particularly in distributed systems and databases, to enhance system stability and data integrity. It comprises maintaining the system's state at predetermined intervals or checkpoints when all active transactions are either finished or not started. To endure system crashes, this saved state–which includes memory and CPU registers–is maintained in steady and non-volatile storage. Restoring the system to the most recent checkpoint minimizes data loss and downtime in the case of a malfunction. Carefully calibrated checkpoint formation frequency reduces system overhead while guaranteeing prompt restoration of recent data.

In database management systems, recovery procedures are crucial for guaranteeing data availability and consistency. Each methodology has pros and downsides that should be taken into account when designing a recovery system.

Log-based Recovery:

Database recovery procedures are methods used to recover data lost as a result of system crashes, transaction errors, viruses, catastrophic failures, improper command execution, and so on. Therefore, methods for recovering from data loss based on delayed and instantaneous updates or data backups can be employed. The availability of a unique file called a system log is crucial to recovery methods. It includes details about each transaction's beginning, ending, and any updates that take place in between. Every transaction that modifies the values of database objects is recorded in the log. To recover from a failed transaction, this information is required.

- **`Start_transaction(T)`**: It will record the entry as the transaction T started.
- **`Read_item(T, X)`**: This will record that transaction T read the data item X.
- **`Write_item(T, X, old_value, new_value)`**: This log entry documents the modification of database item X's value from **`old_value`** to **`new_value`** by transaction T. Sometimes the new value is referred to as an afterimage of X, whereas the old value is called a before image of X.
- **`Commit(T)`**: This log line indicates that transaction T has successfully finished all database accesses, allowing its impact to be committed–that is, permanently

recorded in the database.

- **`Abort(T)`**: This denotes that transaction T is aborted due to some failure.
- **`Checkpoint`**: Through the use of a checkpoint mechanism, all prior logs are permanently kept on a storage disc and deleted from the system. A checkpoint designates a time before all transactions were committed, and the database management system was in a consistent state. When a transaction T's database-accessing actions are completed successfully, the transaction reaches its commit point and will no longer abort (end without finishing). The transaction is stored in the database permanently after it is committed. Writing a commit entry to the log and writing the log to the disc are always required steps in the commit process. When a system crashes, all transactions T that have written a **`start_transaction(T)`** entry into the log but have not yet written a commit(T) entry are looked up in the log; these transactions might need to be rolled back during the recovery process to reverse their impact on the database.

When a transaction T's database-accessing actions are completed successfully, the transaction reaches its commit point and will no longer abort (end without finishing). The transaction is stored in the database permanently after it is committed. Writing a commit entry to the log and writing the log to the disc are always required steps in the commit process. When a system crashes, all transactions T that have written a **`start_transaction(T)`** entry into the log but have not yet written a commit(T) entry are found in the item's log; these transactions might need to be rolled back during the recovery process to reverse their impact on the database.

- **Undoing:** The recovery manager has the ability to reverse a transaction's operations if it crashes. Setting the value of item x in the database to old-value entails looking over a transaction for the log entry **`write_item(T, x, old_value, new_value)`**. Deferred updates and instantaneous updates are the two main methods for recovering from non-catastrophic transaction failures.
- **Deferred Update:** Until a transaction reaches its commit point, this method does not physically change the database on the disc. All transaction updates are tracked in the local transaction workspace prior to commit. **UNDO** is not required if a transaction fails before it reaches its commit point because it will not alter the database in any way. Because the effects of the actions stored in the local transaction workspace might not have been registered in the database yet, it might be necessary to REDO those effects. Therefore, the No-undo/redo technique is another name for a deferred update.
- **Immediate Update:** Certain operations of a transaction may update the database in the instant update before the transaction reaches its commit point. Recovery is still feasible, though, because these actions are first documented in a log-on disc before being applied to the database. We need to both undo and redo a transaction because if it fails to reach its commit point, its operation must be reversed, or rolled back. This method is called the

"undo/redo algorithm."

- **Caching:** This involves caching into main memory buffers one or more disc pages containing data items that need to be changed, updating them in memory, and then writing them back to the disc. The DBMS is responsible for managing a group of in-memory buffers known as the DBMS cache, which is used to store these buffers. To maintain track of which database objects are present in the buffer, utilize a directory. Every buffer has a dirty bit, which is 0 if the buffer is not altered otherwise, 1 if altered.
- **Shadow Paging:** It offers endurance and atomicity. A directory containing n entries is created, with the ith entry pointing to the link's ith database page. The current directory is copied into a shadow directory when a transaction starts to execute. A shadow page is designated for any modifications to a page, and once the page is ready to be made durable, all references to the original are updated to point to the new replacement page.
- **Backward Recovery:** Backward recovery can also be referred to by the terms "`Rollback`" and "`UNDO`". This method can be useful when a backup of the data is not accessible, and changes made before need to be reversed. The database is restored to its original state using the backward recovery approach, which also removes any alterations that were not needed. During the backward recovery, all the modifications made during the preceding traction are undone. Stated differently, it reverses incorrect database alterations and reprocesses legitimate transactions.
- **Forward Recovery:** Forwarding recovery is referred to as "roll forward" and "`REDO`." This forward recovery technique helps when a database needs to be updated and all changes confirmed. To carry over those changes, a few unsuccessful transactions in this database are applied to the database. Stated differently, the database is recovered using stored information and legitimate transactions determined by their historical saves.

Backup Techniques:

Different kinds of backup techniques exist. Following is a list of a few of them.

- **Complete backup:** A predetermined time period is used to back up the metadata–including full-text catalogs, necessary to restore the entire database, including data and database.
- **Differential Backup:** This type of backup keeps track of modifications to the data made since the last complete database backup. A differential backup holds the most recent version of the modified data in cases where certain data has changed significantly since the last full database backup. We must first restore a complete database backup to do this.
- **Transaction Log Backup:** This includes a backup of all database activities, including a log of each and every statement that has been run. It is a database

backup that includes every transaction that has ever occurred in the transaction log. This allows the database to be restored to a certain point in time. If the data files are lost but not a single committed transaction is lost, it is also possible to create a backup from a transaction log.

Conclusion

The ACID characteristics of a DBMS aid in the construction of an effective and faultless database.

The basis and four pillars of a strong database are analogous to the four ACID features. These characteristics enable a database to handle transactions accurately and maintain consistent, safe, and accurate data.

So, be sure to utilize the ACID features effectively if you want to create a robust, prosperous database.

The practice of carrying out several transactions concurrently without experiencing data loss or inconsistencies is known as concurrency control. We have gone over the comprehensive concurrency control guidance in this post. We now understand what concurrent execution in database management systems is, as well as transaction states. Also covered were the fundamentals of concurrency control and the significance of utilizing concurrency techniques.

We have seen a variety of approaches, such as lock-based protocols, time-stamp-based protocols, and optimistic concurrency control protocols to manage concurrency in transactions. Concurrency control prevents inconsistent data, minimizes dirty reads, maximizes efficiency, encourages data sharing, safeguards atomicity, and prevents conflicts, all of which contribute to the smooth and accurate operation of the database.

Database systems must be failsafe if data consistency and availability are to be guaranteed at all times. Using a variety of recovery strategies, including rollback/undo, commit/redo, and checkpoint recovery, may be necessary to restore database consistency. These systems keep an eye on and control modifications to data by utilizing system and transaction logs. The specific needs and limitations of the database system dictate the best recovery strategy. Reduction of data loss, preservation of data integrity, and guaranteeing database management system dependability depend on the proper design of recovery techniques.

In the next chapter, we will have a detailed discussion on data warehousing and business intelligence.

Questions

1. Define and discuss different states of transactions with Diagram.
2. Explain various types of Locks in concurrency control with a suitable example.
3. Illustrate the lost update problem with a suitable example.
4. Explain in detail the timestamp-based concurrency control techniques with a suitable example.
5. What is a 2-phase locking protocol? How does it guarantee serializability?
6. Describe Wait/Die & Wound/Wait protocols in concurrency control.
7. Explain the ARIES recovery method. When does a system recover from a crash? In what order must a transaction be undone and redone? Why is this order important?
8. Why is concurrency control needed? Explain the problems that would arise when concurrency control is not provided by the database system.
9. Explain Grant and Revoke commands with examples.
10. Check whether the given schedule is serializable or not using a precedence graph. Explain with the algorithm. S1:R1(X) R2(Z) R1(Z) R3(X) R3(Y) W1(X) W3(Y) R2(Y) W2(Z) W2(Y).

CHAPTER 7
Data Warehousing and Business Intelligence

Introduction

To help and facilitate analysis, especially on analytics, the business intelligence teams use a specific kind of data management system known as a data warehouse. Data warehouses are frequently used for search and analysis purposes containing huge amounts of historical information. For instance, application log files and transaction apps are among the various sources from which the data in a data warehouse is collected.

A lot of data from multiple sources comes together to be kept centrally in one place called a data warehouse. Organizations can make more informed decisions as they can gain key insights into their business based on their analytical possibilities with this information. Over time, it accumulates a body of past records which can be greatly useful for business analysts or even data scientists.

A data warehouse can be regarded as an organization's "single source of truth" due to these features."

A data warehouse is a sizable, central repository for data created to facilitate business intelligence-related operations. This is why; a data warehouse is a very effective decision support tool because it's capable of organizing and presenting information in a way that it can be easily accessed and analyzed. Through the extract, transform, and load (ETL) processes, it acts as a central repository of this disparate data compiled from several sources. Data loading, transformation, and extraction make up data warehousing. Data may usually be extracted from a multitude of sources by a company, including spreadsheets, text files, databases, APIs, web scraping, and IoT devices. Subsequently, the extracted data is converted into common forms for easy analysis and stored in data warehouses for quick access as needed.

Structure

In this chapter, we will cover the following topics:

- Data Warehouse Architecture
- Extract, Transform, Load (ETL) Processes
- Data Mining and Analytics
- Business Intelligence (BI) Tools and Dashboards
- Reporting and Decision Support Systems

Data Warehouse

As part of data management systems, massive amounts of data are kept in the data warehouses for further processing and analysis. Think of it as a large warehouse where cars, or sources of data, release their data. The information is then organized into countless rows of tidy stacked shelves, making it easier to find the exact thing you're looking for later. According to DW 2.0, the Architecture for the Next Generation of Data Warehousing, the capacity to store "integrated granular historical data" was the advanced data warehouse introduced at the time of their creation.

Translating that into everyday language, data warehouses are excellent at storing data that are:

- **Integrated**: Bringing together information from several databases and sources.
- **Granular**: Holding incredibly comprehensive data that has numerous applications.
- **Historical**: Having the capacity to store an unbroken record of data spanning many years.

Three options are available to us for storing this data: Data warehouses that are cloud-based, hybrid, and located on-site.

- On-premise data warehouses are housed on real servers that are owned and operated by your business. Cloud data warehouses, such as Amazon Redshift, are online and need payment for server space that is managed by a third party. Businesses that are gradually moving to the cloud utilize hybrid data warehouses, which combine on-premise and cloud computing.
- As all the data is kept in one location, data warehouses process data using an approach known as online analytical processing (OLAP), which is intended for complicated queries.
- One way to look at it is as a technique to quickly obtain information about the relationships between different sets of data when you visit your data

warehouse. OLAP facilitates this process by arranging and navigating the many rows of shelves.

- As the questions you ask about your data to make decisions are rarely easy, this is perfect for business intelligence. Data warehouses use OLAP which greatly increases the efficiency of answering these difficult inquiries. They now serve as the basis for numerous effective business intelligence solutions as a result.
- Aspects: storage, software, and labor: You must consider the necessary expenditure for each of the three when deciding whether to deploy a data warehouse.
- Choosing storage is not too difficult. You have three options for hosting your data warehouse: on-premises, in the cloud, or hybrid. Some people believe that on-premises hosting is becoming obsolete. Cloud hosting is far more flexible and less expensive because you're renting space on someone else's server. There's no maintenance to be done; you can grow and shrink as needed, and every year, a new set of features is added. Hybrid hosting, as previously indicated, bridges the gap between these two strategies and is the recommended option for businesses moving from on-premises to cloud hosting.
- You need to utilize a kind of software known as ETL software to get data into your data warehouse. The process of extracting, preparing the data for use, and then, loading it into a data warehouse is known as extract, transform, and load, or ETL.
- These days, we advocate for and observe an increasing number of businesses utilizing extract, load, and transform (ELT) as an alternative to ETL. Businesses frequently take data out of the original source, put it into a data lake, and then utilize data warehouses to change the data.
- Data warehouses are not self-sufficient. Data warehouses are "full-fledged architectures," requiring professionals to set up and maintain, hence labor is an important component in maintaining one.
- All of this work is aimed at centralizing and organizing data to make it easier to understand. Business intelligence technologies are useful in this situation. In essence, they act as a layer that queries, analyzes, and visualizes your data on top of the data warehouses.

The Evolution of Data Warehouses

- There was a huge need for redundancy in these early data warehouses. Most organizations cater to their diverse user base across numerous DSS environments. Even though the DSS environments shared a large amount of data, each environment's data collection, processing, and integration were frequently repeated.

- Data warehouses have developed from information repositories supporting typical BI platforms into broad analytics infrastructures supporting a wide range of applications, including performance management and operational analytics, as they have become more efficient.
- Enterprise data warehouse (EDW) iterations have advanced over time to provide the business with incrementally more value.

Components of Data Warehousing

The following are the main elements of data warehousing:

- The systems that generate data are known as data sources; they can be either internal or external. First-, second- and third-party sources are the three groups into which they can be separated. Several well-known types of data sources include relational databases, flat files and XML datasets, web scraping, web servers, APIs, feeds, and data streams.
- Data is gathered from multiple sources, formatted according to a common format, and then loaded into a data warehouse using ETL (extract, transform, and load) technologies. ETL tools are typically used to process event data that is sent in real-time. One such instance is Microsoft SQL Server Integration Services.
- All of the data is housed in one place in a data warehouse. The data warehouse is designed to manage massive amounts of data and is best suited for analytics. One of the most well-known data warehouse examples is Azure Synapse Analytics.
- The data kept in a data warehouse can be accessed, retrieved, and evaluated with the assistance of business intelligence tools. These include data visualization tools, dashboards, and reporting tools, most notably Microsoft Power BI.

Advantages of Data Warehousing

Some of the advantages are:

- It offers a comprehensive perspective of the data, making businesses easier to recognize trends, opportunities, and patterns to improve overall decision-making.
- Consistent, accurate, and up-to-date data is preserved in a central repository.
- Faster decision-making is made possible for organizations by easy and quick data retrieval, which provides faster access to information.
- Combining data from several sources reduces the cost of data analysis and maintenance.

- Owing to its capacity to handle massive volumes of data, it offers a broad choice of scalable solutions for businesses of all sizes.

Benefits of a Data Warehouse

The primary benefit that data warehouses offer is that they allow companies to examine large amounts of variable data and retain historical information, both of which can be very valuable.

According to this definition, the four unique characteristics of the data warehouses are

- **Subject-focused:** Information about certain subjects or functional areas (like sales).
- **Merged:** Numerous data kinds from disparate sources are harmonized by data warehouses.
- **Not Erratic:** Once kept in a data warehouse, data is time-independent, consistent, and unchanging.
- **Change Analysis:** Data warehouse analysis concentrates on changes throughout time.

A well-designed data warehouse will process queries very quickly, with high throughput, and allow enough flexibility for end users to "slice and dice" or minimize the volume of data for closer scrutiny to meet a variety of demands irrespective of high level, detailed level, or fine level. Middleware BI environments that offer reports, dashboards, and other interfaces to end users are functionally supported by the data warehouse.

Data Warehouse Architecture

The particular requirements of the organization define the basic architecture of a data warehouse. Typical architectural designs comprise:

- **Simple:** Raw data, summary data, and Metadata are all kept in the warehouse›s central repository, which is the same fundamental layout for all data warehouses. On one end of the repository, data sources feed it, while on the other, end users access it for mining, reporting, and analysis.
- **Simple with a Staging Area:** It is necessary to clean and analyze operational data before storing it in a warehouse. Even though this can be done programmatically, many data warehouses include a staging space for data before it enters the warehouse to facilitate data preparation.
- **Hub and Spoke**: By establishing data marts between the central repository and end users, a firm can customize its data warehouse to support several business

lines. When the data is ready for use, it is transferred to the appropriate data mart.

- **Sandboxes:** Companies can swiftly and informally investigate new datasets or methods of data analysis in sandboxes–private, protected spaces–without having to follow the official guidelines and procedures of a data warehouse.

Business Intelligence

BI collects, evaluates, and presents data used for business decisions. Data is gathered from many sources, cleansed, transformed using different tools and techniques, and assembled together. Thereafter, it is given to the decision-makers in an understandable format, that is, short. This aids companies to make informed choices that improve customer satisfaction and increase high-output growth through BI. In addition, this assists organizations in predicting possible risks or hurdles that they encounter thus enabling them to take preventive measures rather than suffering financial problems. It can be used as a way of performing several tasks:

Data Collection

At this stage, data is collected from a variety of sources in one place making it easier to analyse. For instance, a retail startup looking at what factors are behind its sales success could pull together data from points of sale systems, customer loyalty programs as well as social network audits. Startups can leverage online reviews, sales statistics, and customer information among other types of data.

Data Analysis

This is the stage where organizations deduce and reveal hidden pieces of information after gathering data. For instance, the retail company could analyze data and determine patterns and trends through statistical analysis, machine learning, and data mining technologies. Using this research, businesses can find out who their most valuable customers are based on demographics, poorly performing products as well as best sellers.

Data Visualization

In practice, its recommendations should be immediately comprehensible to business managers as well as other stakeholders. This means that one can easily represent such figures aesthetically and understandably using charts, graphs, or dashboards among other data visualization tools. The retail industry, for example, may opt for a dashboard that gives historical sales trends per product type or target market.

Reports

Reporting includes preparing regular updates that consolidate details from various sources into an overview; while providing insights to those requesting the analysis results. Thus, these reports help in decision-making and locating areas requiring improvements. A case in point is when a retailer produces a weekly sales report discussing what is selling fast from those that are not selling at all.

Performance Management

The objective of this phase is to improve the use of data provided through data analysis. This could mean coming up with new strategies or methods or modifying existing ones. For example, depending on information obtained via data analysis, the retail company might choose to increase its marketing expenditure or change its pricing policy to reach certain customer demographics more effectively.

Data Warehousing in Business Intelligence

The foundation of data storage in business intelligence is provided by data warehouses. Complex inquiries and the comparison of different data sets are the foundation of business intelligence, which is used to inform everything from routine choices to organizational-wide emphasis shifts.

The three main components of business intelligence are data wrangling, data storage, and data analysis, which enable this. Extract, transform, load (ETL) technologies–which we'll go into more depth about later usually help with data wrangling, and business intelligence tools–like Chartio–are used for data analysis. Data warehouses, which act as the facilitator of data storage utilizing OLAP, hold this process together. They simplify, combine, and convert data to facilitate analysis. Although they constitute the foundation of data storage, data warehouses are not the only technologies used in data storage. Before realizing they need a data warehouse, many businesses go through a hierarchy of data storage. A comprehensive data analytics solution is created by combining the complementary technologies of data warehousing and business intelligence. The data is managed and stored in the data warehouse after the insights are taken using BI technology.

Data warehousing combines information from various sources into one place that can be easily extracted, transformed, and loaded as necessary. All these have been covered in data warehousing when it comes to delivering insights using BI tools. By utilizing business intelligence, businesses are able to evaluate the data stored in the data warehouse to gain meaningful information. When armed with this information, decision-makers are better placed to take informed actions toward organizational growth. Business users can access and review such databases without any technical skills necessary due to self-service analytical capabilities offered by business intelligence systems such as Microsoft Power BI. For instance, a marketing department at a retail store may use Microsoft Power BI to examine sales details kept within a data warehouse to create reports on purchasing trends and the behavior of customers. Users can create dynamic dashboards to visualize sales trends with low-code features. This frees the team from reliance on IT teams and enables them to make data-driven decisions in real time.

Cloud Data Warehouse

This collects and stores data from various data sources using the cloud.

On-premises servers were used in the construction of the first data warehouses. These on-site data warehouses still have a lot of benefits today. They can frequently provide better latency, security, data sovereignty, and governance. They are less elastic and necessitate intricate forecasting to grow the data warehouse for future requirements. These data warehouses can be quite difficult to manage.

However, a few benefits of cloud data warehouses are as follows:

- Support for high or fluctuating compute or storage requirements that are elastic and scale-out
- Easy to use
- Easier management Process
- Economic

The greatest cloud data warehouses are fully managed and self-sufficient, that is, anyone can set one up and begin using it with minimal effort. Running your cloud data warehouse on-premises, behind your data center firewall, and compliant with data sovereignty and security regulations, is a simple approach to begin your cloud data warehouse migration.

Additionally, the majority of cloud data warehouses have a pay-as-you-go business model which saves clients even more money.

Modern Data Warehouse

Those many needs are met by a modern data architecture, which offers a mechanism to handle workloads, analysis, and all data kinds. It is made up of architectural designs with all required parts combined to function as a unit in accordance with industry best practices. A converged database that makes managing various data types easier; support for SQL, machine learning, self-service data ingestion, graph, transformation services, and spatial processing; multiple analytics options that facilitate using data without moving it; automated management for straightforward provisioning, scaling, and administration are some of the features of a modern data warehouse.

In a manner that traditional warehouses are unable to, a modern data warehouse may effectively streamline data workflows. This implies that everyone may work more productively and pursue the creative activity that advances the company, without endless delays and complications, including analysts, data engineers, data scientists, and IT teams.

Designing a Data Warehouse

An organization must first decide on the scope, define its unique business requirements, and write a conceptual design before designing a data warehouse. The company can then, start working on the data warehouse's logical and physical design. The relationships between the things are part of the logical design, and the most effective means of storing and retrieving the objects is part of the physical design. The methods for backup, recovery, and transit are also included in the physical design.

The following needs to be considered in any data warehouse design:

- The data warehouse's supporting systems environment
- Kinds of data transformations
- Relationships inside and between data groups
- Data content
- Frequency of data refreshes

The end users' needs are a key component of the design. Instead of viewing data as individual transactions, most end users are more interested in conducting analyses and viewing data as a whole. However, unless a certain need emerges, end customers frequently don't know what they want. Planning should therefore involve significant research to foresee needs. Finally, to keep up with the changing needs of end users, the design of the data warehouse should be flexible enough to grow and adapt.

The Cloud and the Data Warehouse

Cloud-based data warehouses provide all the features and advantages of on-premises data warehouses along with the extra advantages of cloud computing, including cost savings, flexibility, scalability, agility, and security. With cloud data warehouses, businesses can concentrate entirely on deriving value from their data, instead of constructing and overseeing the software and hardware infrastructure needed to support the data warehouse.

When handling massive amounts of data from numerous sources, organizations employ data lakes as well as data warehouses. Depending on how the organization plans to use the data, it will determine when to use each. The ideal applications for each are as follows:

- A plethora of unprocessed, heterogeneous data is stored in data lakes for potential use later. In a data lake, raw data from many sources, such as social media, IoT devices, mobile apps, and line-of-business applications is stored. The individual conducting the study determines the format, selection, integrity, and structure of the multiple datasets at that point. A data lake may be the best option for businesses that require inexpensive storage for unstructured, unformatted data from several sources that they plan to utilize at some point in the future.
- Data analysis is the primary purpose of the data warehouse. Data that has been prepared for analysis–gathered, contextualized, and transformed–is processed analytically in a data warehouse to produce analysis-based insights. Large amounts of data from numerous sources can also be handled by a data warehouse with ease. A data warehouse is usually the best option for enterprises that want complex data analytics or analysis that utilizes historical data from various sources within the firm.

ETL (Extracting, Transforming, and Loading Data)

The three procedures of extracting, converting, and loading data into a single, consistent database from many sources are together referred to as ETL. This data source is usually a data warehouse containing prepared information that can be processed to obtain analytical insights. An essential component of data management is ETL.

When ETL first started, data analysis and computing were its main uses. ETL is currently widely used by businesses to support business intelligence using a variety of big data analytics and machine learning procedures. ETL guarantees data cleanliness and consistency throughout enterprises in addition to making data access easier for analysis and further processing. ETL is also used by organizations to enhance the quality of the data, store old data, and obtain a unified picture of all the data across the company.

ETL is being utilized today to improve decision-making and end-user service across many industries, including healthcare, manufacturing, and finance.

ETL Processes

Extract, Transform, and Load are three different processes of ETL.

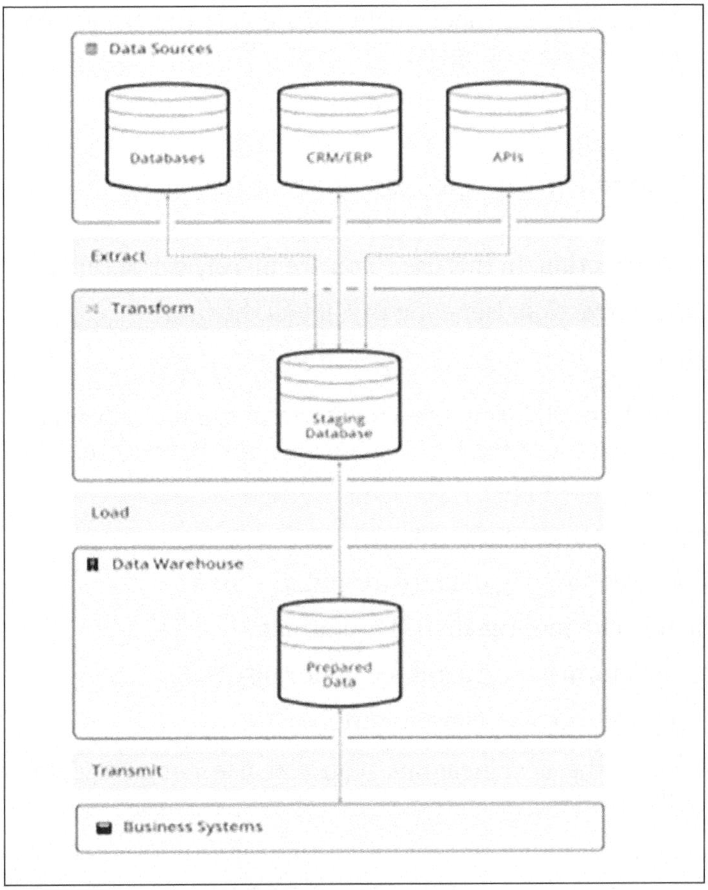

Figure 7.1: *ETL process*

Step 1: Extract

During this stage, unprocessed data is taken out of several sources and kept in one repository. Among the sources of raw data are:

- Systems for managing customer relationships (CRM)
- Internet of Things (IoT) sensors and machine data
- Web pages
- Email archives
- ERP (enterprise resource planning) systems
- Data from APIs
- SQL or NoSQL servers

The source data is available in a variety of forms, including tables, JSON, and XML, and can be organized, unstructured, or semi-structured. Validating the data and eliminating or flagging the erroneous data are steps in the extraction process. There are several methods for extracting data:

- **Online Extraction:** To extract the data, establish a direct connection with the data source
- **Offline Extraction:** Extracted to a different staging location rather than being extracted straight from the data source
- **Gradual extraction:** In this case, you are merely extracting the modified data
- **Complete extraction:** Here you extract all the info

Step 2: Transform

Data must be transformed during the Transform phase into a format that enables its loading into unified data sources. In a staging area, raw data is processed at this phase. The following tasks may be part of the processing:

- Eliminating redundant information
- Verifying and purifying data to prevent mistakes
- Converting data into the necessary format
- Editing data formats to guarantee uniformity
- Filtering to get rid of irrelevant info

Moreover, based on the specifications, you can use complex data transformation methods. As an illustration:

- Data joining
- Data derivation and creation of new values
- Data splitting into different columns
- Data encryption to abide by data privacy rules
- Data summarising to minimize the size of the data collection

Step 3: Load

The last step is to load the transformed data from the staging area into the data warehouse when the data extraction and processing stages are finished. This is a well-defined, automated, and continuous process, with batch loading typically occurring. These are some techniques for loading data:

- **The full loading of data:** Usually, this loading takes place during the first load. The data set must be extracted and transformed from the data source to the data warehouse.
- **The gradual loading of data:** Loading only updated data between the target and source systems regularly. The time and date of the last data extraction should be stored by the ETL system.

- **Loading in batches:** If the data collection is too big, then load it in batches regularly.
- **Incremental load streaming:** With one important disclaimer, this data streams continually. This loading style works best with smaller data sets.

ETL Use Cases

The common use cases in ETL are:

- **Data Warehousing and Business Intelligence (BI)**
  Gather, examine, and arrange data for corporate reporting, OLAP (online analytical processing), and dashboard creation, among other business intelligence duties.
- **Cloud Migration**
  When businesses move their systems and data to or from on-premises data centers to cloud settings, ETL processes extract, transform, and load data into cloud storage and databases.
- **Machine Learning and Artificial Intelligence**
  Accurate machine learning models and tasks related to classification and clustering can be produced using enormous data sets. The performance of machine learning models can be greatly accelerated by the high-quality data stored in data warehouses.
- **IoT Data Integration**
  IoT data integration is crucial for various industries, including manufacturing, healthcare, and logistics, where real-time data analysis can lead to improved operational efficiency and decision-making.
- **Market Data Integration**
  Numerous websites, including social networks, third-party portals, and online analytics platforms, may contain marketing data. This data may be collected, thanks to ETL, which enables analysis and visualization of the results of their marketing campaigns.

ETL Tools and Benefits

When building ETL pipelines, ETL tools enable the tasks involved in these three stages to be automated. Among the leading providers of ETL goods and services are Microsoft, AWS, Google, IBM, and Oracle. Several instances of ETL software tools are:

- Informatica
- Matillion
- Talend
- Fivetran

Benefits of ETL

The following are the benefits of ETL:

- **Improve Data Quality**

  Often containing errors, duplicates, and missing numbers, the original data hinders the ability to derive meaningful business insights. Organizations can enhance the quality of their data by using ETL solutions, which offer automatic data cleaning processes like deleting errors, substituting missing information, and eliminating duplicates. It enables them to consistently keep a uniform data collection on hand for a variety of organizational needs.

- **Enhance Performance**

  Easy and quick access to the data is made possible by the converted data in a data warehouse. Additional features that improve performance, including symmetric multiprocessing and parallel processing, can also be included in ETL programs. Without requiring data processing, it enables business intelligence (BI) tools to query the data warehouse directly. As a result, the tools can produce reports and other findings more quickly.

- **Reduce Unnecessary Costs**

  It takes a lot of time and resources to maintain data from many sources. For organizations, it will also result in needless maintenance expenses. When raw data is in consolidated data sources, it can be deleted or preserved in a different central repository. As a result, you're saving money and making it simpler to save data in a central repository.

- **Improves Productivity**

  ETL systems, in contrast to manual methods, automate all stages of the process, from data extraction to creating business value. This helps businesses to concentrate on enhancing their brand rather than carrying out tedious and time-consuming duties.

- **Ensures Data Security**

  The required data security and privacy are provided via encryption, data backup, recovery techniques, and data access controls built into ETL technologies. This function lowers the organization's risk of unwanted access and cyber threats.

- **Provide Data Visualization**

  An intuitive user interface for data visualization and access is offered by ETL tools. It anyone complete necessary activities even with no programming experience. Certain tools allow you to drag and drop objects.

Challenges for ETL Processes

Even while ETL is a normal procedure in any context with a lot of data, it has its own set of difficulties.

- **High Data Complexity and Volume**
  It is possible to find vast volumes of intricately aggregated data. ETL extraction and transformation may be slowed down as a result, or you may need to combine techniques.

- **High Network Latency**
  When a lot of data needs to be extracted and loaded, network latency might become a hurdle for the ETL process's performance.

- **Lack of Enough Computing Resources**
  If the ETL system isn't getting enough CPU power, it can slow down processes, memory, and storage. On the other hand, depending on the resource requirements, cloud-based ETL systems can frequently scale resources up or down.

- **Maintenance**
  Data from unprocessed sources is frequently erratic. Data formats can also change over time. Requests for more functionality, such as extra data columns, may arise. Because of this, ETL workflows must adapt often to meet these demands, which could result in extra expenses and overhead for the business.

- **Future Requirements**
  In ETL, transformation is the most important phase. Depending on the necessary transformation procedures, this task may demand a lot of time and resources. Underestimating the requirements for transformation will result in erroneous and incomplete transformed data which prevents the data from being loaded into the data warehouse.
  This is where a lot of ETL procedures go wrong. Most importantly, you must specify the precise specifications for data transformation.

- **Lack of Training and Awareness**
  Businesses may need to ensure that their employees have the necessary training to manage ETL data pipelines. To ensure data safety, they should also be educated to handle the data properly and according to established rules.

ETL Tool for Data Integration

Streamlining ETL Data Integration: The Advantages of Automation, Flexibility, and Improved Data Quality.

Companies use a range of apps and systems, so information is stored in several databases. As a result, important information is not as clearly shown or visible. An

ETL tool offers a structured approach and the capacity to accomplish data integration between various databases and systems. As a result, there is less need for complicated and unstructured custom approaches, and crucial business data is more coherent.

ETL solutions give businesses of all sizes a strong, practical, and affordable means of integrating vital business data from a variety of data sources. Because ETL can automate data integration, enhance data quality, and scale to meet the expanding data requirements of the entire organization, it is an essential part of many data warehousing and business intelligence projects. Concerning retailers who aim at a wide range of data usage and need to be ahead of the competition, the ETL system must be taken as a priceless asset.

ETL Process Example

Transforming retail database and adding it to a data warehouse:

For instance, an example of a use case would be a retail organization trying to enhance data management and analyze sales records from multiple shop locations. Using this information to develop a comprehensive perspective of how it operates the company could reallocate resources to grow its business. In this case, the steps of ETL procedure are as follows: :

- **Data Extraction:** One can imagine the retail business taking out sales information from different flat files and storing databases like those found in inventory management or point-of-sale systems.
- **Data Transformation:** In relation to the ETL process, extracted data is then cleaned, converted as well as standardized in its format thus getting rid of any errors or duplication that could have been made while collecting and gathering such information. It might involve deleting unwanted details, ensuring that data is formatted consistently, or creating calculated fields for further analysis
- **Data Loading:** Following the data transformation, it is then loaded into a database for future uses and storage during this step in the ETL process. The data warehouse has been tuned to accommodate various data types and their corresponding use cases.
- **Data Analysis:** Retail businesses would be able to carry out a range of data analytics after importing the data, including figuring out which products are selling well at which shop locations, what days and hours are the busiest, and which promotions have been the most effective. This might enable the business to make better-informed business decisions.

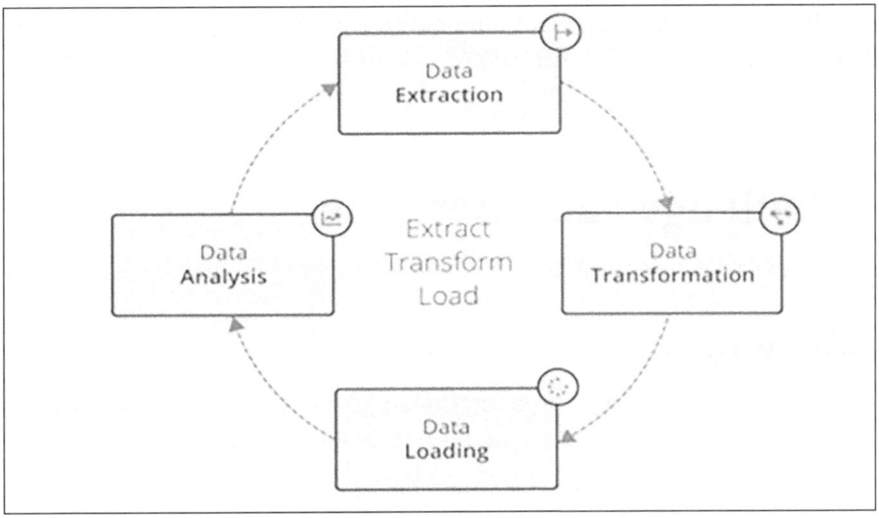

Figure 7.2: ETL Process

ETL Tool Example

The following are the examples of ETL tools that are discussed in detail:

Transforming and Mapping CSV Files

When a company wants to do a normal import routine–like importing data in bulk with or without data transformation–or when a flat file import routine is lacking, this is another typical ETL scenario that calls for using an ETL tool. Plain text and CSV (delimited or fixed width) files are examples of flat files; they do not communicate back and forth between applications as an API does. This means that the following scenarios call for the use of extract transform load solutions with flat files:

- When regular or minimal changes are needed for the data in your application, or when an import procedure is in place for a particular dataset.
- The first synchronization or one-time import of a substantial amount of data.

Examine the situation where a new eCommerce website is put into service to synchronize data with an ERP system. Bulk product uploads are typically started by utilizing CSV files and the eCommerce platforms' import routine, especially if 10,000+ products need to be uploaded. However, these uploads are prone to human processing errors. It could be a costly manual process if there is no ETL tool in place. Errors may arise, for instance, during the first synchronization of bulk uploads. The CSV file could be rejected if there are missing entries in a necessary field or there might be multiple commas or commas in the wrong location. Consequently, in the absence of ETL software, a worker would have to locate the CSV file by hand, make the necessary changes, and then, re-import the file, hoping that the formatting would not be lost.

Import problems and error risks are eliminated with an ETL tool. Data from the CSV file will be dynamically extracted transformed to make it compatible with the target system or database, and then loaded to the database location. This will ultimately save a business, money and time.

ETL Challenges and Benefits

Common issues faced by companies during the ETL implementation process are:

ETL Challenges

ETL may be hard, but it enables organizations to have insights from their data that is helpful in decision-making and become more efficient and streamlined.

- **Data Quality:** Ensuring that the data being extracted is accurate and complete is a challenge for most organizations. Data inconsistency or errors due to incorrect or incomplete information in the data warehouse can greatly affect the quality of the company's data thus being very costly.
- **Data Transformation:** This procedure makes business performance however negative due to its complexity and length.
- **Data Integration:** It may not be easy to integrate information from various applications and platforms which requires exactness for every piece of information loaded into the data warehouse.
- **Scalability:** This will mean an increase in how much data is available as it comes from diverse sources when organizations expand. Hence, this would result in more intricate and difficult-to-manage ETL processes posing scalability challenges for accommodating changing business needs.
- **Data Privacy and Security**: To make the data secure is one of the biggest challenges during the ETL process so we must design the methods and plan to secure the data.
- **Latency:** When data volume rises, an ETL process can take longer to complete, affecting decision-making or real-time data analysis.

Data Mining and Analytics

Transforming the input data into meaningful information is known as Data Mining. For example, a software corporation may use the computer languages R or Python to look for patterns in data to get more understanding of its customers, products, internal processes, and other subjects. This helps businesses identify critical information sets and compare them with past data. This method may lead to better decision-making and strategy. It can also help achieve other objectives, such as effective boosting of marketing and sales.

Although the terms data mining, machine learning, and data analysis are frequently used synonymously, they are not the same. Both machine learning and data mining employ patterns and analytics, while data mining looks for patterns already there in the data. Machine learning can then predict future results by incorporating the previously presented variables, patterns, or rules into the data analysis. In data mining, the laws or patterns aren't usually obvious. In machine learning applications, the machine is frequently given a rule or variable so that it can understand the data better. Data mining requires human involvement, but machine learning is meant to be initiated by a person and subsequently learned on its own. However, machine learning techniques are widely used in data mining to automate tasks. To assist businesses better in understanding their customers and potential sales outcomes, business intelligence operations frequently incorporate data mining, data analysis, artificial intelligence, machine learning, and related approaches.

Steps in the Data Mining Process

Today, practically every business uses data mining, so it's important to understand the process and how it could enhance decision-making. The following is a description of each step in the data mining process.

Business Understanding

Understanding the underlying company goals and how they are converted into a data mining challenge and strategy is the first step toward success in data mining. Understanding a company's ultimate goal is necessary to develop a data mining technique that works. For example, a store might use data mining to learn more about its customers. When the supermarket determines which products customers are most likely to buy, it has valuable business knowledge.

Data Understanding

When you know what a business requires, it's time to begin information gathering. Organizations can handle, organize, store, and gather data in a multitude of complex ways. The data mining process involves getting to know the data, identifying issues, learning new information, and looking at subsets of the data. For example, a supermarket may use a reward program that enables customers to provide their phone number during a transaction, giving the store access to the customer's past purchases.

Data Preparation

Typically, it entails transforming data in computer languages into a format that can be quantified and used by users. When preparing data for modeling, it is crucial to transform and clean the data.

Modeling

During the modeling stage, patterns in the data are found using mathematical models. Businesses can use multiple approaches to analyze the same collection of data. Although modeling requires some trial and error, it is nevertheless an important step in the data mining process.

Evaluation

The outcomes will give a list of pertinent consumer purchases that the company may utilize for its objectives and operational planning. Based on the performance of the product and sales, the managers evaluate the product and services. This will also help them to decide the future of the product or make any changes to reform.

Deployment

Deployment can be as simple or complex as a company decides is necessary, depending on the volume and kind of data. For instance, it could entail creating a single report or creating a routine data mining process. After the data mining process is over, an organization can make final decisions and the required modifications.

Data Mining Techniques in Business Analytics

In particular, how does data mining function in corporate settings? Continue reading to discover five practical methods that many companies employ.

Classification

Using this intricate data mining approach, the characteristics of the data are organized into distinct groups. Supermarket data miners, for instance, might use categorization to classify the many kinds of items that customers purchase, such as baked goods, meat, fruit, and more. These divisions assist the company in understanding the priorities of its customers when they shop.

Clustering

Since this method includes putting data sets in groups according to commonalities, it is similar to classification. Because cluster groups are more versatile than classification groups, they are a better choice for data mining. Simple cluster groups in the grocery example consist of food and non-food products.

Association Rules

Following trends based on linked variables is the goal of association in data mining.

This could imply that, in the supermarket scenario, a large number of consumers who purchase a particular item might also purchase a related second item. The company then gains the ability to combine specific items. When you shop online and come across a "people also bought this" area, you may run into association.

Regression Analysis

Planning and modeling to determine the probability of a given variable are done using regression analysis. The supermarket might, for example, predict pricing points based on consumer demand, industry competition, and product availability. The link between variables in a data collection can be found via regression analysis.

Anomaly and Outlier Detection

Finding a broad pattern alone may not be sufficient for many data mining scenarios. It can also be necessary for you to recognize and comprehend outliers in your data. For instance, if most grocery patrons are typically female, but one week in February is disproportionately male, the company can utilize anomaly detection to look into that outlier and determine what's causing it.

Data Mining Phases

The following are the different stages in data mining:

- **Data Collection:** Data is located and collected that is pertinent to an analytics application. The data may be located in a data warehouse, a data lake, or several source systems. Data lakes, which combine structured and unstructured data, are becoming more and more common in big data contexts.
- **Preparation of Data**: This phase includes several tasks like pre-processing and data exploration, followed by data purification to address errors and other issues with the data quality. In general, this is where raw data is gathered from multiple sources and transformed into a standard format that can be handled and examined.
- **Data Extraction:** Following preparation, the data is mined using the relevant data mining methods. In machine learning applications, the algorithms must frequently be trained on sample data sets to find the desired information before being applied to the entire collection of data. Several of these algorithms are:
    - **Learning:** Occasionally, an association learning rule is employed to ascertain the relationship among variables in a dataset.
    - **Classification**: Using a classification strategy, variables or objects in a data set are grouped into predefined classes or groups. Artificial neural

networks, statistics, decision trees, and linear programming are all used in data mining.

  - **Clustering**: Using a clustering strategy, items can be meaningfully grouped together based on shared qualities. In contrast to classification, which places objects in predefined categories, clustering places objects in classes that it develops.
  - **Prediction**: The prediction approach is used to forecast the relationship between independent and dependent variables as well as independent variables alone.
  - **K-nearest neighbor (KNN)**: The K-nearest neighbor (KNN) algorithm is a non-parametric technique that groups data points according to how close they are to each other and to other available data.

- **Data Interpretation and Analysis**: Depending on the nature of the research, data scientists can look at any interesting data relationships, such as correlations, association rules, or sequential patterns. Analytical models that support decision-making and other business endeavors are created using data mining results. Business executives and users are informed of the findings through data storytelling and visualization techniques.

Data Mining and Data Analysis

- **Purpose:** Technologies must be used to analyze data and generate hypotheses that will support the creation of data-driven decisions. Data mining is not limited to using only "sophisticated machine learning algorithms." It encompasses a broader range of techniques, including statistical analysis, association rule mining, and clustering, which might not always involve complex machine-learning models.
- **Data Structure:** Structured data is the primary source for most data mining studies. This is important because a specialist in data mining develops algorithms to identify patterns in data so they may be further examined. Since it is based on mathematical and scientific principles, having access to organized data guarantees data accuracy and clarity for subsequent studies. The data could be as simple as a few numerical values or as intricate as a matrix made up of hundreds of variables and millions of observations. Data mining's ultimate objective is to provide potentially useful discoveries that analysts can act upon.

  Conversely, organized, semi-structured, and unstructured data can be used for data analytics. Additionally, unlike data mining specialists, data analysts are not in charge of creating algorithms. Rather, they have to make deductions by analyzing the patterns in the data. Future organizational plans then take advantage of the newfound information.

- **Forecasting:** Businesses can better understand the current state of affairs and get a historical perspective with the help of data mining. However, data analysis is proactive in helping users avoid disasters by predicting outcomes and establishing preventative remedies for a range of future scenarios.
  It is critical to recognize that these are connected to high-tech processes despite their variances. Without data mining, it would not have been possible to extract data patterns for future predictions, which would have made data analytics impossible. Without data analytics, data mining would be pointless because structured data on its own is not a very useful tool without an accompanying action plan.
- **Visualization Tools:** Data mining usually does not include visualization tools like bar charts, graphs, and GIPs among its tools. The visualization of results, on the other hand, is what drives data analysis since without a good representation of the data, all the work that goes into data analysis would be in vain.

BI Tools and Dashboards

A wide range of techniques, processes, technologies, and architectures are used by business intelligence platforms to facilitate the extraction and ingestion of massive volumes of unprocessed and heterogeneous data into data warehouses where information may subsequently be queried. BI tools make it easier to create reports, dashboards, and data visualizations by processing and preparing raw data for analysis. Dashboards that are customizable in BI and visualization technologies ensure that the most pertinent data is shown first. What-if scenarios can be investigated by business managers to reduce risk and provide guidance for in-the-moment decisions. Future trends can be predicted using machine learning algorithms, and recurrent trends can be found by cross-referencing existing data.

Managers can see the whole picture of the company more when data sources are centrally located. Additionally, business users can read reports at any time, from any location in the globe, through data integration with mobile devices, which facilitates real-time decision-making. The goal of BI data visualization tools is to make analysis more efficient so that the typical user can see, comprehend, and make inferences from their data. The findings enable companies to make better decisions more quickly, spot patterns and prospects for new revenue streams, boost productivity, establish KPIs, and spot business possibilities.

Business Intelligence Tools

A few of the most widely used business intelligence technologies are reporting, data mining, dashboards, visualizations, ETL, and OLAP. Features of business intelligence tools may consist of any mix of the following:

- **Spreadsheets:** They are available as downloaded software and as web-based formats; they arrange data in a tabular fashion that is simple to query and format.
- **Dashboards:** A type of real-time user interface where data visualizations reflecting the present state of the data are displayed
- **Tools for Data Mining**: To find patterns in data, data mining uses artificial intelligence (AI), machine learning, statistics, and database systems. Ad hoc data analytics is an analysis method intended to provide prompt answers to certain queries.
- **Online Analytical Processing (OLAP):** Multi-dimensional analytical queries can be performed using OLAP business intelligence products' computation mechanism. Software that adapts desktop business intelligence for mobile devices is known as mobile BI.
- **Real-time Business Intelligence (BI):** A sophisticated enterprise analytics methodology that uses business transaction data to feed a real-time data warehouse, providing users with information in real time.
- **Operational Business Intelligence (BI):** A data analysis technique that automatically incorporates real-time data into an operational system for instant usage using real-time business analytics.
- **SaaS BI:** Applications as a Service Business intelligence software solutions are delivered via a cloud-based, subscription-based paradigm known as BI (SaaS BI).
- **Open Source BI (OSBI):** Business intelligence software programs that don't need software license purchases.
- **Collaborative Business Intelligence:** Refers to the integration of collaboration tools with business intelligence software to optimize the sharing process.
- **Location Intelligence:** Applications that link spatial surroundings to corporate data are known as location intelligence (LI) programs.
- **Software for Data Visualization**: Gives visual context, which makes it easier to find patterns and correlations.
- **Software for Reporting and Queries:** Features for sorting, filtering, displaying, reporting, and querying data.
- **Software for Self-service Data Preparation**: Cleans and gets ready data for analysis
- **Data Warehousing Tools:** A consolidated repository for data storage is created by integrating data retrieval from many sources. This repository can later be retrieved for analysis. UML is a modeling language primarily used for designing and documenting software systems, not specifically data warehouses. For data warehousing, developers generally use data modeling languages or techniques

such as Entity-Relationship diagrams (ERDs) or dimensional modeling to design the structure and relationships within the data warehouse.

- **Business Performance Management**: Assesses how well methods are implemented to achieve organizational objectives are working.
- **Process Mining:** A group of methods known as "process mining" enables the examination of operational processes using event logs.

Importance of Business Intelligence Tools

Prior to the competition catching up, future consumer patterns and marketplaces can be identified by historical data analysis. By identifying and getting rid of excess stock, managers can cut manufacturing costs by analyzing data from inventory systems. Additionally, data analytics dashboards can enhance the work experience for employees by offering well-defined work parameters and duties with a focus on results.

The amount of raw data we currently have access to is only as beneficial as our ability to quickly and fully understand it. Modern firms use data for all aspects of their operations, including processes, productivity, profitability, and marketing. Business intelligence (BI) tools can help establish links between different departments within the firm through using visual data visualization and quick decision-making.

The capacity of BI tools to improve exploratory data analysis and make data more "human friendly" is another benefit. Since humans are visual beings, data visualizations are among the most popular ways that business intelligence (BI) technologies present data. Business users can monitor trends, patterns, and anomalies and make more informed decisions using BI technologies to convert cryptic, tiresome, massive data into vibrant, interactive data visualizations.

Business Intelligence Tools

The ideal business intelligence tools for your company will depend on several aspects, such as your target audience, reporting requirements, storage demands, security specifications, and cost. All of the greatest BI tools and platforms have features that assist businesses in focusing on the most pertinent information by presenting it in an actionable manner, even though each platform offers a different set of tools.

A comparison list of some of the most popular business intelligence systems are mentioned here:

- **HEAVY.AI BI Tools:** The boundaries of big data analytics' speed and scalability can be redefined, thanks to AI-enabled accelerated analytics. With interactive dashboards that can query, visualize, and process billion-row datasets, users can connect and cross-filter multi-dimensional data visually.

Utilizing high-performance computing users may leverage HeavyDB—the fastest open-source SQL engine in the world—to achieve visual data discovery, feature engineering, model inspection, and other real-time insights, going beyond the capabilities of standard business intelligence tools.

Based on the requirements of your company, HEAVY.AI offers various pricing tiers that can be used on-site, in the cloud, or hosted by HEAVY.AI. LARGE. For individuals who are just starting out, AI Free is a fully functional alternative with data and sharing constraints.

- **Microsoft BI Tools:** On their Power BI platform, Microsoft Power BI tool provides visualization, analysis, and reporting capabilities for data sourced locally or in the cloud. Additionally included are interactive dashboards, augmented analytics, data preparation, and visual-based discovery. Microsoft stores are the intended audience.
- **AWS BI Tools:** Built for the cloud, Amazon QuickSight BI tool is a scalable, serverless, embeddable, machine learning-powered BI service. QuickSight provides vast scalability without infrastructure or capacity limits, accessibility from any device, natural language responses from queries, machine learning-powered insights, and interactive BI dashboard publication.
- **SAP BI Tool:** SAP BusinessObjects is a complete business intelligence suite that includes real-time analytics, self-service reporting, streamlined workflow, full visibility, predictive modeling, cloud-based analytics, collaborative reporting, credential management for administrators, and more. Business users can also customize the dashboard to access all their BI tools in one place.
- **Tableau BI Tool:** Tableau is a Salesforce BI Tool that offers business intelligence tools hosted by Tableau, used on-site or in the cloud. The intended audience consists of mid-sized and large businesses from a range of sectors. Tableau is a communication tool that uses artificial intelligence and natural language processing. It also has drag-and-drop buttons for live visual analytics, supports a variety of data sources, makes dashboard sharing simple, and supports a wide variety of data sources.
- **Domo BI Tool:** The scalable architecture of Domo's cloud-based platform is intended to complement current data lakes, warehouses, and BI tools. Any cloud, on-premises system or proprietary system can connect data. Domo combines data visualization, cloud data warehouse, and ETL functionality in one location. The analytics suite can be extensively customized with code to automate and standardize business procedures.
- **Oracle BI Tools:** An addition to Oracle's popular Business Intelligence Enterprise Edition suite, Oracle Cloud Analytics provides self-service workforce analytics, support for Natural Language Processing and embedded analytics, collaborative reporting, an intuitive interface, support for embedded

analytics, data connectors, preparation, and visualization capabilities, and machine learning and predictive analytics capabilities.

- **Sigma BI Tool:** Sigma provides drag-and-drop dashboards, data preparation, ad hoc analysis capabilities, a live cloud data warehouse connection, security and governance management, unified spreadsheets, data visualizations, scenario modeling, collaborative data sharing, text for simple data storytelling, and scalable access to billions of rows of reliable data in the cloud data warehouse in real time.
- **Zoho Analytics:** With the help of Zoho Cloud BI, businesses can turn raw data into insightful reports and dashboards on a single, unified platform. Users can also track key business metrics, forecast business trends, identify outliers, uncover hidden insights, collaborate online, integrate and prepare data for analysis, and connect business applications and cloud databases.

Most BI tools on the previous list are proprietary, subscription-based programs. For smaller teams with tighter budgets, free and open-source business intelligence (BI) technologies are further offered. Apache Hive, BIRT Project, D3.js, KNIME, Orange, Pentaho, R, TACTIC, Superset, Grafana, JasperReports, Palo, Pentaho, BILM, Datacopia, icCube, InetSoft, and Splunk are a few of the best open source or free BI tools available.

Over the past ten years, business intelligence has expanded rapidly and doesn't appear to be slowing down. The automotive, public sector, pharmaceutical, oil and gas (see energy business intelligence), utilities, media and advertising, telecom, investment management, logistics, and many other key industries now use BI software. BI tools are an essential component of contemporary firms, and as corporate competition increases, they will only get better.

BI Dashboard

A BI dashboard is a type of business intelligence tool that allows users to track, analyze, and report on metrics and other key performance indicators. Business intelligence dashboards frequently display data as graphs, charts, and maps to help stakeholders comprehend, share, and work together. The best business intelligence dashboards make it simple to combine data from several sources and explore and analyze that data directly within the dashboard.

Benefits of BI Dashboard

BI dashboards' primary advantage is their ability to assist organizations in finding answers and insights that enable them to make more informed decisions based on data.

- **Transform Raw Data into Business Insights:** Actionable insights are generated from raw data gathered from many sources by a true business intelligence dashboard. This means that a contemporary data analytics platform and a data integration platform must be part of an end-to-end solution for the dashboard to be developed.
- **Improve Data Literacy:** All people within an organization may more readily comprehend and engage with data, thanks to BI dashboards that are based on controlled, trusted data. This promotes a more data-driven culture throughout your company.

Here, we go over five essential best practices for building a top-notch business information dashboard.

- **Compile Information:** Gather raw data and transform it into clean, analytics-ready information long before you can build a data dashboard. Integrating various forms of data into standardized formats kept in a data lake or data warehouse entails combining data from a range of sources and carrying out data replication, ingestion, and transformation.
- **State Objectives**: Ensure that the business objective you're attempting to assess, analyze, and optimize is well defined. Are you attempting to find new geographic markets to enter, for instance, or figuring out which stage of your marketing funnel requires the most attention?
- **Maintain Graphics**: Simple visualizations are required so that data can be easily formulated in the form of graphics.. Choose the graphs, charts, and maps that best suite by taking the time to determine the KPIs and relationships that matter most upfront.
- **Permit Experimentation and Cooperation**: Explore the dashboards and discover new insights, thanks to self-service BI. Instead of being restricted to linear searches, the greatest solutions provide an associative engine that lets users freely explore every link inside the data.
- **Make Use of AI**: Augmented analytics, which leverages AI and machine learning to support human intuition by providing insights and analyses, enabling search and natural language interaction, is a feature of contemporary BI dashboards.

Decision Support Systems (DSS)

Organizations are increasingly using Decision Support Systems (DSS) to efficiently exploit data. A decision support system (DSS) is a software-based tool that helps decision-makers solve difficult situations and reach well-informed decisions. These systems combine modeling tools, business intelligence, and data analytics to give a comprehensive picture of the business environment.

Types of Decision Support System

The different types of information systems are:

- **DSS Based on Data:** Focus lies in gaining entry to and modifying extensive repositories of organized data, frequently consisting of internal business data or external data in the form of time series.
- **DSS Based on Models:** These DSS comprise systems that use representational models, optimization models, and accounting and financial models. They emphasize manipulating and gaining access to a model. Although Power points out that some OLAP systems that enable sophisticated data analysis may be categorized as hybrid DSS systems; they often make use of basic statistical and analytical methods. Decision-makers supply the data and parameters for model-driven DSS, although Power points out that these are typically not data-intensive.
- **Knowledge-driven DSS:** These systems advise or suggest actions for managers to take. These systems, which are often referred to as suggestion, consultation, or advisory systems, offer specific domain-specific problem-solving knowledge. Usually, they are employed for jobs that would require a human expert, such as classification, configuration, diagnosis, interpretation, planning, and prediction. To create relationships between data items, these systems are frequently used in conjunction with data mining to sort through databases.
- **Document-based DSS:** For document retrieval and analysis, these systems combine processing and storage technologies. One example might be a search engine.
- **Group-based and Communication-driven DSS:** Group DSS concentrates on assisting groups of decision-makers in analyzing problem scenarios and carrying out group decision-making tasks, whereas communication-driven DSS emphasizes coordination, communication, and collaboration to assist individuals working on a shared task.

Components of a Decision Support System

Three main parts make up decision support systems: the user interface, software system, and database.

- **DSS Repository:** The database draws on a wide variety of sources including information created by apps, data that is internal to the company, and external data that is either mined from the internet or obtained from other parties. It could be anything from a small standalone DSS database to a large-scale data warehouse based on need.

- **DSS Program:** A model serves as the foundation for the software system (containing decision context and user criteria). The DSS's goal determine the quantity and variety of models. Frequently employed models comprise:
- **Models of Statistics**: Relationships between occurrences and factors associated with those events are established using these models. They could be used, for instance, to examine sales in connection to geography or climate.
- **Models for Sensitivity Analysis:** These models are employed in "what-if" scenarios.
  Models for optimization analysis. These models help in finding the optimal value of a target variable with respect to other variables.
- **Models for Prediction:** These include regression models, time series analysis, and other planning as well as business situation analysis models.
- **Models of Sensitivity for Backward Analysis:** Identify a goal for one variable and calculate how it will affect the values that other variables should have to reach this goal, whereas such methods are also known as goal-driven analysis.

Key Components of a DSS

The following are the key components of a DSS system:

- **Data Repository:** Gathered data from different sources which may be historical or current ones kept in one place.
- **Analytics Engines:** Performs calculations based on inputted data using statistical methods for decision-making, predictive modelling, and so forth.
- **User Interface:** Allows managers to interact with the system; view reports and ask questions.
- **Visualization Tools / Data Presentation Tools:** Dashboards, charts, and graphs that clearly represent complex information visually
- **Reporting Functionality:** Automatically generate reports that can be shared among stakeholders.
- **What-If Analysis (WIA):** The ability to run multiple scenarios and determine what they mean in terms of impact.

Applications of DSS

The following are the applications of a DSS system:

- **Financial Decision-Making:** DSS helps enterprises to optimize their holdings and investments by supporting them in the areas of financial planning, budgeting, and forecasting.

- **Supply Chain Management:** It enables demand forecasting, logistics planning, and inventory management.
- **Marketing and Sales:** DSS aids the activities of analyzing market trends, campaign performance optimization, as well as customer segmentation.
- **Healthcare:** In the practice of medicine, DSS assists healthcare providers in making accurate diagnoses for patients and choosing the best course of action.
- **Risk Management:** Many businesses rely on DSS to identify and manage risks. Data analysis can be done using DSS to evaluate risks that would be managed.

Data Analytics and DSS

Data analytics work hand in hand with DSS. Data analytics's major focus lies on the management as well as extraction of insights from data while DSS converts such insights into choices that may be implemented. This happens as follows:

1. **Data Preparation:** These are various data analytic procedures which include integration, transformation, and cleansing among others that get raw data ready for further analysis. This represents what comes out of all this; clear structured data that is very insightful for reports and analyses produced by DSS.

   Data analytics is looking for patterns and trends in data to obtain insight. DSS utilizes this insight for decision-makers to give them a complete understanding of the prevailing circumstances and potential outcomes.
2. **Making Decisions:** Decision makers can use DSS data to evaluate their options, assess the risks involved in those options, and make informed decisions.
3. **Monitoring and Feedback:** DSS often includes decision-impact tracking monitoring tools. This allows the process of analytics to make improvements for subsequent decision-making.

Challenges and Considerations

Despite these numerous advantages of data analytics and DSS, some disadvantages to be considered are as follows:

- **Data Security and Privacy:** As data becomes more important, it is vital that sensitive information is protected.
- **Data Quality:** Invaluable insights depend on accurate and reliable data; however, poor information quality may lead to incorrect judgments.
- **Skill Gap:** Effective utilization of IA personnel requires skilled analysts or scientists who can provide valuable insights from such large volumes of information

- **Integration:** Integrating DSS into existing IT architectures could be challenging as well as time-consuming.
- **Ethical Concerns:** Ethical issues such as bias, fairness, and misuse of information arise when using such techniques as data analytics.

Decision Support System and Business Intelligence

Comparison between Decision Support Systems (DSS) and Business Intelligence (BI) requires understanding the goals, priorities, and functions of both.

Purpose and Focus

Designed to assist personal decision-making, DSS gives recommendations and detailed information for users to make wise choices. DSS provides insights into either current challenges faced or solutions for helping operational decision-making.

BI, on the other hand, has broader applications for business strategic planning. It entails processes, tools, and technologies that enable managers and executives to have access to data-driven insights.

BI helps an organization analyze huge volumes of data from various sources to identify trends, patterns as well as opportunities that promote business growth.

Functionality

Existence of functional differences between DSS and BI: Data warehousing is important when it comes to business intelligence. It can also be defined as the practice of integrating data from various sources into a single central repository, which in turn facilitates the analysis of such information. This way, an organization's departments or divisions can view their data from a unified perspective. In addition, reporting is another feature that makes up BI. Standardized reports are created through custom queries and predefined metrics that users can employ. Since these reports show stakeholders how different key performance indicators (KPIs) affect options, they contain valuable information.

Data visualization is also an essential part of BI capabilities; this technique allows complex data to be presented using charts, graphs, dashboards, and other visual aids so that patterns and trends in the data may be detected by consumers more easily.

Nonetheless, although it may include some reporting or visualization features; DSS is more about giving specific information for individual decisions than an analysis tool with comprehensive evaluation skills or presentation skills.

Decision Support System: Examples

Decision support systems are used by several industries.

- **To Simplify the Path:** By analyzing multiple alternatives a DDS can help plan an optimal route between two points. These systems can avoid traffic bottlenecks by tracking traffic in real time. By using an advanced gate routing algorithm to automatically allocate arriving aircraft to the next available gate, American Airlines saves hundreds of gallons of fuel each year and minimizes taxi times.
- **Crop Scheduling:** DSS is a tool used by farmers to assist them choose when to plant, fertilize, and harvest their crops. Every aspect of Bayer Crop Science's operation has been analyzed and decision support systems implemented, including the development of "virtual factories" to conduct "what-if" studies at its maize production facilities.
- **DSS for Clinical Use:** By using these systems, physicians may diagnose patients more accurately and produce better results. A system that uses cloud computing, machine learning, and predictive analytics has been created by Fresenius Medical Care to proactively detect potentially life-threatening complications in renal dialysis patients.
- **Dashboards for ERPs:** Managers can monitor performance metrics with the aid of these technologies.

Conclusion

Integrating data from various data sources into a single source is known as ETL. Three steps are involved: loading, manipulating, and extracting data. ETL is essential to most use cases in the competitive corporate climate of today, including data warehousing, creating ML and AI applications, market data integration, and cloud migration. ETL does provide several issues, though, which you should be aware of and take the appropriate action to mitigate.

Although data mining and data analysis are used in tandem, understanding their key differences can help organizations make the most of these tools. By collecting the outputs from the data mining process and building the entire data model for the stakeholders, data analytics aims to provide answers to queries or address business issues. Data analysis aims to provide unquestionable insights that a corporation may utilize to make better decisions by testing ideas.

The ability to leverage the immense potential of data for well-informed decision-making represents an unparalleled competitive advantage that no company should undervalue. The future of enterprises in a variety of industries will be significantly impacted by the synergy between data analytics and DSS as the volume and complexity of data continue to soar.

It is crucial for businesses as well as data analysts and technology enthusiasts to appreciate the dissimilarities between business intelligence (BI) and decision support systems (DSS). BI has a broader scope since it supports strategic decision-making with deep insights obtained from available data while DSS emphasizes individual decision-making by furnishing specialized information. In the next chapter, we will discuss distributed database systems and the benefits of distributed database systems over database systems.

Questions

1. How does a data warehouse differ from a database? Differentiate among a data mart, an ODS, and an EDW.
2. Describe the data warehousing process and its major components.
3. What issues should be considered when deciding which architecture to use in developing a data warehouse? List the 10 most important factors.
4. Define knowledge management and describe its purposes. Distinguish between knowledge and data.
5. Define KMS and describe its capabilities.
6. Discuss and define the various steps of ETL with the help of an example.
7. How is the BI process used in Private and Public Intelligence?
8. Distinguish between OLTP and OLAP.
9. Explain data mining and the various processes of data mining.
10. Explain the various strategic techniques used in implementing BI.
11. Explain in detail the extract/transform/load (ETL) design of an automated warehouse.
12. Explain the requisite for implementing business intelligence software on the web.
13. Explain the role of BI in the healthcare industry.

CHAPTER 8
Distributed Databases and NoSQL

Introduction

Logically related data are stored and processed across networked computer systems under the control of a distributed database management system (DDBMS), where data and processing are dispersed among multiple sites.

A distributed database spreads out across two or more physically separate locations and keeps a logically connected database. A computer network connects the locations. On the other hand, the distributed processing system divides the processing tasks among multiple locations while utilizing a single-site database. A database in a distributed database system is made up of multiple components or database fragments. The database fragments can be copied between different sites and are spread over different locations. The local database process for each database fragment is in charge of managing it.

Structure

In this chapter, the following topics will be discussed:

- Distributed Database Design Principles
- Replication and Synchronization Techniques
- Consistency Models (ACID, BASE)
- Scalability and Partitioning in Distributed Systems
- Distributed Transaction Management

Evolution of DDBMS

Employing a centralized database necessitated keeping company data in one single location, typically on a mainframe computer. Dumb terminals were used to access data. When rapidly evolving events demanded quicker response times and similarly quick access to information, the centralized system proved ineffective. However, it did perform well in meeting the structured information needs of corporations. Decision makers were not well served by the sluggish flow from information requests to approval to specialist to user in a dynamic setting.

The following are the various variables that shaped the development of the DDBMS. Demand for data access has increased due to the following factors:

- The increasing use of wireless digital devices, such as PDAs and smartphones like the iPhone and BlackBerry, has led to the maintenance of the repository for distributed data.
- The internet is becoming a more popular platform for data distribution and access. These gadgets demand a variety of data exchanges in numerous types (data, speech, video, music, images, and more) and access data from geographically separated sites. Data replication strategies akin to those found in distributed databases are frequently used to meet performance and fault tolerance requirements, even if distributed data access does not always imply distributed databases.
- The rapid expansion of businesses offering "application as a service" offerings. For businesses looking to outsource their application development, operations, and maintenance, this new kind of service offers remote application services. The company's data is typically kept centrally on servers and isn't always shared. This kind of service might not need fully distributed data capabilities, just like wireless data access. However, other considerations like performance and failure tolerance sometimes call for the adoption of data replication strategies akin to those seen in distributed databases.
- The growing emphasis on data analysis gave rise to data warehousing and data mining. Data replication and distributed queries are two methods that a data warehouse uses, even though it isn't typically a distributed database.

Distributed Database Design Concepts

The design concepts and principles apply to both distributed and centralized databases. However, the distributed database approach raises three additional problems: data fragmentation, data replication, and data allocation. The existing statement incorrectly links data allocation to the third issue. Data allocation refers to deciding where to store the fragments or replicas of data across different sites in the distributed system. This is directly related to one of the core challenges of distributed databases: determining the optimal placement of data for performance, availability, and load balancing.

Data Fragmentation:

A single item can be divided into two or more segments or fragments, thanks to data fragmentation. A table, a system database, or a user's database could be the object. Every piece can be kept on any computer network at any location. The distributed data catalog (DDC) contains data fragmentation information that the TP retrieves to handle user requests.

The strategies for data fragmentation that are covered here are table-level and include breaking a table up into logical sections. Three different kinds of data fragmentation strategies horizontal, vertical, and mixed will be covered.

The splitting of a relation into subsets (fragments) of tuples (rows) is known as horizontal fragmentation. Every fragment has a distinct row and is kept at a different node. The distinctive rows, however, share the same characteristics (columns). Each fragment, with the **WHERE** clause focused on a single attribute, is essentially the same as a **SELECT** query. A relation is said to be vertically fragmented when it is divided into attribute (column) subsets. Except for the key column, which is shared by all fragments, each subset (fragment) is kept at a different node and contains distinct columns. This is SQL's version of the **PROJECT** statement.

When horizontal and vertical techniques are combined, it is referred to as mixed fragmentation. Put otherwise, a table can be split into multiple horizontal groups, each of which contains a portion of the attributes.

To illustrate the fragmentation strategies, let's use the student table. The table contains the attributes **Roll_No**, **Name**, **City**, **Branch**, **Mobile_No**, and **Branch**.

Roll_No	Name	City	Mobile_no	Address
1	Amit	Dehradun	77777	CSE
2	Hitesh	Bijnor	11111	ECE
3	Jagdish	Bengaluru	22222	CSE
4	Parisha	Bengaluru	33333	BFA
5	Shrey	Delhi	44444	CSE

Table 8.1: *Student details*

Horizontal Fragmentation:

Suppose the department conducts a placement drive and for this activity, only CSE students are eligible, in such case, we will do the horizontal; fragmentation by applying select operation with a condition branch= CSE.

SQL Query:

```
Select * from student where branch= 'CSE'; ---------(1)
```

Roll_No	Name	City	Mobile_no	Address
1	Amit	Dehradun	77777	CSE
3	Jagdish	Bengaluru	22222	CSE
5	Shrey	Delhi	44444	CSE

Table 8.2: *Output of Query 1*

Vertical Fragmentation:

If the department wants to retrieve the name and roll no of all the students from the student table, then it will only fetch the **name** and **roll_no** attribute from the student table using the select function; this is called vertical fragmentation.

SQL Query:

```
Select Roll_no, Name from student; ---------(2)
```

Roll_No	Name
1	Amit
2	Hitesh
3	Jagdish
4	Parisha
5	Shrey

***Table 8.3**: Output of Query 2*

Mixed Fragmentation

If we mix the select and project functions, then it will be called mixed fragmentation. For example, now want the **name** and **roll_no** of all those students whose branch is CSE. In this case, we must use select as well as project operation.

SQL Query:

```
Select Roll_no, Name from student where branch='CSE'; ---------(3)
```

Roll_No	Name
1	Amit
3	Jagdish
5	Shrey

***Table 8.4**: Output of Query 3*

Centralized Database Management System Bottleneck

The following are the major bottlenecks of a centralized database management system:

- A decline in performance as a result of more distant locations spread over longer distances.
- The high expense of running and maintaining sizable central (mainframe) database systems.

- Reliability issues brought on by the requirement for data replication and reliance on a single location (single point of failure syndrome).
- Scalability issues relating to the physical restrictions (power, temperature conditioning, and power consumption) imposed by a single location.
- The database's organizational rigidity might not be able to support the agility and flexibility needed by today's multinational organizations.

Distributed Processing and Distributed Databases

Logical processing for a database is divided between two or more geographically separate locations linked by a network. On one computer, for instance, the data input/ output, data selection, and data validation may be completed; on a different computer, a report based on the data may be generated.

- Although a distributed database is not necessary for distributed processing, distributed processing is necessary for a distributed database (each database fragment is controlled by its own local database process).
- A single database housed on a single machine may serve as the foundation for distributed processing. Copies of the database processing functions, or portions of them, must be distributed to each data storage location for distributed data management to take place.
- A network is necessary to link all parts of distributed databases and distributed processing.

Advantages of DDBMS

The advantages are listed here:

- Data are found close to the site with the highest demand. A distributed database system lowers the cost of data access by distributing the data to meet business requirements.
- Fast access to the data, end customers frequently only have access to a portion of the company's data that is locally kept.
- Faster process of data, by processing data at multiple locations in the distributed database, the burden is shared among the participating sites.
- The network can accommodate new sites without interfering with the functionality of existing sites.
- Better correspondence. Local sites encourage better communication between departments and between customers and corporate staff.
- Lower running expenses. Installing workstations on a network is less expensive

than updating a mainframe. With low-cost PCs, development work may be completed faster and more affordably than with mainframes.

- Interface that is easy to use. All the participating sites have an intuitive graphical user interface (GUI). The GUI makes it easier for end users to learn and use.
- A lower risk of a single point of failure. The workload is divided among the remaining workstations in the event of a computer failure. Additionally, data is parsed across several sites.
- Processor autonomy. Any copy of the data that is accessible to the end user is processed upon request.

Disadvantages of DDBMS

Here are the disadvantages of DDBMS:

- The intricacy of control and management. Applications need to be able to combine data from several sites and identify where the data is located. To stop database degradation brought on by data anomalies, database managers need to be able to coordinate database operations.
- The challenge of technology. It is necessary to handle and resolve issues related to data integrity, transaction management, concurrency control, security, backup, recovery, query optimization, access path selection, and other related issues.
- Safety. When data is spread across several locations, there is a higher chance of security breaches. Data management will be divided among many individuals at multiple locations.
- Absence of guidelines. At the database level, there are no established communication methods. For example, different database manufacturers use different and incompatible tools or procedures to control how data and processing are distributed inside a DDBMS.
- A greater need for infrastructure and storage. The need for many data copies at several locations necessitates the need for more disc storage.
- Higher price for training. In a distributed architecture, training expenses are typically higher than in a centralized model; in certain cases, they can even completely outweigh hardware and operating savings.
- Price. The operation of distributed databases necessitates duplicate infrastructure (people, software, licensing, physical location, and environment).

Characteristics of Distributed Database Management Systems

DDBMS controls how logically linked data is stored and processed across networked computer systems when data and processing tasks are dispersed over multiple sites. To qualify as distributed, a database management system needs to have at least the following features:

- An application interface that allows communication between the distributed database's application programs, end users, and other DBMSs.
- Validation to examine data requests for accuracy of syntax.
- Transformation to break down intricate requests into discrete parts that make up a data request.
- Optimizing queries to determine the most effective access plan. (Which database segments does the query need to access, and how should any updates to the data be synchronized?)
- Mapping to pinpoint the position of both local and distant data components.
- I/O interface for writing to and reading from permanent local storage.
- Formatting to get the data ready for an application program or display to the user.
- Data privacy protection through security for both local and distant databases.
- Backup and DR to guarantee the database's accessibility and recoverability in the event of a failure.
- Backup and DR to guarantee the database's accessibility and recoverability in the event of a failure.
- Concurrency control, which allows the DDBMS to manage concurrent data access and guarantee data consistency across database fragments.
- Transaction management, which ensures data is transferred between consistent states. Synchronization of local and distant transactions as well as transactions between several dispersed segments are included in this activity.

Components of DDBMS

The following are the various DDBMS components:

- Workstation computers or other distant objects (sites or nodes) that are a part of the network system. The distributed system is independent of hardware.
- The hardware and software components of each workstation or device that are part of the network. All the sites can communicate and share data with each other in the network.

- Communication is independent of media; all the media should support the communication.
- Each node has a transaction manager and transaction coordinator. The transaction manager is responsible for transactions initiated and executed at the node while the transaction coordinator is responsible for communicating with other nodes.

The distributed database system will operate in accordance with the protocols.

- Interface that connects data processors (DPs) and transaction processors (TPs) to the network to transfer commands and data.
- Route retrieved data to the relevant TPs (DP side) and synchronize all data received from DPs (TP side).
- A distributed database system should have functions like concurrency, backup and DR, Security, and recovery.

Data Replication

It is possible to store fragment copies in multiple locations to meet different information needs. The cornerstone of contemporary data management is database replication, which guarantees data availability and dependability. It entails making and keeping duplicates of a database across several places. The basic goal of database replication is to keep consistent copies of the data across several servers or locations to guarantee data availability, dependability, and performance. Additionally, we need to be mindful of the following crucial database replication factors.

- Data synchronization
- Load balancing
- High availability
- Types of replication
- Disaster recovery
- Data distribution
- Security
- Conflict resolution

Assume that database A is split up into A1 and A2 fragments. In a distributed database that is replicated, the situation illustrated in the subsequent figure can occur: Fragment A1 is kept at sites S1 and S2, and fragment A2 at sites S2 and S3.

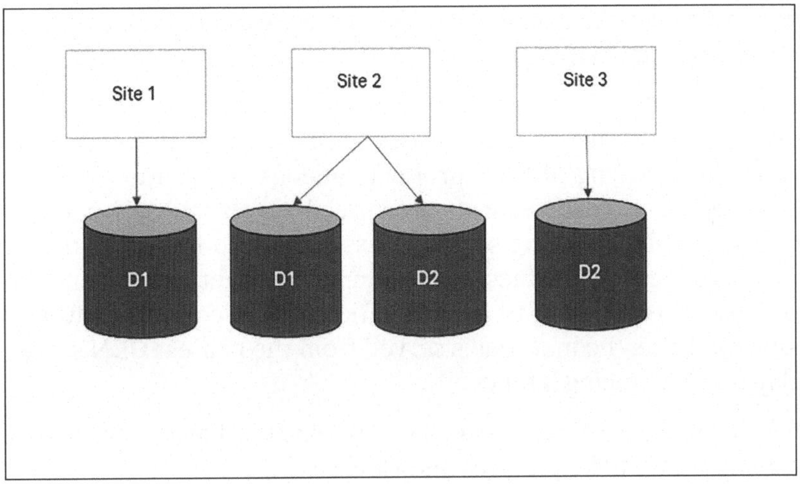

Figure 8.1: *Data Replication*

Types of Database Replication

Changes made in the source database are instantly reflected in the target databases when replication is done synchronously. For applications like financial systems, where data consistency is crucial, this is essential.

- **Asynchronous replication**: Asynchronous replication is a method of maximizing swiftness in which lags are introduced between updating the source and its reflection on the target. Imagine an online news site that uses asynchronous replication to ensure that it can publish the newest articles even if there is a network failure, for instance.

That being said, let's now consider some advantages of database replication within this framework as we have learned it. However, not before we familiarize ourselves with why replication is an essential tool for data management using real-life stories.

Among other things, Database replication guarantees system downtime prevention which results in high availability. Replications such as online banking systems can be configured in such a way that clients will always be in a position to retrieve their accounts even when servers are undergoing maintenance or having some problems.

High availability is the main benefit of database replication. Despite things such as hardware failures, maintenance activities, and more importantly other factors that might cause servers to go down; information could still be accessed from them.

For example, high levels of availability are achieved through replication for healthcare providers who always want to ensure that patient records and medical data are easily accessible all the time. In situations involving emergencies, one would necessarily need to refer to patient histories and medical files quickly as well as easily.

This process makes sure that medical officers are always provided with information despite how the system stands.

- **System Scalability:** It is a way of balancing loads by replication, which is utilized for even distribution of web traffic among big e-commerce websites and faster browsing of their product catalogs. Replication brings about load balancing where read requests are spread across multiple copies. This helps performance by reducing server stress leading to improved user experience with faster response times. For example, Content delivery networks (CDN) make use of replication to achieve efficient web content delivery. When one visits a website, the material is served from the nearest CDN server to reduce delay thus enhancing latency.

  This enhances surfing, especially on websites having loads of media and dynamic content like pictures and videos.

- **Rapid Restoration:** When servers go down or data gets corrupted, replication can quickly restore it. Replication is also employed by a hospital's patient management system to ensure that such records are always present even if there happens to be sudden loss of data.

  Replication is an integral part of disaster recovery plans. Replicated data is the quickest way to restore it in case of corruption, accidental deletion, or server failure.

  For example, replication serves as a disaster recovery mechanism for banks. The finance industry needs data integrity. This means that during transactions and account updates, there are always replicated copies of the most critical financial information such as those related to transactions and clients' accounts. The replicated data provides a strong failover in case of data loss incidents leading to fast recovery without much monetary loss.

- **Geographical Distribution:** It is important for international applications. Therefore, social media companies use replication to save user information at different points across continents such as Asia, Africa, and Europe among others to reduce latency and ensure a smooth flow of operations on their websites. For such businesses which serve worldwide clientele to run smoothly, they must have geographical distribution. For instance, replication reduces delays hence prompt service delivery through enabling storage and retrieval of data from various centers positioned within diverse geographical regions. Illustration: Social media companies apply duplication technology to ensure that they have a seamless global user experience.

  Copying data to regional servers, so that users from different geographical areas can access their own content with the least possible latency, creates an immersive and interactive audience experience. Millions of social media updates, pictures, and videos have been published. Practical replication models among other instances show that replication is still relevant in all cases and industries.

Significance of Database Replication

The significance of database replication is underscored by the following key points for modern data management.

- Database Replication Focuses on Data Availability
- Better information availability
- Backup and Disaster Recovery
- Load balancing
- Performance Improvement
- Accuracy and consistency
- Global data accessibility

In addition, for example, replication affords malleable systems to enable such changes as opening new data centers or redistributing workloads.

- **Better Security:** Regarding increased security, data loss risks, and breaches are minimized by replication through multiple backups. It equally allows trust distribution of data across various domains thus ensuring adherence to several laws and policies.
- **Real-time Data Integration and Analysis:** This is critical in real-time decision-making. Thus, replication enables one to integrate as well as analyze information in actual time from many systems. For any businesses such as financial institutions or e-commerce platforms that rely on real-time data to run, this immediacy is a must-have.

Database replication in different database management systems.

There are various methods of replicating databases used by different Database Management Systems. All the database management systems are unlike each other, and they have separate mechanisms for copying data.

- **MySQL Replication**: To guarantee worldwide access to posts, a well-known blogging platform uses MySQL replication. The platform's needs determine whether to use master-slave or master-master replication.
- **PostgreSQL Replication**: PostgreSQL provides a range of replication options and is renowned for its versatility. A multinational e-commerce business may use PostgreSQL's streaming replication feature to effectively share product data among local databases.
- **SQL server Replication**: Transactional, merge, and snapshot replication are among the functionalities specific to the Microsoft SQL server. To ensure

HR data consistency, a major firm may use SQL server replication to keep personnel records synchronized across several sites.

- **MongoDB Replication**: Replication strategies differ for NoSQL databases, such as MongoDB. MongoDB replica sets can be used by content management systems to guarantee that articles and multimedia material are always accessible, even in the event of server failures.
- **Oracle Replication:** Streams and GoldenGate are two of the many replication choices that Oracle, a popular commercial database, provides. To comply with regulatory standards, an enterprise financial system uses Oracle's replication technology to synchronize vital financial data across data centers.
  Businesses using technology stacks must comprehend the replication capabilities of various DBMSs.

Types of Replication

There are three types of replication:

- Statement-based replication
- Write-Ahead log
- Row-based replication

Statement-based Replication

Every write command (**`INSERT`**, **`UPDATE`**, **`DELETE`**) that the leader executes in this approach is logged and forwarded to the follower, who then executes it on its node. This approach has a lot of drawbacks even though it seems like a smart one. Any non-deterministic function, such as the **`RAND ()`** or **`NOW()`** functions, can, for instance, produce distinct writes on the leader and follower. Furthermore, an unforeseen outcome could occur on the follower node if a write statement (such as **`UPDATE`**) depends on an earlier write (such as **`INSERT`**) and both reach the follower out of sequence (which might occur in an asynchronous application). Moreover, a write may get lost in the network, and followers are unable to contact the leader regarding a lost write. Once more, this leads to inconsistent data.

Sending a fixed return value when a leader sends something to a follower can help combat non-determinism, but it's still challenging to handle all edge circumstances. To prevent write errors or out-of-order writes, VoltDB employs deterministic transactions in conjunction with statement-based replication.

Write-Ahead Log(WAL)

Every query that is received by a system is recorded in an append-only log file, sometimes referred to as a write-ahead log file, even before the query is executed. You can replicate data to follower nodes using this log file.

Oracle and PostgreSQL both use this data replication technique. The problem with WAL is that its log specifies the data at a very basic level, including the bytes that were altered in each of the leader's disc blocks. As a result, it is connected to a storage engine closely. This virtually eliminates the possibility of upgrading the software versions of the leader and follower independently (a rolling upgrade). Downtime is required for these upgrades.

Row-Based Replication

Row-based replication comprises a series of records that describe writes at the row level. For instance, information about all new column values is contained in a row insertion. An update provides the new values for every column, while a delete comprises the information to identify the rows that need to be destroyed.

All rows that are engaged in a transaction more than once are recorded in the log. This is how MySQL's binlog operates.

Row-based replication is not affected by the same problems as WAL since it does not require information about bytes at a specific point on the disc. Additionally, because data is transferred from the leader to the follower using offsets of logs, out-of-order problems are avoided.

Replication Lag Issues with Single-Leader Replication

Asynchronous replication is preferable because it has shorter write latency and higher system availability than synchronous replication. However, it merely provides eventual consistency (all writes will ultimately reach all their followers, but no one can predict when) when it comes to read consistency from a follower (for read scalability).

Different results may occur if the same query is executed concurrently on the leader and follower. Replication lag is the cause of this disparity (Write from the master is yet to reach the slave). Usually measured in microseconds, this latency can increase to minutes if the system is operating at nearly full capacity or if there is a network issue affecting the connection between the leader and their followers. Users of your application may have unpleasant experiences as a result of these replication lag-related discrepancies. The problems that result from replication latency are as follows:

- The inconsistent way that reads follows writes
- Variations in the same query's results for repeated reads/Violation of casualty
- Inconsistency behavior for reads after writes

Have these abnormalities ever caught your attention?

- After submitting changes to your profile and reloading your social media page, are you still seeing the same outdated version of your profile? After that, a second refresh shows the most recent modifications to your profile.

- Leaving a remark on a post that vanishes after a page refresh and reappears in the following one?
- Your bank is sending you an SMS indicating that the fund transfer was accomplished, but your bank app still displays the old balance. (Happy moment) Later, the page refreshes, and the right balance appears.

The asynchronous follower's replication latency is the cause of all these oddities. Since followers provided the read, they could not have received any fresh information. One way to deal with these anomalies is to shift all read requests to followers after a certain amount of time (like a minute or two) has passed, however, this complicates the program. Since only the user can change their own profile, social media platforms have the option to fulfill read requests for both the leader's own profile and for other users' profiles from followers. This strategy doesn't work for other writers and readers who prefer to leave comments. Additionally, it is ineffective for cross-device reads following writes.

Transactions

Transactions are absolutely used in distributed systems, and in fact, they are crucial for maintaining data consistency and integrity in such environments. The statement is misleading in suggesting that transactions aren't used in distributed systems due to performance and availability concerns.

The ACID Model

Having worked with relational databases, many developers are familiar with ACID (Atomicity, Consistency, Isolation, Durability) transactions. As a result, the ACID consistency model has long been accepted. The primary assurance offered by ACID is the provision of a secure environment for your data to function. The abbreviation ACID represents:

- **Atomicity**: Every transactional operation is either successful or reversed.
- **Consistency**: The database is in a consistent state at the completion or rollback of a transaction; no logical corruptions or partial changes exist.
- **Isolation**: There is no competition between transactions. The database manages disputed access to data so that transactions seem to proceed in order.
- **Durability**: Despite failures, the effects of implementing a transaction remain irreversible.

Use Cases for ACID Databases

In fields where data storage is strictly regulated, such as banking, healthcare, and government administration, ACID-compliant databases are commonly utilized. An ACID-compliant database will always retrieve up-to-date data, and customers of a bank, for example, don't have to worry about their account balances appearing inaccurately. Because of their reliability and convenience to use, ACID-compliant databases are also widely used by small and medium-sized businesses. These organizations handle relatively small amounts of data, so they can overlook the overhead that ACID compliance adds to database operations, such as the time it takes to complete lengthy JOINs.

All SQL engines (Oracle, MySQL, PostgreSQL, and MS SQL server are a few examples), Neo4j, and MongoDB are popular examples of ACID-compliant databases. Generally, you can determine if a database complies with ACID by looking for a statement on ACID compliance on the database's website.

When a transaction satisfies the ACID properties, its data is stable and consistent (technical term for write consistency) on disc, which may entail several different memory locations.

For application developers, write consistency is great, but it also means sophisticated locking, which is usually a heavyweight pattern for most use cases.

Most graph databases, including Neo4j, employ the ACID consistency model in NoSQL technologies to guarantee the security and consistency of the data being stored.

The BASE Model

ACID transactions are significantly more cautious (that is, they worry more about data safety) than the domain demands for several domains and use cases.

Maintaining ACID compliance is quite expensive (for example, the overhead of 2 Phased Commit/2PC protocols) in some NoSQL databases where performance depends on large-scale sharing and horizontal scale-out (MPP) when a transaction spans potentially hundreds of instances. Because of this, the BASE (basically available, soft state, and eventually consistent) transaction model is frequently used in NoSQL databases whose performance greatly depends on horizontal scaling. (Notably, by supporting ACID transactions, the .NET-based RavenDB has defied the general tendency among aggregate databases.)

- **Basic Availability**: Working all the time instead of ideal.
- **Soft-state**: Stores don't need to be write-consistent or for many copies to always be mutually consistent.
- **Eventual Consistency**: Later, stores show consistency (for example, lazily at read time).

Use Cases for BASE Databases

Several BASE-compliant databases such as BigTable (Google) and DynamoDB (Amazon), were started as projects by these businesses to solve this problem. Smaller businesses may also have some specific use cases for BASE-compliant databases. To avoid a potential migration process later, a firm that anticipates a rapid growth in the volume of data it processes could choose to employ a database that complies with BASE standards.

Several well-known databases that adhere to BASE standards are BigTable, DynamoDB, Cassandra, and Hadoop. Often, browsing through a database's website will reveal if it is BASE-compliant.

Although availability is crucial for scalability, a BASE data store cannot ensure consistency of replicated data at write time. Compared to ACID, the BASE consistency model offers a somewhat laxer guarantee: data will remain consistent in the future, either at read time (like Riak) or consistently over time, but only for specific processed historical snapshots (like Datomic).

Other stores that follow the BASE model are not regarded as the principal system of record and are easily rebuildable from the original sources, in addition to the MPP NoSQL use cases. These consist of document stores in certain situations, aggregate stores, and key-value stores (which are frequently used to cache data).

ACID vs. BASE Databases

Comparing the qualities of ACID and BASE in the context of databases is like tasting the flavors of two amazing cuisines. Everyone has advantages and strengths. You can choose the best one for your data demands by being aware of these.

Consider the debate over "ACID vs. BASE" as an intriguing exploration of various data management techniques rather than as a war.

This trip seeks to identify a model that best fits your database by striking a balance between flexibility and durability.

Atomicity vs. Basically Available

Atomicity is very essential as per the following:

- **Uncompromising Reliability:** Atomicity is essential in situations like financial transactions when even a small mistake can have serious repercussions.
- **Consistent State Assurance:** It ensures that transactions are either executed completely or not at all to maintain a consistent database state.

Consistency vs. Soft State

Consistency focuses on the following areas:

- **Immutable Rules and Standards:** Consistency ensures that every transaction transitioning from one valid state to another changes the database.

- **Dependable and Error-Free**: For systems, such as accounting software or medical records, even the slightest discrepancies can mean serious problems.

Soft State

The soft state of the BASE model focuses on the following areas:

- **Flexibility:** This approach is best suited for situations where the data keeps changing constantly such as real-time analytics or streaming services.
- **Durability and Scale:** A little consistency tolerance provided by soft state increases how much the system can handle by way of big data and traffic.

The Interplay of Predictability and Adaptability

The Consistency vs, Soft State argument in ACID vs. BASE demonstrates a tradeoff between strong data integrity and immediate adaptability to changes. The ultimate goal of having a consistent environment remains unchanged but when talking about soft state, it is more flexible and scalable as these temporary errors are allowed for whereas consistency leads to increased availability and flexibility through zero tolerance for any error.

To design a database management system, it is crucial to understand the trade-offs concerning consistency versus a soft state that is unique to you. This involves a compromise between the flexibility of Soft State and the rigidity of Consistency. It also increases your understanding of the ACID vs. BASE debate and helps you to choose practical and successful approaches to data management.

Isolation vs. Eventual Consistency: Balancing Independence and Cohesion

Meanwhile, by comparing Isolation (from ACID) versus Eventual Consistency (from BASE) in the ACID versus BASE story, there is an absorbing attempt at achieving balance. In the same way, one contrasts a noisy café full of activity that is ever-changing with a scholar in his library who only speaks when he has something vital to say. Every person employs different ways of managing interactions and information flow.

Isolation: Ensuring Independent Transactions

In other words, isolation can be compared to providing soundproof booths to everyone in a noisy room under ACID model settings. This means that every transaction works independently from others according to database terminology without interfering with them. Imagine editing a document together with others. By isolating your changes from those made by other people avoids potential chaos.

- **Transaction Integrity:** Sometimes like what happens in financial trading systems transactions must be processed concurrently but without any interference whatsoever.

- **Preventing Data Conflicts**: It ensures no abnormalities in data by preventing simultaneous operations from distorting transactions' accuracy and consistency.

Durability

It represents an unshakable commitment by the database to keep data intact regardless of any calamity that may occur.

The Meaning of Durability in ACID

Durability under ACID means that metaphorically speaking, whenever a transaction takes place, its effects are irreversible. Thus, even if there is a power blackout, system crash, or other unforeseen interruption, such information will remain permanently saved and cannot be lost. For durability could mean writing a letter then putting it into an indestructible safe.

- **Immutable Transactions**: Transactions are not reversible once completed. This is crucial because the loss of financial transactions or legal documents could have far-reaching implications.
- **Ensuring Data Safety:** To make the description of a completely successful transaction safe and sound, durability provides databases with a strong foundation of trust and dependability.

Durability in Modern Databases

Nonetheless, as a concept under the ACID paradigm, durability is important for all database systems. In this data-driven world today, it is necessary to be assured that data will not be lost or tampered with. Durable data ensures that operation continuity is maintained for personal, corporate, or even sensitive government information.

- **Building User Trust:** This helps create and maintain people's reliability on the quality of their data when they are certain that their information is secure and immutable.
- **Foundation for Robust Systems:** Durability is required in the creation of strong and dependable databases since they can withstand adverse events without any data loss.

The Universal Value of Durability

Nevertheless, durability is an aspect of the ACID model that shows its applicability beyond the ACID versus BASE argument. It serves as a testament to why regardless of database models or technologies used; permanent and reliable data remains essential.

As technology advances, the importance of durability increases when protecting our digital legacy; therefore, every database architecture should bear this in mind.

System Design and Use Cases

In terms of the "ACID vs. BASE" folklore a system designer would be wise enough to customize system architecture and identify appropriate use cases for each one as if he were choosing the right tools for a task, thus matching the advantages and characteristics of each model with unique application needs or goals.

System Design with ACID:

In this step, we will ensure the safety with precision:

- **Financial Systems:** Banks and other financial institutions utilize the ACID model to ensure the accuracy and dependability of all their transactions including deposits and transfers.
- **E-commerce Platforms:** Ensuring correctness in payment processing, order management as well as inventory control.

System Design with BASE:

In the BASE system, the following are the very immersive areas:

- **Social Media Platforms:** Where rapidity and availability surpass sameness immediately for millions of likes, comments, and postings.
- **Content Distribution Networks (CDNs):** Such networks help distribute enormous numbers of content globally conveniently.
- **Big Data Analytics:** These are systems that must handle huge datasets that are to be analyzed instantly while some eventual consistency may be tolerated.

ACID vs. BASE:

- **Scalability Requirements:** BASE models are frequently more scalable, so they are appropriate for applications that foresee rapid expansion or expansive, dispersed systems.
- **Data Consistency Requirements:** BASE is appropriate for applications where eventual consistency is acceptable, while ACID is preferred for systems that cannot tolerate inconsistency.

Network Partitions and Failures:

It depends on the following factors:

- **Failures are Handled Precisely**: In case of a network failure or split, ACID-compliant systems may suspend their operations to ensure data consistency and integrity. This approach can be likened to closing the castle gates until the danger has passed.

- **Recovery and Consistency**: The system restarts operations when network problems are fixed, guaranteeing that all data is consistent and unaltered.
- **After-Failure Consistency over Time**: BASE systems achieve eventual consistency by resolving discrepancies due to disruption once the problem has been fixed on the net.

Navigating Network Challenges:

The following are the various challenges that arise in the network:

- **System Resilience**: In dispersed contexts where network partitions are more frequent, BASE models may provide more resilience, guaranteeing continued operation.
- **Recovery and Integrity**: Even when networks get partitioned, ACID systems ensure that there will be data integrity once they recover though less available.

Partitioning in Distributed Systems

In the context of distributed systems and databases, partitioning is a process that involves splitting a huge dataset or task into smaller partitions that are easy to manage. Each partition in a distributed computing system has its own node or machine associated with it and forms part of either workload or data.

Partitioning can Improve Availability, Scalability, and Performance.

- **Data Distribution:** In such a distributed system, the dataset can be divided and spread across multiple nodes or processors. Every node must process some portion of the data as well as store it. Since different nodes can already be working on separate partitions concurrently; it therefore enables parallel processing which enhances speed and shortens processing time.
- **Load Balancing:** It helps to transfer the load from one node to another load and due to that, each node will share an almost equal amount of load.
- **Scalability:** It allows us to increase or decrease the size of nodes that will not affect the performance of the system.
- **Fault Tolerance and High Availability:** Data will be available even after any failure occurs.
- **Data Locality:** Data will be processed at a local level first to reduce the communication cost among the nodes.

Let's talk about a few popular data storage-level partitioning strategies.

Data Partitioning

The technique of dividing a large data set into several smaller ones and allocating the duty of storing and processing these smaller data sets to several distinct nodes within a distributed system is known as data partitioning.

Types of data partitioning:

- Vertical data partitioning
- Horizontal data partitioning

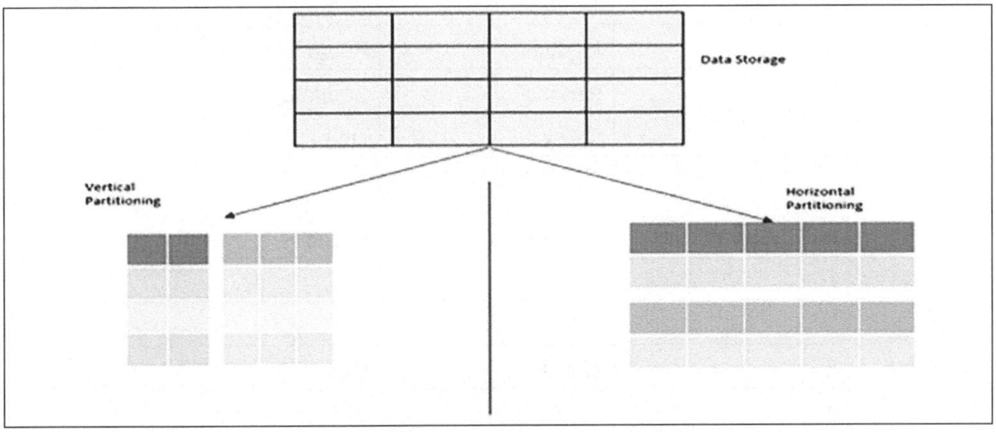

Figure 8.2: *Communication Network*

Vertical Data Partitioning

This method of data partition is known as vertical data partition, column partition, or column-based partitioning and refers to the division of a table along columns. For instance, this approach may involve a situation in which columns with similar characteristics or access patterns are placed in different divisions.

Normalization is one of the ways to perform vertical partitioning. Therefore, let us take the example of vertical data partitioning within an institution's student information management system.

The student table will be used in this example. It has the **`Roll_No`**, name, city, branch, and **`mobile_no`** attributes.

Roll_No	**Name**	**City**	**Mobile_no**	**Address**
1	Ravi	Dehradun	77777	CSE
2	Tanupriya	Bijnor	11111	ECE
3	Jagdish	Bengaluru	22222	CSE
4	Parisha	Bengaluru	33333	BFA
5	Shrey	Delhi	44444	CSE

Table 8.5: *University Student Details*

Through vertical data partitioning, we can divide our table depending on logical relationships between columns. Suppose we decide to do so by dividing the "student" table into two partitions: "student1" and "student2".

Roll_No	Name	City
1	Ravi	Dehradun
2	Tanupriya	Bijnor
3	Jagdish	Bengaluru
4	Parisha	Bengaluru
5	Shrey	Delhi

Table 8.6: *student1*

Roll_No	Mobile_no	Address
1	77777	CSE
2	11111	ECE
3	22222	CSE
4	33333	BFA
5	44444	CSE

Table 8.7: *Student2*

By splitting the table vertically, we can achieve the following benefits:

- **Improved Performance:** The improved query performance is achieved by accessing a lesser amount of data read. For example, if queries primarily involve retrieving personal information about students like name and city, then one could directly access the 'Student1' partition.
- **Reduced Storage Overhead:** In case, the "Address" column is relatively large but not frequently accessed, it can be stored separately in the "student2" partition which reduces storage overhead for queries that don't require it.
- **Enhanced Data Security:** By separating the address column into a separate partition, we get better control over permission to access sensitive order data. The student1 partition will have wider accessibility whereas strict security measures shall apply to the student2 partition.
- **Reduced Data Management:** To meet your specific application requirements, this involves vertical division of student table data based on a logical grouping of columns for optimal data access, storage, and security. The choice of the most appropriate vertical partitioning technique should consider relationships between columns and patterns of their usage.
- **Security and Privacy Requirements:** Vertical partitioning helps in better application of privacy as well as safety measures for data. To lower the

chances of unauthorized access or data leakage, separate partitions could be used for private or sensitive columns with more stringent access controls and encryption techniques.

Remember, not all cases require vertical partitioning. The choice of whether to do vertical partitioning or not depends on the data model itself, access patterns, and individual application-specific requirements.

In some cases, the best way of achieving the needed performance, scalability as well as data management requirements, might be a combination of vertical and horizontal partitioning or any other alternative data partitioning methods.

Vertical data partitioning involves dividing data into user profiles, product catalogs, customer-related information in e-commerce, patient records, medical data in health care, and more.

Horizontal Partitioning

Splitting a table into several smaller tables; each containing a portion of the original table rows is called horizontal data partitioning. These subsets are then stored by other nodes.

There are various commonly used methods for horizontal data partitioning such as:

- Partitioning by range
- Hash Function
- Consistent hashing

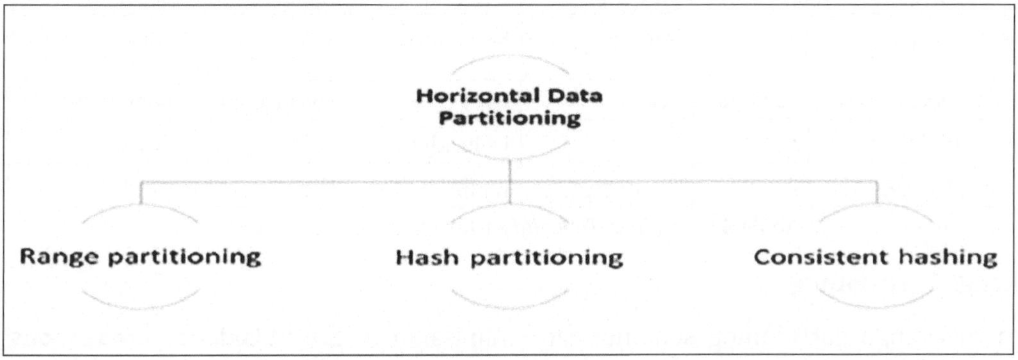

Figure 8.3. *Horizontal data partitioning techniques*

In the range partitioning method, the data is separated into partitions based on predetermined range criteria. Each partition has a range of values that satisfy this specified range requirement. The benefit of this partitioning lies when we must logically group the data according to an interval of values for a particular column.

Let's take an example of the student database where we can use range partitioning to illustrate it further. We have a table called "**`Student admission details`**" with the following columns: **`Admission date`**, **`Roll_No`**, **`Name`**, **`City`**, **`Mobile_no`**, and **`Address`**.

Admission date	Roll_No	Name	City	Mobile_no	Address
10/07/2022	1	Ravi	Dehradun	77777	CSE
15/07/2022	2	Tanupriya	Bijnor	11111	ECE
17/07/2023	3	Jagdish	Bengaluru	22222	CSE
19/07/2023	4	Parisha	Bengaluru	33333	BFA
10/07/2024	5	Shrey	Delhi	44444	CSE

Table 8.8: *Student admission details*

To apply range partitioning, we can partition the "**`student admission`**" table based on the **"`Admission date`"** column, which represents the date of admission. That will divide the data into three partitions based on the following ranges:

- **Partition 1** (Recent admissions): Includes admissions from the last 30 days
- **Partition 2** (Previous Year): Includes admissions from 31 days to 365 days ago
- **Partition 3** (Older more than 1 year): Includes admissions older than 365 days

Admission date	Roll_No	Name	City	Mobile_no	Address
10/07/2024	5	Shrey	Delhi	44444	CSE

Admission date	Roll_No	Name	City	Mobile_no	Address
17/07/2023	3	Jagdish	Bengaluru	22222	CSE
19/07/2023	4	Parisha	Bengaluru	33333	BFA

Admission date	Roll_No	Name	City	Mobile_no	Address
10/07/2022	1	Ravi	Dehradun	77777	CSE
15/07/2022	2	Tanupriya	Bijnor	11111	ECE

Table 8.9*: Student Table (after horizontal partitioning)*

Range Partitioning

In this range partitioning scheme, each admission in the **"`Student admissions`"** table will be stored in the corresponding partition based on its admission date. New admissions will be added to the **"`Recent admissions`"** partition, and as time progresses, admissions will move from one partition to another based on their age.

Google's BigTable and Apache HBase seem to leverage Range Partitioning.

It is not feasible to run effective range queries with range partitioning using keys other than the partition key. Furthermore, when a large range is spread across several nodes, the query performance will suffer. If one range has more data than another, range partitioning may also lead to an unequal distribution of the data.

Data is split into partitions using the hash partitioning approach, which divides the data according to a hash function applied to a particular column or group of columns. The partitioning key's hash value is used to assign each record to a partition. The Hash function output should be divided equally among its partitions when considering hash partitioning objectives.

Let's consider an example of hash partitioning in the context of a student database. We have a table called "**`student`**" with the following columns: "**`Roll_No`**," "**`Name`**," and "**`City`**."

`Roll_No`	**`Name`**	**`City`**
1	Ravi	Dehradun
2	Tanupriya	Bijnor
3	Jagdish	Bengaluru
4	Parisha	Bengaluru
5	Shrey	Delhi

Table 8.10: *Hash Partitioning*

To use hash partitioning, we decided to divide the "**`student`**" table based on the column called "**`Roll_No`**". Steps involved in the process of partitioning involved:

- **Number of Partitions:** Here decide the number of partitions required during fragmentation. Here we have taken three partitions.
- **Define a Hash Function**: Pick a hash function that uses the "**`Roll_No`**" column to get a hash value. Data should be equally divided among all the partitions.

In consistent hashing, the number of partitions and load is going to be redistributed as per the changing requirements. The process of redistribution is done dynamically. This has been done by mapping data to partitions using a ring-like structure and a hash function.

For instance, let's take an example from a distributed caching system to illustrate consistent hashing. Suppose there is a distributed cache with four cache nodes named A, B, C, and D. Every cache node is a partition representation.

Assigning Nodes on the Ring:

- To represent all possible hash values in a cyclic manner, we make up a circle (hash ring).
- The multiple places on the ring for each cache node's identifier are calculated using this particular hashing algorithm.

Mapping Data to Nodes:

- The same hash function is used to hash the key whenever a fresh piece of data needs to be stored or retrieved.
- The associated cache node is then found by mapping the generated hash value onto the hash ring.
- We proceed clockwise until we reach the first cache node, starting from the spot on the ring where the hash value is located.
- From that cache node, the data item is subsequently saved or retrieved.

Adding or Removing Nodes:

- The hash function is used to determine a new cache node's location on the hash ring, such as node E when it is added to the system.
- The existing cache nodes' placements are changed to disperse the load equally.
- Less data must be redistributed because just a portion of the keys need to be remapped to the new node.

Handling Node Failures:

- If a node fails (say, node C), the keys associated with that node are divided up among the other nodes.
- Once more, a subset of the keys requires remapping because some of the keys from the failed node can be assumed by the already active nodes.

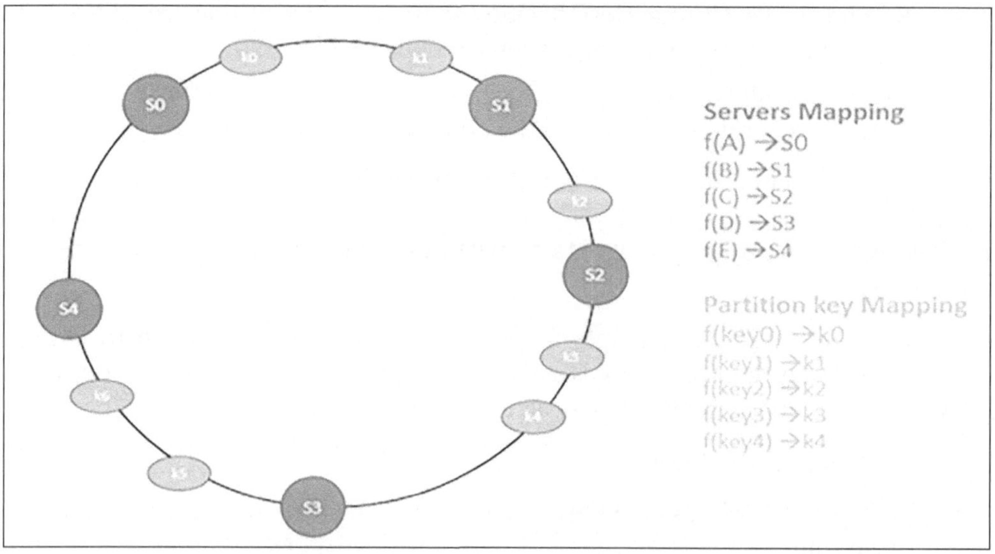

***Figure 8.4**: Consistent Hashing Ring*

Consistent hashing ensures that data distribution among cache nodes doesn't change when nodes are added or withdrawn from the system. This enables scalability and fault tolerance while reducing the impact on the data that is already in existence.

In distributed systems where data partitioning and load balancing are essential for performance and scalability, such as distributed caches, distributed databases, and content delivery networks (CDNs), the consistent hashing technique is frequently employed.

Request Routing:

For rebalancing, different partitions are assigned to different nodes. It's difficult to determine the IP address of a node that performed the read operation.

Another name for this issue is "service discovery." Here are several methods for solving this issue:

- Permit clients to make requests to any network node. The request is forwarded to the node that does have the relevant data if that node does not already have it.
- There is a routing tier in the second strategy. The routing layer receives all requests and then chooses which node to connect to process them.
- The information about partitioning and which partition is connected to which node is already known to the clients. As a result, they can get in touch with the node that holds the necessary data directly.

The primary difficulty with each of these methods is figuring out how these parts are informed about changes to the node partitioning.

ZooKeeper:

Many distributed data systems require a separate management server, such as ZooKeeper, to track changes inside the cluster. Every node connects to ZooKeeper to obtain the information, and Zookeeper maintains track of every mapping in the network. ZooKeeper is updated and notifies the routing tier of any changes to the partitioning or additions or deletions of nodes. ZooKeeper is used by HBase, Kafka, and SolrCloud.

Distributed Transactions

The interbank money transfer scenario is a common example of a distributed transaction. Let's say A must send money to B through a different bank. Since the situation involves data from two banks, a distributed transaction is the only way to ensure the ACID of the transfer rather than relying on a local transaction in a single database.

When a transaction is distributed, it indicates that its coordinator, resource manager, and transaction initiator are all situated on separate distributed system nodes. The A-$100 operation and the B+$100 operation are not situated on the same node in the interbank transfer scenarios. Distributed transactions basically seek to guarantee that data operations are carried out correctly in a distributed environment.

In a distributed context, distributed transactions adhere to the BASE (Basically Available, Soft state, and eventually consistent) theory to address availability, performance, and degraded service requirements while lowering consistency and isolation requirements:

- Fundamental accessibility
- Comfortable condition
- Final coherence

Distributed transactions, however, also adhere to some extent to the ACID definition.

- **Atomicity**: Rigorous adherence
- **Consistency**: After a transaction is finished, consistency is rigidly adhered to; but, consistency inside the transaction can be suitably eased.
- **Isolation**: No interference from concurrent transactions; a safe degree of transparency regarding transaction intermediate results.
- **Durability**: The changes made by the distributed transactions, should exist in the systems until and unless no further changes are made in the database.

Distributed Transaction Management

Since the full ACID guarantees cannot be met, there isn't a perfect answer for every business issue in distributed transactions. As a result, in real-world applications, we should select the distributed transaction solution that best fits the various business requirements.

Two-stage commitment/XA:

The X/Open organization has suggested the XA specification for distributed transactions. The interface between a (local) Resource Manager (RM) and a (global) Transaction Manager (TM) is primarily defined by the XA specification. According to the XA specification, local databases like MySQL perform the RM function.

There are two phases to XA:

- **Phase 1 (prepare)**: Every participating RM is ready to lock in the necessary resources and carry out their transactions. The participants notify TM that they are prepared when they are.
- **Phase 2 (commit/rollback)**: All participants receive a commit command from

the transaction manager (TM) once it has verified that each participant (RM) is prepared.

Currently, practically all widely used databases–including MySQL, Oracle, SQL Server, and Postgres–support XA transactions.

One or more resource managers (RM), one transaction manager (TM), and one application program (AP) make up an XA transaction.

The transaction is finally successfully rolled back if the preparation phase operation of any participant fails. DTM will call xa rollback of each child transaction to roll back. The characteristics of XA transactions include:

- Long resource locking and low concurrency
- Easy to comprehend and create

Refer to DTM if readers would like to examine XA in more detail.

The main reason distributed transactions are utilized is that spreading your database over several nodes–possibly even across several regions–offers several benefits. Among these benefits are:

- **Straightforward Horizontal Scaling**
  Adding nodes is a simpler way to increase database capacity than upgrading the hardware on a single machine. This is typically less expensive and easier as well.
- **Higher Availability**
  When your database is spread over several nodes and one of them fails, the remaining nodes can usually handle your workloads, and your application won't be impacted. On the other hand, if your whole database is stored on a single system and that machine experiences a problem or goes offline, your application won't work again until the machine is fixed.
- **Better User Experience**
  When set up correctly, a distributed database can frequently provide better performance since numerous machines can share the workload. Data can also be placed geographically close to the users who require it most in multi-region settings, which reduces user latency when they access the application.

Moreover, the benefits of database distribution are so great that, at some size, database distribution becomes practically mandatory.

Distributing the database, however, can complicate certain of the transactions that are a crucial component of mission-critical workloads for most businesses.

Distributed Transactions and Consistency Challenges

Because we require a mechanism to ensure that every database node is consistent with every other node, distributed transactions are more complicated than transactions on a single-instance database.

The following diagram shows an example of a possible distributed transaction issue. Suppose we have an application that is trying to commit a transaction to three different database nodes (maybe all three nodes are replicating the same data, or maybe the transaction impacts several rows, each of which is stored on a different node). The transaction is shown in the diagram as being successfully written to the first two nodes, but it fails to write to the third, either because of a node problem or a network disconnect. As a result, the first two nodes and the third node enter a condition of inconsistency.

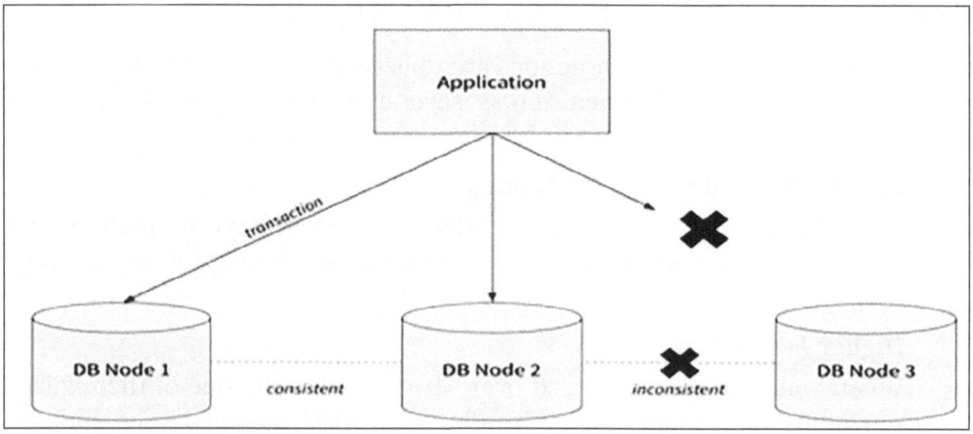

Figure 8.5: *A potential problem with distributed transactions*

Undoubtedly, inconsistent data in a database can lead to several issues, especially with workloads involving transactions (such as payment processing systems). Let's examine some practical instances of distributed transaction patterns in the real world.

Distributed Transaction Patterns: Real-world Examples

This strategy is feasible and will guarantee consistency between the two database nodes. It does, however, have a few notable drawbacks.

The Two-phase Commit Patterns

The way the two-phase commit pattern operates is that database nodes are synchronized in two stages: preparation and execution of the commit for each node. The transaction won't be finished until both phases have been successfully completed. This is a diagram showing how it appears in a basic two-node setup:

First, both nodes' resources must be locked while the two stages are finished. Other database activities cannot access those locked resources, which can soon lead to a performance bottleneck at scale.

Second, it is not very fault-tolerant and gets more complex with every extra node added. Even if every other node is available and able to complete the transaction, it will fail if only one of them goes down. As a result, one of the main benefits of sharing your database is eliminated because the system would eventually become unresponsive if even one node failed.

Active-passive Replicas

Using an active-passive configuration, where a single node serves writes and is supported by one or more read-only replicas, is an additional method for managing transactions in a distributed system.

This method provides a few key benefits over the two-phase pattern. When set up correctly, it can be more fault-tolerant; if the active node fails, one of the passive nodes can take over as the active node to continue operations. This switchover usually takes some time and may cause a brief service interruption, but it can be automated to reduce downtime.

However, there are also several drawbacks to this strategy. Once more, we are overlooking some of the initial justifications for utilizing a distributed system. Write tasks must entirely be handled by the active node; they cannot be divided among machines. As a result, even if the database includes three nodes (in the preceding architecture), the performance constraints of the one active node still limit its write performance.

It could also be difficult to scale. Adding more active nodes would require some system for resolving consistency issues between the active nodes as they occur but adding more passive nodes is quite simple.

Multi-active Distributed Transactions

A multi-active system, where every database node is active and supports both reads and writes, is arguably the best way to handle dispersed transactions.

Since there aren't many real-world systems that can do this, we'll use CockroachDB as an example here. Every database node in CockroachDB is operational and ready to handle reads and writes. The Raft consensus mechanism solves the consistency issue across active nodes. This means that even if a node (or, depending on your settings, many nodes, AZs, or even entire regions) goes down, your database can still function because transactions can be committed if most nodes agree on them.

Crucially, the database software automatically manages the complexity of sending transactions to various nodes and maintaining consistency as nodes are added and removed. CockroachDB can be used in much the same way as a single-instance Postgres database by application developers.

We don't have enough room to cover the whole intricate history of multi-active systems here. Learn more about a distributed transaction's lifecycle in CockroachDB.

Finally, the multi-active strategy fulfills the real potential of a distributed database by providing fault tolerance, high availability, and easy horizontal scaling without compromising consistency.

Conclusion

Database replication in today's data-driven world is not only a strategic advantage but also an inevitable technology. It is a critical component of any company's data management plan as it improves safety, performance, and dependability. Replication or duplication helps data available anytime and accessed from anywhere.

Fragmentation is also useful to categorize the database based on the user requirement so that the burden will be lesser and processing will be faster. Users get the results faster as compared to the regular process.

ACID properties are a very crucial property of a database where we can ensure atomicity, consistency, isolation, and durability. BASE is beneficial in distributed transactions where we can easily manage a huge amount of data. In the next chapter, we are going to discuss another important aspect related to database systems, that is, database security and privacy.

Questions

1. Mention the advantages and disadvantages of distributed DBMS
2. Explain the phases of query processing in a distributed database.
3. Compare Parallel and Distributed databases.
4. State the use of the NoSQL database system.
5. Draw and Explain Distributed Database System Architecture.
6. Differentiate between SQL and NoSQL databases.
7. Discuss in detail about database, collection, and document in MongoDB by taking appropriate examples.
8. How to Query for null or missing fields in MongoDB? Discuss with example.
9. What are the challenges of using NoSQL databases?

10. Explain NoSQL and describe the four types of NoSQL databases.
11. Elaborate on the causes that led to the emergence of NoSQL.
12. Explain the Document Database with an example. Elaborate on the various use cases for document databases.
13. Give a comparative study of RDBMS over KeyValue Store and Document-based database.
14. Give instances when the Key value database and document-based are to be used and when to be avoided.

CHAPTER 9
Data Security and Privacy

Introduction

It is a procedure to guard against unauthorized use, access, disclosure, disruption, alteration, and destruction of data. Information security is a common term used to describe it. Access control and encryption are two examples of non-technical and technological approaches that can be used to secure data. To put it succinctly, data security is essentially about safeguarding your existing data. The three main areas of data privacy are data collection, use, and sharing.

The right to decide how their personal information is collected, used, and disclosed is known as data privacy. Data privacy is viewed by an organization as pertaining to the data management policies and processes that are implemented. Having a solid data privacy policy is essential to keeping clients' trust.

Structure

In this chapter, we will cover these topics:

- Authentication and Authorization Methods
- Data Encryption and Hashing Algorithms
- Security Best Practices for Databases
- GDPR, HIPAA, and Other Data Privacy Regulations
- Database Auditing and Monitoring

Security and Privacy

Data privacy emphasizes people's rights to prevent businesses and governments from using their personal information without permission. With the ease with which we can now access nearly any information, people's concerns about their personal data are at an all-time high. One way that organizations are changing is by taking data privacy seriously. For instance, in many states and nations, businesses must get consent before collecting and using client data for marketing initiatives. To share that data with outside companies for advertising, they also want consent from the respective individual or company.

Data security guards against employees, rogue individuals, or harmful software gaining unauthorized access to private data. To put it another way, if a company or other entity has authority over data, what steps are they taking to ensure that they don't run the danger of data theft or loss?

Regarding data security, one thing to keep in mind is that these initiatives call for constant attention and observation. Since the threat landscape is dynamic, you cannot afford to implement procedures once and then forget about them.

Key Similarities:

These are some topics that are related to both data security and data privacy.

- **Data Protection**

  Data protection is the focus of both. For this reason, a lot of people confuse these terms. Ultimately, the aim is to guarantee the security of the data. Companies and customers want their data to be used only for the purposes for which it was designed.

- **Identical Rules**

  Regulations governing the collection, use, and sharing of information by organizations with third parties may be necessary for both data security and privacy. These laws are essential in preventing information from falling into the wrong hands.

- **Data Policy**

  Data security and privacy are core components of any complete data policy that an organization wishes to have. You cannot completely handle the constantly changing risks and issues associated with data management without these elements.

After resolving some of the typical confusion, let's examine how these terms differ from one another.

Key Differences:

The following are the key differences between Data Privacy and Data Security:

Data Privacy and Data Security

There's still more to think about after you've established how these phrases relate to one another and their fundamental distinctions. Your plan needs to consider the additional elements and documentation requirements when compliance is taken into account. Data privacy goes beyond ensuring that consumers and clients are at ease. The rise of global privacy laws like the CCPA and GDPR, coupled with data breach notifications, means that it is increasingly important to treat privacy as a paramount concern for businesses that have to engage in more efforts to ensure compliance. This implies proper planning and continual effort. Data security entails taking protective measures against digital information; it's not merely an idea. In terms of compliance, data protection is needed to build trust among customers and potential clients.

Both are not the same thing, however, data security does not necessarily mean data privacy. Effective management of information requires both conceptual understanding and organizational policy implementation. If you must follow a framework in your company, then think about how these requirements might change your operations.

The Significance of Data Security

It is amazing how much information firms manage. For business purposes each online transaction, such as clicks or purchases, develops usable data points, this flood of information necessitates its greater safeguarding.

- **Volume of Data**

  Businesses, as they move online, are dealing with an unprecedented amount of data. This knowledge-wading pool is being facilitated by the growing use of IoT devices that generate data constantly and every interaction with customers.

- **Potential Risks**

  Every organization aspiring to safeguard its assets and reputation has to understand what it will face if data is not protected. In today's world, organizations are handling more and more huge amounts of information hence security is becoming more important than ever. Let's deduce why modern enterprises desiring success should consider data privacy and security to be a priority.

- **Legal Implications**

  Strict data privacy laws are being enacted across all countries including California Consumer Privacy Act (CCPA) and European Union General Data Protection Regulation (GDPR). Serious fines run in millions or even billions of dollars if privacy laws are violated depending on the seriousness of the impact and the number of people affected by the breach.

- **Financial Consequences**

  Data breaches can have immediate financial repercussions in addition to legal charges such as the expense of fixing the incident and paying impacted customers. Customers may lose their trust in business and select competitors leading to long-term sales slump.

- **Reputational Damage**

  A single data breach can destroy years of built-up trust. When a corporation has a bad reputation for privacy policies, it is hard to regain the public's trust. In the era of social media, online markets, reviews, and news about a data breach being spread fast might lead to a degradation of brand image.

Customers' loyalty and trust: What happens to their data? Trust can be built through open discussions on data usage as well as protection policies. The companies must value the privacy of the customers and protect their confidential data so that companies can win their customers' trust which will lead to loyalty.

A Competitive Advantage

If a business has solid guidelines on data privacy and security, then it can easily outshine other players in an industry where competitors offer similar products or services. Once they have a secured database, businesses should not worry about possible breaches and hence can explore new offers and models based on data.

Therefore, there are serious consequences for ignoring data security and privacy. Also, there are significant potential benefits for companies that implement safe procedures.

The issues around safeguarding data security and privacy are:

Therefore, here is a summary of what ought to be done to ensure data security and privacy in an organization.

The first step towards ensuring that your data is safe and cannot be stolen by unauthorized persons is to encrypt it. Encrypted data cannot be understood by anyone who does not have a decryption key.

- **Secure Data Storage**

  Ensure that servers are located in places with strict access restrictions. Use well-known cloud services that have excellent security reputations. Ensure that your backups are both secure and regularly updated.

- **Employee Training**

  Helping your employees fully understand the gravity of data threats and what they contribute toward averting data mishaps will go a long way. Employees should be educated on responsible handling of data, detecting threats, and safe online behaviors. Regular updates should also be made as cyber threat technology advances so as to encompass these developments in the training materials.

- **Regular Security Audits**

  To identify weaknesses that can be improved upon, regular checks on safety measures should be carried out. Seek assistance from external security professionals for objective and thorough assessments.

Authentication and Authorization Methods

The importance of authentication and authorization must also be considered in any safe access control project. However, there is a widespread perception that these terms are interchangeable. What's more, multiple ways of implementing them have been proposed, thus making things difficult for the developers to follow through.

If you're feeling overwhelmed as a developer who is confused about how to differentiate between authentication and authorization as well as the various implementation ways available, take heart; you're not alone in this. This section will delve into the differences between AuthN and AuthZ and equip you with information about their different techniques.

Authentication:

Authentication (AuthN) is a process that confirms that an entity is actually what it claims to be. Identity authentication refers to the process of verifying the identity of an individual or service. Authentication processes typically use one of three methods to verify someone's identity:

- Something the user knows (for example, passwords or security questions)
- Something the user has (for example, physical devices like USB security tokens or mobile phones)
- Something the user is (such as biometric authentication or certification-based authentication)

Authorization:

It concerns itself with the level of accessibility a user or service will be able to enjoy. Authorization is also used in technology to say 'yes' to an action or agreement with data. Identity is required for authorization and authentication.

On the other hand, authorization uses confirmed identity to regulate access while authentication confirms the identity before allowing it.

- **Role-based Authorization:** Here a user can only access resources based on their role within an organization such as "manager" as an employee hence giving them some privileges that other employees may not have.

- **Attribute-based Authorization:** This provides access control based on certain characteristics of a user for example, file access may be restricted only to those who maintain specific security levels or belong to one department.
- **Rule-based Authorization:** This involves granting permissions using pre-set rules such as only users logged in between actual business hours being allowed into a particular resource.
- **Context-based Authorization:** which permits access based on the context of the request, for instance, if a request comes from a particular location or device, then it becomes relevant.

Authentication Methods

The most widely used authentication methods are:

Basic Authentication

Basic Authentication is a simple way whereby the user supplies their username and password in the HTTP header of every request. The server authenticates this identity and admits if it is genuine. This HTTP-based approach employs Base64 format to code usernames and passwords, which are found in an HTTP header. However, sensitive credentials can travel between systems unencrypted, making it essential to use Secure Sockets Layer (SSL) and Transport Layer Security (TLS) channels when sharing data between multiple web applications.

With Basic Authentication, login credentials are sent in the request headers with each request. Usernames and passwords are concatenated together using a : symbol to form a single string, which is then encoded using base64. This method is stateless and suitable for API calls along with simple authenticated sessions that does not require any dedicated sessions.

Advantages:

The following are the advantages of basic authentication:

- Faster authentication due to fewer operations involved
- Easy Implementation Widely supported by browsers

Disadvantages:

The following are the disadvantages of basic authentication:

- It is not the same as the encryption technique and can be easily decoded since it's sent in plain text. Secure socket layer and HTTPs are essential.
- Every time credentials are going to be recorded.
- Logout options are only applicable when giving the correct credentials.

Session-Based Authentication

The introduction of session-based authentication was motivated by the challenge posed by the stateless nature of HTTP protocol that requires repeated authorization from users for each new request. A token is generated by the server upon successful authentication during session-based authentication and sent to a client which stores it in a cookie and sends it back with each subsequent request. This token is used by the server to authenticate the user and returns requested information. Logging out means deleting the session ID held in the cookie.

Advantages

The following are the advantages of session-based authentication.

- **Ease of Implementation:** Session-based authentication has relatively easy implementations that do not need complex cryptographic operations.
- **Scalability:** For instance, in a load-balanced environment, sessions can be scaled horizontally across multiple servers making it possible to cater for many concurrent users at once.
- **Security:** Session-based authentication can protect against cross-site request forgery (CSRF) attacks, which are requests sent by an attacker to a website on behalf of an authenticated user, using a session ID stored in a cookie.
- **Logout Functionality:** To implement a logout functionality via session-based authentication does not require many steps; just erase the session ID which was saved as a cookie.

Disadvantages

The following are the disadvantages of session-based authentication.

- **Session Fixation Attacks:** The most common way attackers perform session fixation attacks is by setting the target's session ID prior to login to take over their session.
- **Session Hijacking Attacks:** One among the many types of online fraud is noted when someone steals your email and webmail login details. This person then uses this information for malicious purposes. To deter such actions from taking place, developers should consider using secure cookies and put constraints on hijacked sessions, such as IP tracking and renewing identity after long inactive periods.
- **Session Management:** Sometimes it may be difficult to manage user sessions, especially where a server needs to maintain a store for sessions so as to keep track of authenticated users.
- **Stateful Servers:** In other words, stateful servers save session information on the server side and must be used in conjunction with session-based

authentication methods. However, this might be limited when there are too many connections.

The difficulty with mobile apps is that whereas on websites one can utilize session-based authentication, the absence of cookies on some devices and the leaking of session information to unauthorized users makes it impossible to implement this in mobile applications.

Unauthorized access is not the only challenge for session-based authentication on mobile platforms. Scalability limits it especially when it comes to session management because sessions are mostly stored in memory. When servers are replicated to multiple instances, all user sessions must be replicated to each server, making it challenging to handle several concurrent users. To address these limitations developers often employ specialized tools for managing sessions or turn to third-party services which can help centralize such functionality as well as distribute session data across multiple servers. Additionally, distributed caching technologies such as Redis or Memcached may be applied so that they store all sessions within a single centralized cache which will reduce the need for replication and simplify the process of managing them. Nonetheless, having a dedicated server for session management may not always be feasible for small to mid-sized applications. In this regard, developers should think about any other authentication approaches that would fit their cases better than this. Thus, scalability requirements should carefully be reviewed by developers before selecting an appropriate method of authentication.

Token-Based Authentication

Nowadays, a lot of people use token-based authentication as their go-to method for accessing websites and online accounts because of the new single-page applications, web APIs, and IoT devices that have been developed. The statelessness of this kind of authentication system does not require storage of any user-related data on the server side. Instead of using usernames and passwords, tokens are employed to authenticate users. Whenever users authenticate themselves, a token is generated by the server for exchange between the client and server to verify the identity of the user. Tokens normally include unique user identifiers and time stamps which mark their expiry dates. Tokens do not need to be saved at the end where they are initiated from by using their signature to validate them thus making requests faster without involving database lookups.

Token-based authentication also fits well with microservices architecture, which has multiple services that require authentication. It is simple to specify how each service can handle both token and token secret at its own discretion. However, there are some drawbacks to using token-based authentication too. XSS attacks exist when tokens get stored on the client side using local Storage or CSRF attacks through cookies. Deleting tokens is impossible just like expiring them only after they expire can prevent attackers from misusing them if leaked until such time expires. It's a good practice though to set short expiry times and utilize refresh tokens which automatically renew expired ones at expiry. Also, another option to overcome this problem is to have a blacklist database that removes the tokens, which adds overhead and violates microservice principles.

JWTs are the most common type of token used for this purpose because they are versatile and easy to use. Other examples of token-based authentication include SWT (Simple Web Tokens).

In general, compared with traditional authentication methods, token-based authentication provides enhanced security, scalability as well as flexibility. It is, however, important to assess potential vulnerabilities and ensure that necessary safety measures are put in place.

SWT vs. JWT

Simple Web Tokens (SWT) and JSON Web Tokens (JWT) are two different ways through which web services and applications can securely exchange information with each other when they want to authenticate their users or keep the records confidential. Unlike JWT which performs payload encryption or digital signatures, SWT was specifically designed for lightweight web scenarios without these types of support. An SWT token consists of three elements: header, payload, and signature. The header has information about the token itself; claims about the authenticated user/client are stored in the payload; while the signature contains a cryptographic hash signed by a secret shared key or asymmetric keys.

SWT and JWT have some important distinctions:

- **Format of an Identifier:** The structure of these tokens is different. A SWT token has three parts: header, payload, and signature which are in key-value pair format while a JWT token has JSON format with three parts, that is, header, payload, and signature.
- **Payload Encryption:** SWT does not have any support for payload encryption whereas JWT uses JSON Web Encryption (JWE) to encrypt the payload. This additional layer of security ensures that sensitive information contained within a token's payload is secure.
- **Signature:** To derive the signature, SWT and JWT employ different algorithms. While HMAC algorithm is used by SWT which requires both the party who generates the token as well as the recipient to share a secret key; JWT supports both symmetric keys such as HMAC which use shared secret between parties and asymmetric keys, for example, RSA or ECDSA.
- **Standardization:** On one hand, JWT is a standardized protocol with defined rules for claims, algorithms, and token formats while on the other side, SWT is not a standardized protocol and has less support compared to JWT.

- **Use Cases:** Unlike Java Web Token which can be used beyond web-based scenarios, Windows Token was designed specifically for web-based applications, such as APIs or web services.

SWT is helpful when authentication and authorization require a lightweight and simple token format that does not require payload encryption. For example, in a company that offers a web API that serves as an interface to its services for third-party developers who can access the service, SWT is used as the token format for authentication. When a user or client wants to get access to an API, it generates SWT tokens containing information about the user or client, such as their ID, authorization level, and permissions. Thereafter, the SWT token must be included in each subsequent request by the user/client through which the API verifies the token signature and authenticates the customer.

The claims on this token claim assert security-wise whether this user can consume these requested services.

This is essentially because JWT provides better security features and flexibility making it more suitable for different uses. Also, SWT may be used in conjunction with other web-based authentication protocols like OAuth to enable secure transmission of client/user credentials between systems.

SSO (Single Sign-On)

In SSO, users do not have to key in their username and password for each application they use but log on once and automatically reach all valid applications without entering the credentials again. This will save you from the hustle of remembering different usernames and passwords since it improves the user experience while working on several applications.

For example, the flow of an SSO process may be as follows:

1. The first Google item is accessed by a user, which sends back a cookie generated by Google Accounts.
2. If a user visits another Google product, they are directed to Google Accounts.
3. On realizing that you have already logged into some authentication-related cookie, Google Accounts will direct you to the necessary product right away.

In simple terms, SSO can be defined as; "a user logs in only once and then obtains access to all other systems without having to authenticate himself/herself at each one of them." Three identities completely trust each other, and these are: identity provider (IdP), service provider (SP), and the end-user.

To get into an SP, a person types his/her IdP password (or any other authentication means). This makes the SP is able to trust the user as well.

There are many ways of implementing SSO, including:

- **Federated SSO**: In this way, an identity provider (IdP) is a third party trusted with authenticating users and sharing their log-in credentials with applications or services they want to access. The IdP acts as a middleman between the application and the user, where the user only needs to sign into it once to use all of his/her authorized applications. For instance, it is commonly known that when using a Google, Facebook, or Microsoft account one can log in into a third-party application using them; hence a third-party application which acts as a service provider while on the other hand Google, Facebook, or Microsoft acts as an identity provider by giving your authentication data respectively to the service provider.
- **Enterprise SSO:** This approach enables single sign-on functionality within an organization across multiple applications and services used in that organization. The user logs in once at an SSO system and then he/she accesses multiple applications and services required. Many organizations use enterprise SSO solutions to provide their staff with consistent access to different applications and services. For illustration, an employee may sign into his or her firm's SSO portal utilizing network login details and then automatically get logged in to email, intranet, HR portal, and other applications that they have been granted authority.
- **Web SSO:** This is used for web-based applications and services where a user logs in at a central authentication server or portal and thereafter, can access any of the web-based applications or services that they are authorized to use. Web SSO is commonly used for accessing web-based applications and services. For instance, as you log into your online banking account you may be redirected to a central authentication server or portal where you enter your credentials. Upon successful authentication, you are then able to access your account as well as any other related service without having to re-enter your credentials.
- **Kerberos SSO:** Kerberos is a network authentication protocol that provides Single Sign-On functionality across networks of computers. With this method, users authenticate once with the Kerberos server so that they can thereafter gain entry into any service or application within the network without typing their passwords again. Kerberos is often used in large enterprises to achieve SSO. For instance, once the user logs into their computer using their network credentials and is authenticated, they obtain automatic access to all authorized applications and services within the network.
- **Mobile SSO**: This approach is for mobile apps and services. They sign in only once by which they can then use any authorized mobile application without re-entering login information. It is one of the commonly applied strategies in mobile apps like social media or banking applications. As an example, you may

enter your bank app with your fingerprint or face recognition, and from then on, everything is automatically signed in without having to fill out username and password details over again.

SAML

SAML (Security Assertion Markup Language) is a widely used standard for implementing federated SSO. In this way, the user attempts to access a protected resource on the service provider's website thus initiating the authentication process in the SAML framework. After that, the service provider directs the user to a different place where this person is asked for his/her secret code. The latter authenticates the user and generates a response where information about the user's authorizations and identity is placed in an assertion of SAML type. Lastly, this assertion is sent back to SP which it uses to let him/her play.

Assertions under SAML have various types, such as authorization assertions, attribute assertions, and authentication assertions therefore allowing control at different levels of resource accessibility. It finds wide application in enterprise environments for implementing SSO, hence supported by notable solutions for identity management.

OAUTH

OAuth stands for Open Authorization. It represents an open standard protocol enabling users to grant third-party apps access to some of their resources without providing login details including usernames/passwords. This way, users can safely permit applications to access their data on their behalf over a secure connection without having to reveal personal credentials over the internet. In web and mobile applications as well as social networking sites like Facebook and other web-based services OAuth is widely adopted.

Here's how it works:

- If a user tries to access the protected resource on the website or app via a third-party app then the OAuth procedure will start.
- The third-party app obliges the user to permit it to access some specific resources, such as profiles, emails, or photos on their behalf.
- If agreed, a third-party app receives an authorization grant that signifies permission given by a user to access the required resources.
- The authorization server of the service provider uses the authorization grant given by the third-party application to get an access token.
- Then, this token is used for accessing users' information by these applications on behalf of service providers.

This occurs when someone desires to register for a new web application with his/her

Google account; it demonstrates OAuth's real-life example. The following is how the flow should be:

- While using the client (the new application), which is one among other clients held by Google, a person tries to sign up for him/herself into that new application via his Google account credentials.
- Upon directing the user to Google's authorization endpoint, they get consent about accessing their Google accounts' data.
- A user who has been authenticated successfully will agree to allow any client to retrieve his/her profile information from Google.
- These are client-side requests made at Google's Authorization Server where they apply for an access token by providing them with what they got from the stages mentioned earlier.
- When a user is authenticated, Google provides the client with an access token and a refresh token that can be used to access the user's data on his/her Google account.

With this token, the client can get information about their name, email address, or contacts in their Google Account without keeping or sharing the password for accessing such accounts. This enhances security and ease of use, especially for those who would like to use their existing accounts to sign up for new applications.

OAuth has had several versions each with different features and improvements. The first version was released in 2007 as OAuth 1.0 which uses a signature-based authentication mechanism requiring clients to sign each request they make using a shared secret key. OAuth 1.0a was released in 2009 which fixed some security issues and added new functionality such as support for mobile devices. OAuth 2.0 is the current version released in 2012; it has a simpler and more adaptable design than its predecessors making it possible for developers to utilize emerging authorization flows like implicit and client credentials flows. OAuth 2.0, on the other hand, is said to be less secure compared to OAuth 1.0 because of its use of bearer tokens which may be stolen and thus used for accessing user data.

The OAuth 2.0 specification's latest version is OAuth 2.1, which was released in September 2021 as a revision of the OAuth 2.0 protocol to enhance the security, privacy, and usability of OAuth 2.0 features. Key adjustments in OAuth 2.1 include more prescriptive security guidance for implementers, elimination of insecure practices, stronger client authentication methods, and improved user consent.

Some popular apps that use OAuth include Twitter (OAuth1.0a), Facebook, Google, LinkedIn, and Microsoft (OAuth2.0).

Open-ID

OpenID is an open standard that enables users to sign on to different web applications and services using their existing online identities. OpenID allows users to log into an application using their preferred online identity, say, their Google, Facebook, or Twitter account instead of creating a new account just for the application.

Imagine you would like to log into an online marketplace through your Facebook account. Using OpenID, the marketplace can confirm your identity and pull in basic profile details from Facebook, such as your name and picture.

Here's how it works:

1. You click the "**Sign in with Facebook**" button on the login page of the marketplace.
2. The marketplace redirects to Facebook's authentication server where a prompt to log in via Facebook account exists.
3. Facebook will issue an ID token once you have logged in successfully.
4. The marketplace, on the other hand, uses this ID token to identify you and gain access to your basic profile information including your name and profile picture.

OpenID is a layer built on top of OAuth2.0 which serves as an authorization framework for accessing protected resources. OpenID Connect is the latest version of OpenID with additional authentication features and improvements over its predecessor.

In summary, OAUTH2.0 is an authorization framework, while Open ID is mainly used for authentication.

OAuth allows third-party clients (for example, Facebook or Google contacts) to access protected resources, leveraging the use of access tokens issued by an authorization server (Facebook or Google Auth server). On the other hand, OpenID allows users to log into another application using their login credentials from an OpenID provider (for example, Google), using its ID token.

MFA/2FA

MFA (Multi-Factor Authentication) and 2FA (Two-Factor Authentication) are security measures that demand several ways of proving somebody's identity before giving him/her access to his/her account or system. Both MFA and 2FA however provide extra security beyond a mere username/password combination that is prone to hacking.

Typically, MFA mandates that the user is supposed to provide at least two different forms of authentication types from three categories: something a user knows such as a password, something the user possesses like a mobile phone or token generator, for example, face-based or fingerprint-based authentication.

MFA purposes that require 2FA are just one of many cases in which there must be two different kinds of authentication factors provided by the users. This usually involves some kind of information (like password) and possession (for example, mobile phone or token generator) on the part of the user.

Here's how 2FA typically works:

1. A username and password are entered by a user to log in to an account.
2. The system then asks for another authentication factor like a code generated by an app on your smartphone or sent via SMS text message.
3. The good thing about 2FA is that even if someone else gets hold of or guesses your secret key they would still need another device with their second level of authentication before he can gain access to your account.

Data Encryption and Hashing Algorithms

What is encryption as you've probably already heard it? To put it simply, it means converting data into a code so that it can only be used by authorized personnel, but there's more to this.

Encryption involves complicated and necessary technology that uses algorithms to change information into a form that cannot be read assuring the security of data during exchange or storage.

In the following sections, we will discuss how encryption works, look at some popular algorithms used, and show you how real-world cases help us understand its practical aspects.

Encryption is like a locked safe for your digital information. When you send data over the internet, in the form of a message or personal details, encryption turns it into code that would be almost impossible for unauthorized people to understand.

It uses an advanced cryptographic technique ensuring that the information only makes sense to the intended recipient alone.

Think about shopping on the web and looking at your bank account balance. Whenever you see "https" in the address bar of your browser, this is an indication that encryption is taking place. What happens is your data gets jumbled up with unbreakable codes while moving from one device to another through a server located on the other end of cyberspace. Anybody who may try and interfere with such text will only get gibberish lines of letters.

This describes how Web-based encryption unfolds step-by-step:

1. When a user enters a website: As soon as you access a secure website (URLs that start with "https://"), your browser requests the server of the site to create a secure connection.

2. Sending of its public key by the server: The browser then goes ahead and requests the website's server to send back its public key.
3. Checking for certificates by the browser: Besides, your browser also gets digital certificates from this message, which are then verified if they are real or not.
4. The use of public keys in encryption: After that, your web browser will use its HTTP/SSL configurations to encrypt the session ID with the help of the RSA encryption algorithm used in SSL protocol.
5. The session key is decrypted by the server: This process is done through decrypting using the private key at the server end.
6. Establishment of secure connection: Therefore, during your visit to this particular site both yours and its servers now have the same session keys which they utilize in coding and decoding all data sent between them.
7. Secure data transfer: At each point in time when transmitting information from your own computer system such as emails from one place to another through the internet whereby such information cannot be intercepted through any possible way unless someone knows how it can be decrypted without anybody else being aware, hence ensuring that all messages remain confidential and tamper-proof.

Most Common Encryption Algorithms

Encryption utilizes mathematical procedures generally known as cryptography algorithms to convert plain text into cipher text. Different encryption algorithms exist due to differing security requirements.

The symmetric encryption algorithm is a popular one. It uses the same secret key for both encryption and decryption, ensuring a straightforward process.

Two of the most common symmetric encryption algorithms are the **Advanced Encryption Standard (AES) and Data Encryption Standard (DES)**. DES, although outdated, was once a prevalent method for encrypting data. On the other hand, AES is currently the industry standard, widely adopted for its robustness against attacks.

RSA (Rivest-Shamir-Adleman) is another widely used Public Key Cryptography **asymmetric encryption algorithm**. In this two sets of keys are used, one is called a public key which is used for encryption, and another one is called a private key which is used for decrypting at the receiver end. One set of public keys and private keys is used for encryption and decryption, for example, if from set public key is used, then the private key will be from this set only.

Examples of Encryption:

Whether sending messages, conducting online transactions, or storing data, you must encrypt information in today's digital space. Here are practical examples of encryption in action:

- **Secure Communication (Public-Key Encryption)**: Asymmetric encryption, with its public and private keys, is commonly used in messaging apps, email services, and online communication platforms to encrypt data and protect user's confidentiality.
- **Online Banking (SSL/TLS Encryption)**: When you access your bank account or make transactions online, encryption ensures the security of your financial information, such as account numbers and transaction details.
- **Virtual Private Networks (VPN) (Tunneling and Data Encryption)**: VPNs utilize a combination of tunneling protocols (like IPSec or OpenVPN) for secure communication and encryption to protect data during transit.
- **File Storage and Cloud Services (AES Encryption)**: Advanced Encryption Standard, with its single encryption key, is commonly employed for file integrity and data stored in the cloud.
- **Government and Military Communications (AES, RSA, etc.)**: Government agencies like NSA (National Security Agency) and military communications often involve several encryption methods, including RSA and other sophisticated algorithms. These technologies protect sensitive information and communications critical to national security.

Hashing Algorithms

"A distinct input data is changed (or 'message') into a full-sized string of characters, which is typically numbers and letters." Hash functions make hash value representations referred to as hash codes. The designs of hashing algorithms are based on speediness and efficiency criteria while producing different hash values when given different inputs.

First of all, pick an appropriate hashing algorithm like SHA-256 or MD5. Then come up with a hash function. The purpose of this part is to produce a fixed-size hash value from the initial message using the selected function.

Now let's consider the type of information you want to be hashed. You could have it as a password, document, or any other kind you possess; thus, apply the earlier hash function to it. For this reason, data is processed to create output that uniquely identifies it in terms of a particular code known as hash value.

The output produced by this routine is called the hash value, which is often expressed in a hexadecimal format having some common number/letter combination length.

Hashing the same data with the same algorithm as well as hash function will always produce the same result for the hashes. This property ensures predictability.

Changing even one character in input data will completely change its corresponding code by a significant amount. In case you may not be sure about what this means, it simply implies that there are unique codes for every set of data used here.

In other words, hash codes serve as unique identifiers for efficient computer comparisons to determine if data are the same or different. The function always creates a fixed-length hash value, regardless of the size of the input data. This standardized format makes storage and comparison easier. You can use or employ a hash sum in specific instances, which is a specialized form of hash value that can condense huge datasets into smaller sizes.

Common Hashing Algorithms

Hashing algorithms can be found in many places in computer science and cryptography with applications, such as ensuring data integrity, storing passwords, and creating digital signatures. The following are some of the most common hashing algorithms:

- **MD5 (Message Digest Algorithm 5):** MD5 produces a 128-bit hash value; this value is usually presented as a 32-character hexadecimal number. However, due to weaknesses that facilitate collision attacks, it is cryptographically broken and unfit for further use.
- **SHA-1 (Secure Hash Algorithm 1):** SHA-1 produces 160-bit hash values. Just like MD5, SHA-1 is also considered weak because it has been vulnerable to various attacks making it outdated.
- **SHA-256, SHA-384, and SHA-512**: They belong to the SHA-2 family and they are more secure than MD5 and SHA-1. SHA_256 gives out a 256-bit hash which has become the standard hashing algorithm used today in digital signatures and certificate generation.
- **SHA-3 (Secure Hash Algorithm 3)**: This latest SHA algorithm, offers a different internal structure from SHA-2 and provides a set of hash functions with distinct output sizes.
- **Whirlpool**: Whirlpool is a hash function that produces a 512-bit hash value. It is not as widely used as other algorithms but is considered secure.

Examples of Hashing:

- In **Data Integrity Verification**, hashing ensures data hasn't been tampered with. Before transmission or storage, the original data hash value (checksum) is calculated and sent along with the data. Upon retrieval, the hash is recalculated and compared, verifying data integrity.
- **For Password Storage**, hashing adds a layer of security by storing password

hash values instead of the actual passwords. During login, the entered password is hashed and compared to the stored hash, minimizing risks in case of a data breach.

- **Digital Signatures** use hashing to create a hash of a message or document, which is then encrypted with a private key. Recipients can verify authenticity using the sender's public key.
- **Caching** stores previously computed results for quick retrieval, using hash values as keys. This optimizes performance, as the cache is consulted using the hash value when a new request matches a prior input.
- Finally, in **blockchain**, each block contains a hash of the previous block, forming an unbroken chain. This design ensures tamper resistance, as altering one block requires changing all subsequent blocks.

Encryption and Hashing

When comparing hashing and encryption, the main difference lies in the reversibility of the process.

Encryption encodes data in such a way that only authorized parties can read it. It uses an algorithm and a key to transform plaintext into ciphertext. Importantly, this process is reversible given the correct key, you can decrypt the ciphertext back into plaintext.

Encryption is used when the information stored needs to be retrieved in its original form, like when you're sending sensitive emails or storing confidential files.

On the other hand, hashing is a one-way function. It takes an input and returns a fixed-size string of bytes, typically a digest. Unlike encryption, hashing doesn't require a key, and the process is irreversible.

You can't get your original message back from the hash value. When you enter your password, the system hashes it and compares the result to the stored hash. If they match, you're granted access.

In encryption, a slight change in plaintext results in a significantly different ciphertext. But with hashing, even a small change in input will generate an entirely different hash. This property, known as the 'avalanche effect', increases security against attacks.

Security Best Practices for Databases

For a safe database system, first, secure the space where the database is kept and only authorized persons can access and use the database. The following are the best practices used to keep the database safe and secure:

- **Differential Database Servers:** Web servers are by definition publicly accessible, but this makes them an obvious target for attackers. If an attack is successful, the attacker might be able to access the website or application's host server, which would give them access to everything else hosted on the server.

This micro-segmentation can stop attackers with more widespread network access from simply moving laterally to acquire access to a database server that might not be visible on the network of a compromised user.

- **Use Database Firewalls:** If the use case permits it, then direct access to the database should be restricted or disallowed. Change management protocols must regulate firewall rule modifications and initiate security monitoring warnings.

  Specialized database technologies such as web application firewall (WAF) solutions, dedicated physical or virtual next-generation firewalls (NGFW), and unique firewalls like the Oracle Audit Vault and Database Firewall, can be implemented by organizations. Businesses with fewer resources can install a more robust version of the operating system firewall on the database server.

- **Secure Database User Access:** The database should be accessed by the fewest number of users, programs, and application programming interfaces. Only after a network or application permission should any access be allowed. Three subcategories comprise this best practice: privileged access, user authorization, and database use for development and operations.

  The admin, or system administrator, is in charge of controlling access to the database. By assigning user accounts to certain database roles, the administrator grants permissions that are specified by roles. Row-level security (RLS), for instance, limits read and write access to data rows according to a user's identity, role memberships, or query execution context.

  Password rotation policies, password storage reduction, and centralized management of identities and permissions are all possible with specialized database security solutions. Smaller businesses may not be able to afford comprehensive access control, but it is still crucial to manage permissions through roles or groups rather than individuals.

Additionally, administrators must strengthen the database access rules:

- Null passwords ought to be prohibited
- Password-containing temporary installation files ought to be removed
- If default accounts are not required, they should be terminated; otherwise, the default passwords should be changed
- All users should have unique IDs to be tracked and logged in
- Applications and users ought to have different accounts

- Regularly, inactive users ought to be disabled or removed
- Logging, reporting, and maybe generating security warnings are all important aspects of elevated database privileges
- Access privileges and user groups should be evaluated regularly
- Accounts ought to automatically lock after a certain amount of unsuccessful login attempts; generally, six unsuccessful tries

Administrators should only be granted a minimal amount of access for the time that is necessary to complete their assigned responsibilities. It is best to offer privileged access momentarily and to continually rescind it. Software called privileged access management (PAM) is used by larger organizations to automate access control. PAM keeps track of actions, prohibits password sharing, and assigns a temporary password to authorized users.

DevOps teams must set up test environments even though they are not usually thought of as users to ensure that programs can access and use databases properly. Regrettably, leveraging production or live database data frequently results in unintentional data leaks.

DevOps should employ the following procedures to prevent problems:

- It is best to keep sensitive data inside the production environment
- Production settings and test environments must be kept apart both physically and conceptually
- Roles and permissions should be used differently in test environments than in production environments
- Access to production environments should only be granted to developers when absolutely essential
- Real production data should never be used in test settings; instead, artificial or anonymized datasets should be used

Harden the Database: The database needs to be protected in the same way that the server is to stop easy exploits and assaults.

Depending on the kind of database platform, database hardening procedures differ, but generally speaking, they involve encrypting sensitive database fields, safeguarding network traffic, and enhancing password protection and access controls.

To stop unnoticed exploitation, all superfluous or unwanted database services and functions should be disabled or eliminated.

It is recommended to enable all database security features offered by the database. Certain controls will be turned on by default, while others might be disabled for particular reasons. Admins can enable dynamic data masking and row-level security for sensitive data wherever possible.

Sensitive data should be kept in separate tables by design, according to DevOps. Administrators should also regularly evaluate the data to find critical information, so they may decide whether to add more security or change the segregated tables. Certain data discovery requirements may be mandated by regulatory or compliance standards, and to demonstrate compliance, they must be implemented, followed, and recorded.

Audit and Continuously Monitor Database Activity: Although DevOps designs with specific expectations, unexpected access, user queries, or data behavior may happen after databases and applications are integrated and put into a production environment. Database logs, data, and activity must be regularly observed and audited by administrators. This includes:

- Records of user logins, in particular, failed and attempted logins
- Locked accounts (due to numerous unsuccessful attempts to log in)
- Elevation of database privileges
- Copying, deleting, or extracting data from databases (especially large-scale modifications or extractions)
- Data access that is controlled or sensitive (may be required for compliance)
- Creation of a new account

Test Database Security: Audits can detect fraudulent activity while it is happening, but companies should test their database deployments before waiting for assaults. Database suppliers must keep an eye out for upgrades, and patch management procedures ought to update databases as quickly as possible.

However, patching only fixes vulnerabilities that have been made public. Risk-identifying security and configuration testing tools, like Oracle's Database Security Assessment Tool, are provided by certain database manufacturers. But these techniques shouldn't be taken for granted because they can't guarantee 100% security. Instead, you should conduct further testing using vulnerability scans and penetration tests, which mimic possible attacks and reveal misconfigurations, accidentally accessible data, and other problems.

Database Data Best Practices: Databases organize data, but the data that is stored inside also needs to be safeguarded. An organization must store only the protected data necessary for the operation of the business in the first phase. Removing superfluous data or superfluous historical information might reduce the amount of risk involved.

The data must then be deliberately managed. Shadowing of protected data outside the system of record must be avoided wherever feasible, and redundancy of protected data should be removed from the system as a whole. Protected data items can have hash functions applied to them before the data needed for matching is stored outside the system. Protected data, including credit card numbers or health information, should be kept separate from personally identifiable information (PII) wherever feasible.

Further security should be achieved by pursuing encryption. Numerous suppliers offer products for encrypting data while it's in use, in transit, or even at rest. DevOps can employ data masking or encryption within the database to hide certain data in tables. Certain encryption solutions go so far as to enable data processing and searching without decryption, ensuring that the data is always safe and secure.

Certain cloud providers, like Oracle, offer encryption key management tools, such as Azure Key Vault or encrypt data by default. Nonetheless, it is the duty of the organizations to guarantee sufficient security during the data transit and storage procedures.

System-related Security Best Practices: A security procedure cannot be regarded as exclusively belonging to database security if it does not relate to databases in particular. This does not, however, lessen the significance of these procedures or the necessity of their implementation to guarantee database security.

- **Physical Security**

  Physical security is important, but it should never be taken for granted. Even the strongest cybersecurity procedures and technologies can be compromised by an attacker's physical access to a data center. The first best practice for basic IT security should be protecting a physical environment that houses servers and network equipment.
  Physical security measures such as cameras, locks, and manned security officers are necessary for on-site data centers. Physical access servers also need to be monitored, tracked, and routinely assessed. When frequent access is not the norm, an alarm ought to be sent out.
  Cloud-hosted assets might not be directly under an organization's physical control, but they are still under its obligation.
  The company still needs to verify that there is sufficient physical security, which is usually satisfied by the cloud provider's adherence to physical security guidelines set forth by organizations, such as IEEE, NIST, ISO, and so on.

- **Use Web Applications and Network Firewalls**

  All IT assets are fundamentally protected by firewalls. Organizations must install web application firewalls and next-generation firewalls (NGFW) in addition to database firewalls to safeguard their networks and the websites and apps that access the database.
  These more all-encompassing firewalls defend the company from threats like distributed denial of service (DDoS) and SQL injection that impact databases and other systems.

- **User Authentication**

  The underlying presumption when databases grant users access is that they have previously undergone identity verification and authentication.

The authentication or identity verification of all users, including visitors, staff members, clients, and administrators, is mandated by security best practices. Insider threat management, user verification, and privileged access management (PAM) are some of the subcategories of user authentication security.

Management of Insider Threats

Certain types of data can be so valuable that criminal organizations can either pay employees to leak the information or even put their own members in bogus employment to obtain access to the information. Organizations should perform background checks on programmers, contractors, security experts, database administrators, and anybody else who might have access to or be able to reroute important information to reduce these insider threat concerns.

Organizations utilize user and entity behavior analytic (UEBA) technologies, UEBA features on other security solutions, and audit logs to search for indications of anomalous or inappropriate behavior after employee IDs have been verified. Remember that most security tools will view stolen credentials used by a hacker as authorized access unless anomalous behavior is noticed. Finally, set up a procedure for deactivating accounts or unused access when staff members change positions or depart the organization.

User Validation

Users need to validate their identities regularly, or even continually in the case of zero trust, to preserve the integrity of a verified identity. While passwords are still the most widely used means of identity verification, some businesses are starting to employ passwordless authentication.

It is recommended that organizations always utilize multi-factor authentication (MFA) for administrators and other privileged accounts. Organizations should think about utilizing physical MFA, such as magnetic cards, USB tokens, and other techniques that are difficult for remote attackers to steal or duplicate, for their most critical data.

Strong passwords and password management should be utilized by organizations that use them:

Password phrases, which are considerably longer passwords, or password complexity, which combines capitalization, numerals, and special characters, ought to be mandated.

At least eight characters must be included in your password; privileged accounts may require more.

- Password hashes ought to be salted and encrypted for storage
- As many as six attempts should be made to get into a regular user account,

and as few as three attempts should be made to enter into privileged or administrator accounts.

- Passwords ought to run out.

By using password managers, businesses may increase password complexity and frequency without having to worry about customers keeping their credentials in unsafe or susceptible places. To stop access from outdated and forgotten users or devices, user access should be refreshed regularly.

Privileged Account Management Abuse of administrator access can result in significant harm, so extra precautions need to be taken to secure admin credentials. Organizations should think about implementing privileged access management (PAM) solutions in addition to stricter password requirements. These tools create temporary passwords with restricted access, requiring authorized users to verify each time they access the database. Privileged access should impose extra guidelines like:

- Don't share passwords
- Every session and activity is recorded, and periodically evaluated
- All user privileges should be monitored

1. **Device Security**

   Every device that uses the network to access the database must be checked and kept an eye out for any potential security breaches. The bare minimum of protection is offered by antivirus software, but for increased security, enterprises frequently use endpoint detection and response (EDR) or extended detection and response (XDR) technologies, which offer more proactive detection.

   Network access control (NAC), whitelisting, and IP and MAC address restrictions should all be used to further restrict admin devices. To lessen the usefulness of compromised credentials to hackers, these procedures restrict the number of devices that are permitted access to sensitive regions.

   All tools, apps, and devices connected to the database's infrastructure (or other sensitive systems) should be documented by the company. In addition, configuration files and source code need to be restricted, available only through secure administrator accounts, and shielded by tools and policies for change control.

   Finally, it's important to monitor every system. Tools for intrusion detection and prevention systems (IDPS) or XDR should be used to monitor networks. Security operations centers (SOCs), managed detection and response (MDR) teams, and security information and event monitoring (SIEM) tools should receive alerts from all security systems.

2. **API Application Security**

   Applications and APIs need to be secured when they connect to the database or other IT resources. Applying vulnerability screening technologies to internally produced websites and applications should be the first step for DevOps. To further protect and monitor systems, larger organizations will implement API security tools and application security solutions.

3. **Update Operating System And Patches**

   Poor maintenance will compromise the effectiveness of the best security systems and tactics. Every system, program, tool, and firmware should have its vulnerabilities and recently issued patches checked for. Regular patch and vulnerability management should be given priority for critical systems, such as those that connect to database systems. Open source libraries and other software supply chain components should be monitored for updates and vulnerabilities.

4. **Business Continuity**

   Issues arise with even the best-laid plans. Regardless of the cause of the problem, a dissatisfied worker, a malevolent hacker, a power outage, or a flood–business continuity and disaster recovery best practices build resilient and quick recovery systems.

   Designs with redundant architectures ensure uptime in the case of a system failure. Using load-balancing servers, which distribute possible loads across several servers, or active-passive redundancy for fail-over recovery can strengthen a server's resilience.

   Backups of data and the system guard against malicious activity or total system failure. Regular backups with strong security are recommended. The 3-2-1 backup guideline, which calls for three backup copies of the data, two different kinds of storage, and at least one copy offsite and offline, is adhered to by best practices. Backups should be encrypted and kept apart from encryption keys; there should be no public access allowed.

   For accelerated system recovery, backups should contain not only the data but also the configurations, software, and settings of the supporting infrastructure. Regular testing of backups for mission-critical infrastructure is necessary to ensure that the procedures are functioning properly and to establish recovery expectations.

Health Insurance Portability and Accountability Act (HIPAA)

Individual health information used, transmitted, and retained for the delivery and payment of healthcare services is protected by the Health Insurance Portability and Accountability Act of 1996 (HIPAA), as amended by the Health Information Technology for Economic and Clinical Health (HITECH) Act. PHI or protected health information is the term used to describe this data.

All health insurance plans, health billing clearinghouses, and healthcare providers (including clinics, hospitals, and doctors' offices) that submit electronic claims to insurers are subject to HIPAA regulations. "HIPAA Covered Entities" is the aggregate term for these organizations. To perform services for a Covered Entity, third parties such as consultants, auditors, lawyers, and other service providers (referred to as "Business Associates") must abide by HIPAA.

PHI is defined by HIPAA as any health information created, received, or maintained by a HIPAA-covered entity, whether it be electronically, orally, or in print. It also includes information that could be used to identify an individual, such as "individual identifiers," and it is connected to a person's past, present, or future physical or mental health condition, the provision or payment of healthcare, or genetic information.

Virtually any information from a person's medical records, records of payments made by or on their behalf for medical services (including insurance claims and reimbursements), or information given to a health care provider about a person's physical or mental health or condition that identifies or can be used to identify the person are all considered personally identifiable information (PHI).

General Data Protection Regulation (GDPR)

The main goal of the General Data Protection Regulation (GDPR), which went into effect in 2018, is to unify data protection laws throughout the European Union. The GDPR significantly improves individuals' rights to privacy and data protection within the EU. Many businesses that operate in the EU or provide goods and services are required to abide by a broad range of standards and duties.

Two levels of sanctions are outlined by GDPR. Tier 1 refers to any form of improper database security measure failure, typically discovered after a data breach. The maximum tier 1 fine is equal to 10 million euros or 2% of a company's worldwide revenue, whichever is higher.

Tier 2 pertains to the gathering and use of data, penalizing businesses that do not get consent prior to gathering and using personal information. Tier 2 fines have a maximum of 20 million euros or 4% of a company's worldwide revenue, whichever is higher.

The GDPR's extraterritorial regulatory oversight and enforcement reach, allows EU regulators to regulate and take enforcement action against any company handling personal data (employee, consumer, or business contact) of EU residents regardless of the company's location or the location of the data processing, is one of the largest and most significant changes.

Data can be a very useful resource, particularly if it contains unique information. Ever since the beginning of time, businesses have dedicated funds and resources to preventing theft of trade secrets and intellectual property. However, in more recent times, personally identifiable information (PII) has emerged as a new kind of data that is becoming more valuable.

Businesses are less diligent about protecting PII than they are about intellectual property. There are primarily two causes for this. First, obtaining customer and employee personal data doesn't take a lot of work or financial sacrifice. The second is that, in contrast to intellectual property, the original copy of personal data remains relatively valuable even if a copy is compromised.

Personal information is still very crucial despite this. Serious repercussions such as identity theft and financial fraud can affect thousands or even millions of people when personally identifiable information gets into the wrong hands. Companies need to reassure customers that they are secure to do business with by accepting full responsibility for protecting personally identifiable information (PII) as consumers become increasingly aware of this threat.

Regulations pertaining to data privacy are relevant in this regard. They not only assist businesses in assuring the public that conducting business (that is, exchanging data) with them is safe, but they also guarantee market justice by penalizing those who neglect their obligations.

Numerous data privacy regulations and standards exist, tailored to certain industries and geographical areas worldwide. Knowing which regulations apply to your company and how to abide by them is essential.

The good news is that most of these rules are fairly similar, so you should be able to comply with them all if you adopt a specific set of security standards.

Database Auditing

Database auditing is the term used to describe keeping an eye on and documenting the activities of a database. Consequently, all database events, such as modifications, queries, and logins are put down in a log file or saved in a database. Log data can be utilized by DBAs and consultants to monitor user behavior, identify problems, detect security violations, and comply with legal requirements. For developers and administrators, different levels, such as application, operating system, or database server can be involved in this type of auditing. In addition, it may involve different databases like object-oriented ones, NoSQL databases, or relational databases.

This is done under database auditing which helps to ensure data integrity while preventing unauthorized access to confidential information. Auditing has the following objectives: troubleshooting; detecting errors/fraudulence; and recording for accountability purposes. This may include alarms by administrators among other methods of audit trails, such as logs and triggers. These logs should be continuously monitored by managers responsible for the database security of any organization to keep an eye on every activity going on in the database and therefore prevent malicious activities from taking place.

Administrators should prioritize the events to be audited according to their priority and customize the auditing process to the unique demands of the organization. By using optimal database auditing techniques, institutions can ensure the accuracy and security of information.

Database Audit Types

Database administrators can perform several types of database audits to monitor different aspects of the database such as:

- **User Audits:** These are audits that observe user activities, such as queries, modifications, and logins. They discover harmful or unauthorized operations; resolve problems with output and evaluate results.
- **Data Audits:** Insertions, updates, and deletions of data are tracked by these audits. Data accuracy is watched over, abnormalities are sought for and compliance with rules is ensured.
- **Security Audits:** How users access tables, views, and stored procedures among other database objects is monitored in these audits. For example, they may be useful in checking who has roles and permissions to the user's table or view, hence ensuring that unauthorized individuals will not enter the system where sensitive information resides.
- **Compliance Audits:** These audit activities monitor compliance with regulations, such as GDPR, PCI-DSS, and HIPAA.

For instance, they check for any security breaches that may occur within an organization's system; ensure proper handling of data; and control access to private/ sensitive information.

These numerous reasons make auditing one's databases vital. First of all, it assists companies secure their data integrity and security. Monitoring what users do with data gives organizations a way of stopping data loss or corruption since unauthorized activity can be identified thus discovering security breaches due to user actions on the data.

Database auditing also helps businesses conform to industry standards and legislation. Several requirements call on organizations to track and report access to confidential data; otherwise, non-compliance might lead them to fines or legal actions.

Lastly, database auditing can be used by administrators to enhance efficiency and solve issues. Through log analysis, organizations can find problems; identify performance bottlenecks; as well as optimize their databases.

However, it is necessary for such database audits. For the successful execution of database auditing processes, establishments had to follow some recommended procedures including:

- Purpose exact audit goals
- Determine the kinds of audits that are required for your organization
- Select the right audit tools and technologies
- Assign responsibilities for auditing tasks
- Review audit logs and reports regularly
- Update and improve auditing practices continuously

While implementing a plan for a database audit, caution needs to be exercised. Consider the following best practices when designing a system of database auditing:

- **Define the Requirements for Auditing:** Specify audit requirements: Initially, determine what types of audits your organization has committed itself to in line with its objectives and legal obligations. This could encompass compliance auditing, data access logging, and monitoring activities of users.
- **Choose the Right Auditing Tool:** There are different options for database auditing tools ranging from third-party software to in-built functionalities. Choose a platform that can give you real-time data and alerts that meet your audit requirements.
- **Find a Starting Point:** Establish a baseline for consistent activity within your database. It will enable you to spot strange behaviors or trends indicative of security risk.
- **Set up Alerts:** Configure alerting systems that will notify you about certain situations, such as unsuccessful login attempts, unauthorized access to data, or its change by an intruder.

- **Check Audit Logs**: To identify irregularities, unusual activities or any security risks go through audit logs regularly. This should help you quickly detect and resolve any security problems.

These best practices created an effective database auditing system that secures your sensitive information, complies with legal requirements, and maintains data integrity.

Database Auditing Tools

A variety of tools are available for implementing database auditors. They include;

- **Native Database Auditing Tools:** Several DBMSs have built-in auditing functionalities that allow observing the behavior of the database.
- **Solutions for Independent Auditing:** There are several other third-party options available that have more sophisticated features, such as alerts, reporting, and real-time monitoring.
- **Security Information and Event Management (SIEM) Tools:** SIEM systems can collect, analyze, and report on various types of data including database logs. They offer a unified platform for managing security incidents and can correlate information from different systems.

Conclusion

Database auditing is an essential tool in ensuring the security and reliability of your data. By observing user activities for signs of security threats, you can take proactive steps toward protecting your personal information against breaches while staying within the confines of the law. Proper tools and best practices will help you identify and prevent breaches and maintain data integrity while providing a secure foundation for business success. It is important to remember that data protection goes beyond mere compliance; it is an important first step in safeguarding your company from the growing cybercrime menace. In the following or the final chapter, we shall look at database administration as well as various cloud services used in managing data.

Questions

1. What are the principles used to incorporate privacy and ethics into our data usage?
2. Explain the various security solutions to manage our data privacy program.
3. What access to the data and do the control mechanisms in place to meet IT security policy or standards?
4. Explain the process of recovery arrangements in the event of an IT infrastructure incident.

5. Differentiate between data security and privacy with the help of a case study.
6. What do organizations need to know about individual rights and data subject access requests (DSAR)?
7. Explain the best way to enforce data privacy without impeding future innovation.
8. What is the Best Way to Enforce Data Privacy in Your Organization?
9. What actions should you take when data security is compromised?
10. Define and discuss the various technology solutions to manage our data protection strategy.
11. Write a case study and analyze it on the various security standards, such as HIPPA, GDPR, and so on.

Chapter 10
Database Administration and Cloud Services

Introduction

The basic concept of cloud computing is that a service provider delivers IT resources, including processing power, database services, applications, and storage, over the Internet at a pay-per-use rate. There are several reasons why organizations are moving to the cloud, but the two main ones are the increased scalability and the potential for cost savings.

DBMS can be utilized in the DBaaS architectural model. For these reasons, the database management system acts as a software backend behind the DBaaS system, enabling users to use the database and its operations as a service.

DBaaS can be useful to several companies regardless of the industry they operate. First, DBaaS is a particularly valuable tool for testing and application development. It enables developers to provision databases quickly thereby saving time and effort. Consequently, the development process is enhanced since the developers do not have to maintain the database infrastructure and worry about database development and testing, they can concentrate on developing and testing applications. Besides, DBaaS supports scalability which allows businesses to rapidly increase or decrease the size of their data storage facilities corresponding to the changing needs of their applications.

Second, the other major use of DBaaS is in business intelligence and data analytics. Thanks to the capability of huge amounts of data that is supported by DBaaS and the ability to perform complex queries with high performance, organizations are able to use DBaaS for data storage, processing, and analyzing valuable information. The advantages of cloud computing over traditional systems enable businesses to cope with changing workloads and the growing volume of data. For the upper management of the enterprise, it is important that there are such analytics as data warehouses, machine learning, and real-time analytics.

The DBA team must also understand the precise cloud services being offered and confirm that they meet its usage requirements. DBAs must comprehend, for instance, problems with latency, size constraints, and any other factors that affect how an organization uses the database.

Structure

In this chapter, we will cover the following topics:

- Database Backup and Recovery Procedures
- Performance Tuning and Optimization in Cloud Environments
- Cloud Database Deployment Models (IaaS, PaaS, SaaS)
- Multi-cloud and Hybrid Cloud Strategies for Databases
- Database as a Service (DBaaS) Offerings and Management Tools

Database Backup and Recovery

The steps for database backup and recovery are outlined in the following checklist and are covered in detail:

1. Create a thorough backup strategy
2. Carry out efficient backup administration
3. Test database restores regularly.
4. Draft and distribute backup and recovery SLAs to all parties involved.
5. Have the database part of the disaster recovery plan (DRP) created and recorded.
6. Stay current with an understanding of database and operating system backup and recovery tools.

DBAs are in charge of creating a thorough backup strategy for the databases under their supervision. All RDBMS types used by the company should be covered by the backup strategy, which should also address the following:

Backup Requirement

The database and associated OS and application components that require backup, either through an online backup or an offline cold backup, must be known to the DBA. The specifics of what must be backed up are as follows:

OS software: As per best practice, OS backups are done periodically as per company policies. It is done at a defined frequency, such as once daily or weekly, as a hardware failure will necessitate a full system restore, beginning with the OS.

- **RDBMS software**: Before applying any fixes or upgrades, the RDBMS software should be backed up.
- **Application software**: This is particularly relevant to OEM versions of Oracle Enterprise Manager, Oracle Application Server, and Oracle E-Business Suite.
- **The submission Using the relevant OS command**: The DBA should finish the first full backup of the apps to disc. Following that, they should plan further. Incremental backups only cover the changes done after the last full backup.
- **Passwords**: Passwords that might be needed for recovery. Ensuring that the default passwords from the RDBMS's initial installation are changed is a smart approach.
- **Every part of an Oracle database**: A database parameter file, also known as a server parameter file (SPFILE), contains details on database control files and other persistent initialization parameters for a database.
- **Database control file(s)**: The control file maintains the state of the database's physical structure.

If it is unavailable, the database will not function. These files must be backed up concurrently with the database's other components. The DBA can set up an automated backup of the parameter file and the control file in later versions of Oracle (9i and higher) to ensure that these are backed up following every backup and any structural changes made to the database. Data files stored in databases should be backed up both online and offline, either using RMAN (Oracle Recovery Manager) or by setting tablespaces to backup mode in Oracle Database versions prior to RMAN's introduction.

- To enable recovery to the point of failure, the DBA ought to attempt to operate all production databases in Archive log mode.
- **Redo log files and archived redo logs**: The DBA must backup redo logs in addition to cold backups. The DBA must manually or automatically archive redo logs and then, back up all archive redo logs while the database is operating in archive log mode and performing an online backup.
- **Oracle network files**: It's crucial to back up every Oracle network file both before and after making changes. When using password files, always ensure to back up before and after making any changes.

MS SQL Server databases:

Maintain distinct plans for system databases, such as master, model, and msdb, full backups are supported by Master. Make a backup of each user database and transaction logs, then configure each user database for the full recovery model.

- **Create a plan for managing VLDB backups:** In Oracle, the DBA can use several channels, optimize backups, and conserve disc space by utilizing compressed backups. They can also use incremental backup procedures with the most recent versions to prevent tracking. To verify if this option is available, the DBA needs to examine the database's version and edition. Should this be ineffective, the DBA may want to think about establishing split mirror backups. The DBA for SQL Server might employ the file or filegroup backup approach and divide the database among several files. Additionally, backups can be written to all devices simultaneously in SQL Server when multiple backup devices are used.
- **Backup schedule**: To prevent the backup from lowering the amount of database server resources that are available and slowing down database user activity, it is best practice to choose a backup window when the database is experiencing the least amount of activity. By parallelizing backups across different channels, the DBA can adjust the backup window; however, to ensure that this option is available, the DBA must first check the version and edition of the database. Setting up a weekly backup cycle is generally the best course of action, with complete backups performed on Friday night or Saturday morning and incremental/differential backups performed during the week. Backups of the transaction logs and archives can be scheduled for every few hours, contingent on the database's volatility.
- **Backup Storage:** Databases running Oracle and MS SQL Server can be easily backed up to tape or disc, either locally or remotely. The backups can then be archived on cloud storage. Creating disc backups, transferring them to tape, and storing the tapes offsite for disaster recovery (DR) are best practices. DBAs can keep two sets of backups using this method: one on tape and one on disc. The backups to the disc are faster, and they give them greater control and better monitoring. If backups are still stored on a disc, the restore process will be quicker and the mean time to recover (MTTR) will be lower.
- **Develop a backup retention policy**–The SLA developed in conjunction with the business-user community should guide the decision on the backup retention policy, which is related to the disc and tape rotation schedule. The owner of the data should indicate how long it will be kept on file. Depending on local rules, the retention duration could range from months to years. To make room for new backups, the DBA should erase older backups. Care should be taken while selecting the data retention policy to ensure that it aligns with the backup media subsystem retention policy and backup recovery plan requirements. The DBA must ensure that the control file record keeps the time instance parameter corresponding to the retention policy if they are not utilizing a catalog.

Effective Backup Management

Following the creation of a strong backup strategy and the completion of preparatory work, the DBA should appropriately manage backups, bearing in mind the following:

- **Automating backups**: Use an OS scheduling tool or set up backups through OEM for Oracle, and spool output to a log file so that faults may be checked. Use Maintenance Plans in SQL Server to arrange backups.
- **Backup Monitoring**: Set up monitoring with the right tools so that if a backup fails, the DBA receives an email or a pager alarm on their cell phone, and the backup should be redone as quickly as feasible.
- **Logs and catalogs**: Periodically check backup catalog data and backup logs for any problems. To display the backup status, use RMAN reporting. For Oracle, periodically exports all catalog schemas and performs an export backup of the RMAN catalog schema after each backup to safeguard the RMAN catalog database. Backup system databases for SQL Server, in particular the master and msdb databases.
- **Maintenance**: Use "delete obsolete" while working with Oracle databases to get rid of backups that don't comply with the company's retention guidelines. Performance concerns will arise as a result of the catalog's continued expansion if outdated backups are not removed. Verifying that the catalog and control file match the physical backups is known as cross-checking (or cross-check backup).
- **Backup Validation**: Check and validate backups without actually restoring any data.
- **Dependencies**: Archive these backups to tape as soon as the disc backup is finished when backing up.

Backup Validation

Consider the following situation: The company's headquarters are located in a flood-prone area, and while the IT system has not been completely destroyed, it has sustained significant damage. The DBAs followed all procedures previously mentioned in this article to create backups to the backup media prior to the event and had them stored offshore. The backup procedure was deemed "effective" by the auditor in the business's most recent IT audit. The remote storage's backup media is retrieved and loaded. A notice stating that integrity problems have rendered the backup media "unreadable" flashes on the screen. Numerous things could have occurred. It is evident, therefore, that a crucial step was missed.

There was never a true test conducted on the restoration from backup media. Due to the existence and operation of a backup procedure, the control was deemed effective.

Furthermore, when the company backed up to the backup media, no errors were ever received.

If the IT staff is unable to restore the data to the system when it is needed, backups are useless. For this task, a DBA should create a thorough plan:

1. **Databases restore:** Testing database restores from disc and tape backups ought to be mandatory.
2. **Validating restores:** Without performing restores, the DBA can assess and verify backups. The "`restore validate database`" command can be used to validate backups; however, it will not restore the database. This is the most effective way to find out whether the backup is reliable and useable before a circumstance arises when it becomes crucial.
3. **Backup Refresh**: Building nonproduction databases from production backups regularly using the proper backup/restore utility instructions is a solid restore procedure.
4. **Backup Audit**: To demonstrate this kind of restore testing, the DBA need to take screenshots, save logs, and provide a narrative explanation of the procedure.
5. **Actual restores**–The DBA should back up the database before beginning any actual restores. The DBA must choose between complete (point-in-time) and incomplete recovery, depending on the kind of loss and accessible backups. Time-based, cancel-based, or change-based incomplete recovery are all possible.
6. **Strategy to recover from database corruption**– To find out if there are any corrupt blocks in an Oracle database, the DBA can enable block checking with the right parameters. This will enable early detection of faulty blocks caused by underlying disc, storage system issues; however, there is a tiny performance overhead. RMAN automatically looks for corrupt blocks when doing a backup. RMAN can be used in Oracle versions later on to fix broken database blocks.

Backup and Recovery SLA

The DBA team is required to create and obtain management approval for a backup and recovery SLA that includes a schedule for recovery and comprehensive information about backup practices. Although the SLA doesn't help with the recovery process itself, it does set expectations for the recovery process among the user community and management, which could provide the team additional time to finish the restoration process.

Disaster Recovery Plan

Databases are an important component of the company's overall DRP, thus the DBA needs to be careful to ensure that they are covered. The components of the recovery plan and the sequence in which the IT team will restore the databases must be understood by all parties involved. All business-critical applications should have a priority tag so that in case of a disaster, teams have a clear understanding of the order to recover such apps.

Recovery Tools

Although it may seem apparent, DBAs are the last and most crucial players in the process because they are required to maintain current knowledge of RDBMS backup and recovery technologies. DBAs may not have time to learn about any new developments in backup and recovery tools during the actual restoration event.

The database administration team's main duties include reviewing all RDBMS types used by the company and creating a thorough backup plan. This will allow for efficient backup management through proactive backup monitoring, failure alerts, and time-saving, seamless backup reruns. For disaster recovery purposes, it is best practice to back up data to a physical disc and then archive it to tape. After a strategy has been developed, it is crucial to regularly test data restoration as part of the backup and restore plan and consider all available options prior to carrying out the restoration or recovery process.

It's critical to verify that the DBA team has a well-defined procedure in place with defined tasks and that they are up to date on the most recent backup and recovery solutions. DBAs have completed a significant portion of their task if they keep adequate backups, regularly monitor them, and guarantee data recovery up to the point required by the business.

IT auditors can validate DBA activities, including testing data recovery, and help data administration teams increase their controls and data recovery procedures. Management can be reassured by the DBA team's and internal audit's ongoing, proactive, and collaborative efforts.

The process of backing up data in case of loss and putting in place safe procedures to enable recovery later is known as data backup and recovery. To ensure that computer data is available in the event of data damage or deletion, data backup necessitates copying and archiving computer data. Only data that has been stored on a dependable backup device can be recovered from a previous point in time.

Not all data and settings on a business operating system can always be restored by backing up the data. For example, extra forms of disaster recovery may be required for computer clusters, database servers, or active directory servers since a backup and recovery might not be able to fully reconstruct them.

Offsite Servers vs. Independent Drives

Offsite servers are good for data recovery since they offer enormous amounts of storage for low costs, especially when weighing the inconvenience they save in the event of an information disaster. In the long term, it's critical to have a secure location to keep data apart from the primary corporate server.

In most cases, data recovery is painless. Furthermore, offshore servers have additional data backups stored on their own disks in the unlikely event that they crash. For this reason, utilizing an offsite server for data backup and recovery is a practical way to secure the data.

Purchasing independent drives is another efficient way to protect a company's data. Terabyte drives are now reasonably priced, especially if procured from high-volume or budget retailers. Data recovery and storage are made simple as these devices are essentially plug-and-play. Furthermore, the market offers a variety of storage quantities.

All large enterprises have standard backup policies, such as daily incremental and transactional log/archive log backups and weekly full backups.

Cloud Backup and Recovery

A data backup technique known as "cloud backup," also known as "online backup," is transferring a copy of primary data to an off-site server via a public or private network. Usually, a third-party service provider (CSP) hosts the server and costs a fee based on the capacity, bandwidth, or user count.

Data is copied during the cloud backup process and then stored on other media or a different storage system for convenient access in the event of a recovery scenario.

Some options include:

- Directly backing up data to a public cloud. Writing the data directly to a cloud infrastructure provider, including Microsoft Azure, IBM Cloud, Google Cloud, and Amazon Web Services (AWS), is required.
- Making a service provider backup of data. In this instance, write data to a CSP that manages a data center and provides backup services.
- SaaS (software as a service) apps that store data in the cloud can use the cloud-to-cloud backup option. This process duplicates data to another Availability Zone or region for fault tolerance and high availability.

This happens in case when you want to upload all the data at once. However, when such tools are implemented not all the servers and databases are cut over to these tools or services at the same time rather they are divided into batches to reduce the load and increase the efficiency. The supplier only uses the network to back up data after the first seeding is finished.

Online data backup systems are frequently based on client software programs that execute according to a timetable set by the service level that was paid for.

Every 24 hours, the program will gather, compress, encrypt, and transport data to the CSP's server if, for example, have contracted with them for daily backups. To minimize the duration of transfers and bandwidth consumption, the CSP might only provide incremental backups subsequent to the initial complete backup.

A lot of cloud services are paid either annually or monthly. Large corporations and SMBs (small and medium-sized organizations) both frequently employ cloud backup services these days. Cloud data backup services are utilized by large enterprises and organizations as an additional option.

Backup vs. Recovery

To put it briefly, backup refers to a copy of the original data that can be used in the event of a database failure, whereas recovery is the process of getting the database back to its original, right state after a failure.

As previously mentioned, a backup is a representative copy of data that contains control files and data files, two crucial components of a database. A comprehensive database backup is necessary since unplanned database failures are inevitable. Two main categories of backup exist:

- **Physical Backup**: This is an exact duplicate of the database's actual files, including the data, control, log, and archived redo logs. The basis of the database recovery process is a copy of the files that store database information in a different location.
- **Logical Backup**: This comprises tables, procedures, views, functions, and other logical data that is taken out of a database. However, since logical backups simply offer structural information, they are neither advised nor helpful on their own.

On the other side, recovery aids in getting the database back to normal in the event of a failure. Because it enables the database to return to a consistent state following an unexpected failure, it increases the dependability of the database.

Log-based recovery is a fully viable option for database recovery. A sequence of records that includes transaction records is called a log. When kept on a reliable storage medium, the history of all transactions aids in the recovery of the database in the event of an error. It includes details about updated values, transaction states, and transactions that are carried out. Each of these bits of data is kept in the order it was executed.

Types of Data Backup

Although the concept of data backup may seem straightforward, putting an efficient and successful plan into practice can be challenging. Applications for backup software are created to lessen the difficulty of carrying out backup and recovery tasks.

Recall that the objective is not backup. It's just a way to get what, which is to shield the company and its consequences of data loss. The following are the most widely used backup types:

- **Full Backup**: This is a straightforward and comprehensive backup process that creates a copy of all the data to a different media set, such as a CD, tape, or disc. This results in an entire copy of all data being made available on a single set of media.

  As it needs a lot of storage space and takes longer to complete, it is usually used in conjunction with an incremental or differential backup.
- **Incremental Backup**: With this method, replicate only the data that has changed since the previous backup. The time and date of each backup activity will be noted and tracked by a backup application. This process uses less storage medium and is faster than a complete backup solution.
- **Differential Backup**: This sort of backup is comparable to the incremental type. In that it copies all modified data from an earlier episode, but each time it runs, it copies all modified data since the last full backup.

Backup and Recovery

The idea behind a backup is to make copies of data so that it backs up in case the original data fails. Primary data failures can be caused by a variety of problems, such as malware, malicious ransomware attacks, software or hardware malfunctions, human error, data corruption, and unintentional data deletion. Therefore, backup copies recover data from a previous point in time to help the company bounce back swiftly from an unforeseen incident.

Keep a copy of data on an alternate means to guard against loss or corruption. The additional backup device could be something as basic as an external hard drive or USB stick, or it could be something more serious like a cloud storage container, tape drive, or disc storage media. Store the alternative medium remotely or in the same place as the source data. It makes sense to use a remote location if this is located in an area where weather-related occurrences are likely to occur.

Make backup copies as often as possible to reduce the amount of data lost between backups for optimal outcomes. This implies that the chances of losing data when recovering from a failure increase with the amount of time that elapses between backup copies. Thus, don't put off creating backup copies for months. Maintaining several copies of data also gives the assurance and flexibility to return systems to a state before malicious attacks harm them by malfunctioning hardware.

Disaster Recovery

Disaster recovery (DR) and business continuity planning are created in tandem as part of security planning in the information technology industry. It describes the strategies and practices aimed at shielding a company or organization from any major repercussions in the event of a negative incident. Examples of such events include building or gadget malfunctions, cyberattacks, and natural catastrophes. When creating plans to enable the company to promptly restore its data, applications, and hardware for business continuity, disaster recovery is crucial. It is occasionally regarded as a part of business continuity. To create a suitable disaster recovery plan, a thorough analysis of the business effect and risk assessment must be prepared. IT services that can assist the company with its vital business operations also assists in establishing the recovery point and recovery time goals.

Three categories can be used to group disaster recovery measures:

- **Preventive Measures**: Seek to stop an incident from happening
- **Corrective Measures**: These are implemented in the event of a crisis or unfavorable occurrence to rectify a system.
- **Detective Measures**: They concentrate on tracking down and identifying unfavorable occurrences.

Even in the worst-case situations, company continuity may be achieved with the aid of any prudent disaster recovery plan. It's also a good idea to conduct routine audits and drills to ensure disaster recovery plans are up to date and being adhered to by each department within the company.

The Importance of Disaster Recovery (DR)

After a crisis, disaster recovery enables the company to continue or restore mission-critical operations promptly. Businesses, nowadays, have a much lower tolerance for downtime since they have grown increasingly dependent on and used to high availability. Therefore, a calamity might have a disastrous impact on the company, particularly in today's fiercely competitive marketplaces. Disaster recovery is becoming a crucial component of business operations since there is a strong likelihood that a corporation will fail following a major data loss. Two metrics are utilized in DR and downtime: recovery time objective (RTO) and recovery point objective (RPO).

- **RTO**: Stands for the longest period the company may resume regular operations following a disaster by retrieving its files from backup storage. RTO, then, is the maximum amount of downtime that the company can tolerate. The company cannot afford to experience more than two hours of downtime if its RTO is two hours.

- **RPO**: The maximum file age the company needs to recover from backup storage to carry on with business as usual following a disaster. RPO will ascertain the minimum frequency of backups. For example, if the RPO for the company is five hours, then the system needs to backup data at least once every five hours.

Consequently, RTO and RPO play a crucial role in assisting in selecting the best disaster recovery practices, plans, and tools for the company. Keeping secondary data accessible when needed will be necessary if the tighter RTO periods must be met.

Recovery-in-place is a fast and efficient way to get data back. To avoid moving the data across a network entails utilizing technology that enables the transition of the backup data files to a live state on a backup appliance. This guards against malfunctions in the server and storage systems.

A complete approach covering networking equipment, power, software and hardware, connection, testing, and disaster recovery planning is necessary to ensure that disaster recovery (DR) can be accomplished within RTO and RPO objectives. Although putting in place a comprehensive disaster recovery plan is a big undertaking, there are a lot of potential advantages.

Data Backup and Disaster Recovery Plan

The company faces the risk of irreversible data loss, needless costs, and extended downtime if it does not have a robust data backup and disaster recovery plan. The following five points make a data backup and disaster recovery plan very compelling:

- **Every Data Point is a Target**: Whether in a Fortune 500 company, a law firm, a dentist, or a pet store, data is always at risk. Hackers, viruses, malware, ransomware assaults, and accidents don't discriminate. They will target the company for several reasons, including retaliating against, obtaining private information, or just because they can.
- **It is Easy to Lose Data**: Rather than being caused by natural disasters, a large amount of data loss is the consequence of device failures or human error.
- **Some Data is Priceless**: If lost, some of the company's data is irreplaceable.

Backup and Recovery Software

A database management system, or DBMS, is a software program that makes database management simple and efficient, enabling it to organize the data correctly. One of the numerous benefits of DBMS is that it makes data storage, manipulation, and retrieval possible. In addition, it protects the data and transactions. Additionally, it might require reliable backup and recovery software, such as NetBackup, Commvault, Cohesity, Rubrik, and so on.

Backup and recovery are not exclusive to disaster recovery. In actuality, both strategies will be part of best practices.

Performance Tuning and Optimization

The improvement of efficiency of any existing cloud infrastructure is what is regarded as cloud performance optimization. The essence of this is to ensure that the resources are being used to their best by overseeing, assessing, and modifying the use of the clouds whenever possible. Like any other system, the tuning of performance is a perpetual aspect that requires routine changes and improvements to keep the cloud environment at optimum performance. An important component of coarse-grain refining of cloud performance is monitoring cloud resource utilization. By constantly assessing the effectiveness of the utilization of cloud-based resources, one can discover interferences or nuisances for better configurations. Such parameters may include CPU usage, RAM states, network de-congestion time, and other related performance assessment instruments like APM software. By monitoring these parameters closely, a problem might be detected and rectified before a critical point is achieved. This means that not to sit back and complain about poor performance but rather do something; upgrading and/or changing the cloud environment. This may mean changing network configurations, improving resource allocation, or adjusting the settings on the applications. Due to the nature of the tasks performed via the cloud, we often have to recalibrate the environment to render the applications functional to the best possible state.

Cloud performance tuning is one of those processes that is undertaken to ensure the best possible performance of cloud infrastructure. Any application that requires cloud resources is sure that all apps are up and running as accords. There needs to be regular maintenance, analysis, and change in the arrangement of cloud systems to maintain their efficiency level. All the same, they are optimal and if anyone is to make optimum use of the cloud infrastructure, cloud performance tuning is something that one has to embrace.

Cloud optimization, which falls under cloud operations practices, seeks to improve the performance, cost efficiency, and reliability of the resources and services in the cloud. The preceding process implies a systematic process of resource design in terms of what computing resources are required together in the right quantity and ensures that each cloud application or workload within the cloud has its right computing resources. Most importantly, helps cut costs whereby management of performance relative to workload performance costs proceeds until the appropriate level of the resources is obtained for the respective use.

There are lower expenses because of fewer instances running idle in cloud resources, greater visibility into costs incurred in usage of the cloud resources, and better use of resources which increases efficiency, which is one of the key benefits of cloud optimization. Less infrastructure can be required for applications to run, therefore easing the management and increasing the efficiency.

This ability is made possible through the effective management of resource consumption through the application metrics.

To carry out cloud optimization, there are aspects that every workload and application will always change with time. Resource allocation using expert knowledge is a traditional approach in which baseline performance is estimated for the resources required. However, in the future, we can see artificial intelligence techniques replacing these manual activities and making it easier and more efficient to manipulate the resources available in the cloud.

Here are the models that can be applied for cloud optimization:

- Appropriately scaling computer services to achieve scalable solutions
- The utilization of spot instances to reduce expenses
- The purchase of reserved instances for long-term savings
- The identification and removal of unwanted resources
- The consolidation of idle resources for increased effectiveness

Cloud Optimization

It is necessary to address cloud performance tuning since this is important in achieving optimal performance of cloud infrastructure. There are several approaches in which we can do this and increase the performance of the cloud and its robustness.

An essential optimization technique is a regular improvement of the system by evaluating and identifying the needed changes and possible bottlenecks. One may, for instance, use performance monitoring systems, such as load tests, to gather pertinent data regarding CPU utilization, memory usage, or even latency. This helps predict certain regions that will need maintenance and helps to change the geographical placement of the data centers. Another pertinent technique is application and workload optimization positioning.

Once we have a basic understanding of the dependencies and requirements of the workload, we can make rational decisions on how to utilize resources and allocate tasks across different instances or locations. This method enhances general performance as it ensures that the necessary resources are spread out amongst the applications thereby reducing the strain on any particular instance.

There is also the possibility of cloud resource performance being affected by ways of data management and storage that need control. Further, other procedures with more storage efficiency and faster data access should be applied. For instance, CDNs can be used to reduce delays encountered by users when they request information, thus improving their experience.

While there are such barriers, cloud performance can be significantly improved by taking active measures including effective workload management, optimization of data location, and system metrics assessment. Likewise, such approaches not only enhance performance but also make it possible for the system to withstand much more strain while delivering optimal user experience. In the best interest of the cloud environment, always review and change its configuration regularly to maximize its benefits and keep up with the inevitable changes in demand.

For businesses that want to expand businesses without increasing costs, optimization of the cloud becomes paramount. It should however be noted that cloud cost optimization is an important aspect of cloud optimization but not the main objective of a cloud optimization strategy.

Cloud optimization also covers measures aimed at ameliorating application performance, collaboration between teams, improving the quality of software, and obtaining feedback over the entire organization continuously. A comprehensive cloud optimization strategy also helps ensure a significant and quick payback on investment once the business transitions to the cloud. Moreover, it helps in the migration of company processes from the premises to the cloud and aids in increasing the productivity of developers.

For businesses that strive to grow changing the approach toward managing cloud resources and expenditures using cloud optimization is vital. Cloud costing helps enterprises allocate cloud resources to use cases without overspending, increases the visibility of cloud costs, and efficiently utilizes or maximizes the potential of cloud resources. Secondly, it can help companies in budgeting and reporting to the management teams.

These benefits are mainly associated with cloud cost optimization. The rest is the understanding of the reason for cloud optimization and is the focus area but one of the critical areas within the broader cloud optimization agenda.

Cloud optimization will pursue elements like measures to improve the application performance, improvement of cross-team cooperation, use of software quality assurance, and collection of feedback on any ongoing interventions within the company. Effective cloud optimization is good as it helps achieve a good return on investment over the long term and within a short month after moving to the cloud. Furthermore, it supports the change of the company's operations from the in-house unit, focuses on the wider cloud unit, and elevates the productivity of the developers.

Continuously monitor and analyze the performance of the monitoring cloud system by tracking down and fixing the abnormalities in performance which provides insights on where to concentrate the resources. Regular performance appraisal helps in determining any issues and bottlenecks that could compromise the proper functioning of the cloud infrastructure. Ensure that the cloud infrastructure is efficient and performance is well managed.

From the analysis, we can say a lot about the trends and patterns of the performance of the cloud system. Better reconstruction of how different parts and resources are utilized is critical in decision-making and in optimizing the system. It would be able to identify areas where resource utilization is high or, where there is a latency and it can use appropriate measures, for instance, increasing resource allocation, to increase efficiency of the system.

Also, thanks to monitoring and analysis, we can assess the cloud performance compared to industry averages and recommendations appropriately. In the search for waste and efficiency of cloud resources, the results of the performance data can be compared to those of other similar organizations to find out how well-managing the cloud resources and which ones need further refinement.

Consistently outperform competitors in cloud performance due to this constant process of monitoring and analysis which ensures that the system is always effective and yields the optimum outcome.

Data analysis and monitoring should go hand in hand as it is crucial in enhancing cloud performance. Efficiency of the system can be monitored and displayed graphically facilitating the understanding of potential aspects of development and appropriate usage of available resources. Through preventive maintenance, ensure that the cloud environment will be functioning optimally which enhances performance and the utilization of resources.

Here we shall examine a few of the most critical components of cloud optimization.

Cost-Effectiveness

Cost cutting is perhaps the most common step toward the optimization of the use of cloud computing resources for most companies. The problem with cloud computing is the likelihood that can incur expenses quickly considering the ease of resource allocation as opposed to the on-premises setup.

The intricacy of cloud service pricing schemes increases this problem. For instance, a menu of services offered by the cloud service provider often contains several prices for the same service depending on time or geographical location.

This problem may be solved with the use of cost monitoring tools provided by the cloud provider, such as Cost Monitoring Tool AWS or Cost Messenger for Azure. Guided by these tools, we will be able to know imposing costs and even tell when it has breached the set costs.

It is noticed however about on-demand services that there is a lack of any proactive measures taken by the cloud service providers to discourage the clients from overstretching the resources offered to them. They do not have tools for managing work in mixed clouds and multi-cloud. Therefore, where most cloud cost optimization is based on native vendor tools, which offer only limited and basic plug-ins, multi-cloud architecture with third-party cost optimization tools is the general state of affairs.

Performance

In a cloud environment, to enhance its performance, it is essential to ensure that the apps and services are running smoothly and swiftly.

Cloud performance, like its cost, is also a complex issue that is dependent on many parameters. An important parameter that needs to be considered is the structure of the cloud's architecture. For instance, geographical distribution (using different geographical places for different users) can introduce delays in cloud design where data is sent to these different places quite regularly.

The cloud vendor/network chosen may affect the performance of this service as well. For some workloads their VM (virtual machine) resource distribution can be more limited; 'serverless computing platforms like AWS Lambda or Azure functions can perform better than the conventional VM environment.

Even though it is not considered cloud-specific, basic characteristics of the source code may greatly affect performance improvements of the cloud. After all, performance testing should always be performed against the application code that has been developed for every single business production stage.

Reliability

Workloads that are provisioned in the cloud may cease to be available due to the existing hosting cloud going down. Over workloads can, from time to time, turn out to be very volatile due to some causes. Since the reliability of the cloud services relies upon them, it is necessary to eliminate such risks.

It is observed that redundancy helps in increasing reliability. It means an organization is running multiple copies of the same workload in different cloud regions or multiple clouds. To achieve the best possible outcomes, attention should also be given to the balance of the redundancy strategy and cost minimization aim because this type of insurance is often expensive.

Holding these strategies can be third-party solutions that provide guaranteed enterprise SLAs although incorporating more than one cloud.

Security

For those who work in cloud environments, accurately identifying security weaknesses and implementing the appropriate security measures is a major challenge. This challenge is possible to surmount through centralized visibility and the application of useful security intelligence.

Cloud systems are built to provide a higher level of security to the users. Ensure that the technology offers both proactive and responsive actions, including:

- Pre-event awareness entails identifying hazards and putting in place the necessary protections in advance of an event. Virtual machine (VM) encryption, VPNs, and container visibility are notable pre-event security measures.
- Post-event awareness: Implement strategies to help detect and react swiftly and efficiently to security incidents. Post-even strategies that are frequently used are automation of compliance, security risk mitigation technologies, and DevSecOps processes.

Cloud Optimization Services and Tools

There are dozens of possible combinations of services and technologies offered by the major public cloud vendors, such as Microsoft Azure, Google Cloud, and Amazon Web Services (AWS), depending on various pricing models. Navigating the sheer volume of offers is challenging for businesses and even highly experienced IT experts.

Thankfully, cloud optimization service providers assist businesses in meeting their cloud optimization needs and goals. Through a cloud optimization service, businesses can find areas in the cloud where they can cut costs, boost productivity, create organizational optimization plans, and manage cloud infrastructure to support ongoing optimization.

Through cloud optimization services, clients can connect with qualified cloud specialists who function as an extension of their existing IT staff. They carry out impartial assessments of the cloud environment and point out important areas where the business might cut expenses.

The following services can benefit in important ways.

Reduce Costs and Invest Smarter

A significant amount of an organization's total cloud investment is consumed in provisioning and redundant infrastructure. A major organization can save a lot of money by streamlining costs across the board, freeing up cash for greater initiatives. To highlight cost efficiencies, an organization can reduce its overall cloud costs by close to 50 percent by optimizing its cloud infrastructure, thereby releasing money for more innovative and expansionary strategic activities.

Increase Visibility

Cloud optimization services render useful, detailed, and significant analysis about how resources are consumed and spent, and where more efficiency could be achieved for each business unit. Thanks to improved visibility, organizations can match their cloud spending to the actual business requirements.

In addition to cutting costs, Cloud optimization services are targeted to appreciate the visibility across the cloud systems. They give business teams the certainty with which they can broadly use the cloud services for their applications.

Access Skills and Expertise

With more companies migrating to the cloud, the technical skill requirements are growing. But many organizations do not have enough internal expertise which creates a skills shortage in cloud computing. With respect to the skills shortage, most organizations have recorded almost twice the levels of caseloads as a result of increased cases and competition for personnel who are already in short supply.

This cloud optimization service can help address the skill gap by granting the internal IT department of any organization to a pool of qualified cloud professionals as well as providing cloud-specific tools.

Cloud Optimization Best Practices

One of the most effective approaches when streamlining the cloud environment is right-sizing to make it possible for organizations to determine the capabilities and the scope of the cloud services needed to support their workloads. Such processes also include making both the type and the size of the execution units according to the workload requirement.

For example, AWS has the spot instances and reserved instances for the effective use of cloud services.

Use of Spot Instances

Spot instances are the most efficient way to use cloud resources for workloads that are not sensitive to real-time. Spot instances are excess cloud providers, such as AWS offering compute capacity available at a very cheap cost in comparison to the on-demand pricing model.

However, in case of an increase in the usage of these resources, the spot instances can be withdrawn rather instantly by the provider. They work perfectly for operations that are unlikely to get interrupted along the way and resumed, for example, batch jobs, data analytics, and development and test environments. It is even possible to perform critical operations that require no interruptions by using automated systems with spot instances.

Reserved Instances

One more effective methodology for the rational management of cloud resources that can result in serious savings is the use of reserved instances. Specifically, these are commitments to pay for certain services for a minimum of 1st - 3rd year in return for lower overall costs from the provider relative to the pay-as-go rates.

Workloads that are consistent and predictable suit us well in reservable instances. This method of reserving resources is within reach with 75% cost limitations emanated when compared with intangible on-demand instances costly models.

Idle Resources

It is considered another effective cloud optimization strategy to merge surplus capacities. There may be some instances that are less utilized at the off-peak hours. Identifying idle resources is one of the key strategies in cloud cost optimization where identifying the resources that are underutilized and doing consolidation of such resources or right-sizing them as per the load helps in reducing the operational cost.

For this, the technologies of load balancing and auto-scaling are fundamental. Load balancing prevents any one server from being excessively loaded by distributing network traffic between several servers and auto-scaling the number of servers that are in an active state according to how overwhelmed they are with users.

Potential Challenges

Some problems that one might consider would emerge in the process and affect the tuning process of cloud performance. As experts in tuning the performance of clouds, we have had several issues that required strategizing. Such problems can range from the allocation of resources to issues of scaling up which could have an impact on the effectiveness of cloud systems overall.

Finding a solution to the problem of making the system scalable is one of the toughest challenges in tuning the performance of clouds. Systems that are not able to function optimally given the high usage of cloud services are destined to have a very limited future. To achieve this, the design and environment should be able to adaptably scale upwards or downwards depending on the variation in the intensity of use of the system.

Additionally, forecasting and preparing for growth is important to prevent the risks of failing to deliver results as expected. The distribution of resources is one of the main barriers against the optimization of a cloud. In a cloud environment, several virtual machines (VMs) share it there underlying physical resources at the same time. Efficient allocation of these resources is required to achieve optimal performance. This means unidirectionally controlling the load on the resources of each virtual machine and in case of excess load allocation providing reallocation of resources to the virtual machines as per the requirement. Improvement in the overall performance of the cloud system could be appreciated due to the proper allocation of resources and distribution of the load across multiple virtual machines (VMs). And finally, some factors like security and compliance impose further constraints in the cloud performance tuning process. It is also crucial to enforce strong security measures like encryption, access control, and regular vulnerability assessments as protection from various possible single threats. Compliance with such industry standards and regulations as GDPR and PCI DSS also implies that the cloud environment has to be diligently configured and monitored. When it comes to cloud performance optimization difficulties also come into play. This process of achieving the goal of optimal cloud performance has some barriers, such as resource allocation, security, and scalability.

Cloud Database Deployment Models

The benefits of having a cloud-based database are obvious for many organizations. They provide security, availability, and scalability. In comparison to custom and on-premises database solutions, there may also be financial savings. But not every cloud database is made equally. Although different levels of cloud computing have historically been described by terms like IaaS, PaaS, and SaaS, how do these terms relate to cloud databases? What should we think about the database as a service (DBaaS) offerings?

In the context of cloud computing, Figure 1 illustrates that the main distinction between software as a service (SaaS), platform as a service (PaaS), and infrastructure as a service (IaaS) is the degree of abstraction over underlying resources and services. It is generally easier and faster for the user to get value from a cloud service the more abstraction the service provider removes from the customer. Additionally, the user would have more authority and responsibility over the environment the less the supplier manages on their behalf.

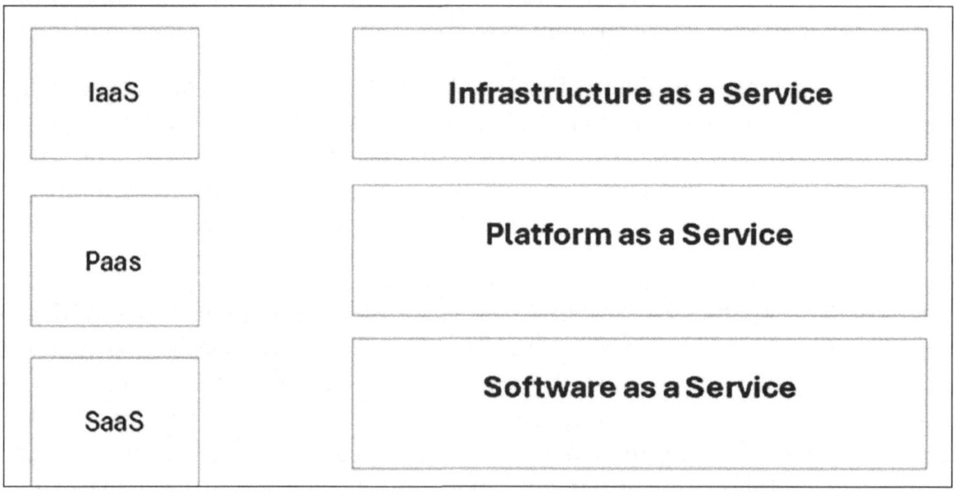

Figure 10.1: *Different levels of abstraction in cloud computing*

The concepts behind this taxonomy of cloud computing also apply to cloud databases. As is the case with most cloud-based products and services, the database choice will depend on the team's go-to-market needs, level of experience and competence, amount of overhead and administrative work ready to do, and level of customization needed.

IaaS (Infrastructure as a Service)

An implementation of an IaaS database on cloud infrastructure is self-managed. It would be in charge of installation, configuration, and continuing maintenance for the operating system, runtime, and database software. Running on-premises would be comparable to the experience, except of using cloud servers and storage. The maximum control over the system is provided by an IaaS database, but that comes with additional duties inherently.

No, we don't need to run own data center with an IaaS database and acquire hardware. But, must choose the infrastructure of a cloud service, install the database on our own, and maintain it within the provider's guidelines.

IaaS gives all the power and the maintenance burden of a traditional database.

Advantages:

The following are the advantages of IaaS:

- Select databases that do not always offer comparable PaaS or SaaS versions have more options when it comes to database(s) while using IaaS.
- Set up database(s) with IaaS so they function as required.
- As with other cloud database choices, IaaS provides almost infinite scalability. IaaS is all that is needed if accustomed to managing the database and are making the switch to avoid managing data center.
- Replicating on-premises database infrastructure in the cloud is made simpler by IaaS.
- Lastly, IaaS offers additional control over OS, database software, and other configuration options.

Disadvantages:

The following are the disadvantages of IaaS:

- Decide to use an IaaS database, will be solely responsible for doing regular maintenance, which includes managing backup, scaling, security, and other issues.
- Team members might require additional database knowledge and cloud credentials in comparison to PaaS and SaaS, particularly in relation to database operations. It will just require a larger crew.
- The setup of an IaaS database could take a long time. Need to compare this to the project's urgency.

PaaS(Platform as a Service)

A database provided as PaaS expands on the benefits of the cloud. Provisioning, configuration, scaling, and other cluster administration operations can be automated with the use of PaaS databases. With PaaS, a team can avoid having to build up and manage infrastructure, as they would have to with IaaS.

In our IaaS-PaaS-SaaS continuum, PaaS is the middle option, and this is how many cloud databases are provided. With cluster automation technologies, they facilitate database management for teams. Users of PaaS must still be somewhat knowledgeable about cluster specifics, such as the quantity and kind of nodes, capacity, and sharding.

The advantages and disadvantages of a PaaS database are:

Advantages:

- Benefits from scalability comparable to those of an IaaS implementation.
- Provisioning, setup, scalability, and other typical tasks are made simpler by the vendor's administration tools for PaaS.
- Additionally, the vendor manages routine administrative duties like patches and updates.

Disadvantages:

- Although there is less of an operational load than with IaaS, it will still need to organize the cluster, define the software version, the quantity and kind of nodes, the size of the instances, and other details.
- Capacity planning is also necessary in order to account for expansion, as well as peak capacity/usage and headroom.
- Still be in charge of some or all software updates when using PaaS.

SaaS (Software as a Service)

For cloud apps, SaaS is undoubtedly the most well-known software delivery model: simply log in and get to work. Everybody uses SaaS apps, often using dozens of them in a single day; examples include Salesforce CRM and Google Docs. When it comes to databases, SaaS is significantly less well-known, but we'll use it to refer to databases that absolve users of all cluster operation responsibilities.

In general, SaaS databases are the simplest to set up and manage. This is so that the service provider can take care of all technical problems as well as planning, provisioning, and other daily duties. Stated differently, the user is not aware of any cluster information because the database is entirely managed by the supplier.

Advantages:

- Most capacity and cluster planning are removed from the plate by SaaS databases.
- It also removes the need for node, node type, and instance size configuration by abstracting away cluster administration.
- SaaS eliminates the need for manual involvement in tasks like scaling and provisioning.
- All software updates take place in the background in a transparent manner.
- Rather than the quantity or size of nodes, the cost of a SaaS database is typically determined by the amount of storage, compute, I/O, or queries that are processed. This indicates that depending on the instance types, the storage-to-compute ratio is not fixed.

Disadvantages:

- As there are fewer readily user-configurable options with this architecture, cost estimation may be more challenging. For many teams, nevertheless, this can still be the most cost-effective choice due to the lighter operational strain.
- Since most databases provided as Software as a Service (SaaS) were designed with the cloud in mind, there isn't a self-managed version available for those who need it.

Multi-Cloud and Hybrid Cloud

A database that is implemented over one or more cloud systems is known as a multi-cloud database.

A multi-cloud database is distributed because it utilizes hardware from at least two distinct cloud providers. Genuinely multi-cloud database, can run one cluster or several clusters, that span several clouds. The application can use true multi-cloud databases similar to that of a single-instance database running on a single cloud.

It is easy to deploy any database over many clouds, even though few database management systems (DBMS) are genuinely cloud-native and can handle multi-cloud in this way. However, the amount of work needed to set up such a system can become more expensive, especially as it develops more complicated. YugabyteDB and CockroachDB are a few examples of multi-cloud environment.

Multi-Cloud vs. Hybrid Cloud

When we talk about multi-cloud, we usually mean using several public clouds (such as AWS, GCP, Azure, and so on.). Operating on a combination of at least one on-premises system and one public and private cloud is referred to as the hybrid cloud. However, in practice, these phrases aren't always used exactly; for example, hybrid cloud systems may be referred to as multi-cloud systems, and vice versa. When a system combines two or more public clouds with a private cloud or on-premises system, it can also be classified as a hybrid cloud or multi-cloud.

Benefits of a Multi-Cloud Database

The particular use case and deployment specifics of a corporation will determine the benefits of a multi-cloud database. However, businesses that use multi-cloud databases typically have an interest in one or more of these commercial objectives:

- **Risk management**

  There are hazards associated with restricting database deployment to a single public cloud, such as but not limited to:

  Although whole-cloud or public cloud region outages are uncommon, they do occur. If deployed on a single public cloud, there's a good chance that a localized problem would take down a whole cloud region because most cloud providers either offer a single data center per region or numerous data centers that are clustered in the same geographic area.

  Furthermore, when something like a regional outage does occur, it can be extremely expensive and disruptive; huge companies may lose millions of dollars due to lost revenue and reputational harm from even a brief outage.

  Technical staff members experience stress as a result of outages, which negatively impacts their work-life balance and, consequently, their productivity and retention. The effects of a regional outage can be severe even with multi-region deployments on a single cloud. Users in the affected region may experience significantly higher latency, and the resulting increase in traffic to other regions may overload the system since fewer machines are now managing the same workload. By choosing one public cloud provider, agreeing to their terms of service and pricing, including any future modifications, or risk having to deal with an expensive and challenging migration in the future.

  Regulations controlling how businesses handle customer data differ by area and are rapidly evolving.

  Ensuring that a multi-cloud database deployment retains its flexibility can help businesses stay compliant and more readily enter new markets.

- **Cost**

  Multi-cloud database deployments can sometimes save expenses. This can happen directly (by taking advantage of offers from a specific cloud's marketplace, for example) or indirectly (by lowering the number of hours needed for database operations when businesses choose managed multi-cloud services).

- **Strategic planning**

  Multi-cloud database deployments are often part of a broader strategic initiative to modernize IT infrastructure and leverage the benefits of cloud computing.

Multi-cloud Data Management Best Practices

Here we discuss the best practices for effective multi-cloud management.

- **Data and Application Portability**

  Critical issues for modern organizations operating multi-cloud architecture include data silos and lack of mobility.

  The main public cloud service providers each have their own proprietary data management APIs, therefore there isn't a straightforward or uniform method for sharing or copying data between public clouds. For this reason, data generated or gathered in public clouds may frequently get isolated within multi-cloud settings. Data portability is a challenge for even open-source enterprises, as they frequently lack a simple method for transferring petabyte-scale data between cloud providers.

  Cross-cloud data-sharing technologies allow enterprises to provide data portability as part of their multi-cloud strategy.

  Cross-cloud solutions facilitate cost-effective, high-bandwidth connectivity and data sharing between public clouds, hence addressing issues with data silos and portability. As an illustration, consider Google's Cross-Cloud Interconnect, which enables users of GCP to create cross-cloud connections with Oracle Cloud Infrastructure, Alibaba Cloud, AWS, and Azure.

  Many businesses already use Kubernetes and containerization to deliver applications when it comes to application portability. Major public cloud providers can also help organizations deploy application workloads in multi-cloud environments or deploy cloud services from one provider onto another's public cloud with ease by providing multi-cloud platform solutions, such as GCP Anthos, Azure Arc, and Amazon EKS Anywhere.

- **Data in the Cloud**

  More data than ever before is being generated and gathered by modern businesses. This data includes transactional data as well as application, event, cloud service, and security logs.

To support use cases such as application performance management, user behavior monitoring, and security incident investigation, enterprise DevOps and SecOps teams analyze this data. However, when pertinent data is siloed across multiple cloud deployments and cannot be analyzed jointly, important context and insights are lost.

To optimize their data collection in multi-cloud environments, businesses must combine and consolidate their data into a single database, data lake, or cloud data platform. From there, it can be safely stored, aggregated, and analyzed to derive insights that facilitate data-driven decision-making.

For Chaos LakeDB, our data lake database that combines the storage capacity of a data lake with the accessibility of a cloud database and the analytical capabilities of a data warehouse, both Amazon S3 and Google Cloud Storage can offer a reliable, scalable, and affordable storage foundation.

- **Security Practices**

  By spreading out databases, cloud services, and application workloads across several public clouds, increase the attack surface of the company, making it easier for cybercriminals to target the infrastructure (using malware, botnets, and zero-day exploits, for example) and raising the possibility of data breaches. Although some advocates of multi-cloud computing assert that distributing resources around public clouds can lessen the likelihood of a cyberattack, there is a chance that a security breach in one cloud could propagate horizontally to other clouds in the multi-cloud setup.

  Organizations must have standardized and coordinated security policies that are applicable to all cloud environments, independent of provider, in order to secure multi-cloud environments efficiently. Additionally, we advise gathering security information from every public cloud and consolidating it into a single repository, such as a security data lake, which may provide constant visibility and thorough monitoring of the whole multi-cloud system from a single interface.

- **Multi-cloud Disaster Recovery**

  Business continuity planning (BCP) for enterprises running mission-critical or customer-facing cloud apps must include IT disaster recovery as a key component. Businesses that use only one cloud frequently rely on the cross-region disaster recovery features provided by public cloud providers such as Azure and AWS; nonetheless, there are valid worries regarding the dependability of this configuration. Here is the reason: During a cloud service outage, some AWS customers run their application workloads in the US-East region and failover to the US-West region, whereas others run in the US-West region and failover to the US-East region. The other region would be severely burdened in the event of a service outage in any of these regions, and there would likely not be enough resources to address it.

Organizations can take advantage of application portability and avoid these restrictions by implementing a multi-cloud disaster recovery strategy, which allows data and apps from one public cloud to be recovered to another in the event of an unplanned outage.

- **Optimize Data Retention to Use Cases**

  Organizations should develop data retention policies based on their operational needs and legal/regulatory compliance when it comes to retaining data in multi-cloud settings.

  Organizations should first perform a thorough inventory of all the data they are creating or gathering, identify the data that is required to support operational goals and processes, and ascertain which data may be subject to data retention requirements as a result of data security and privacy regulations.

  From there, businesses may set up data retention guidelines to guarantee that vital information is safely and affordably kept for the necessary amount of time to satisfy legal compliance goals and analytical use cases.

  Large-volume modern organizations sometimes encounter trade-offs where potentially valuable data is prematurely lost to lower data retention costs, as well as data retention constraints. Organizations can achieve unlimited cost-effective data retention that supports compliance objectives and analytics use cases like application performance monitoring, multi-cloud observability, and advanced persistent threat hunting by centralizing data in GCS or Amazon S3 and indexing it with Chaos LakeDB.

Multi-cloud vs. Hybrid Cloud Data Management

Although multi-cloud and hybrid-cloud data management share many similarities, it's crucial to comprehend their differences as well. Whereas a hybrid cloud computing system uses a combination of on-premise data centers, private cloud, and public cloud infrastructure, a multi-cloud computing environment runs databases, applications, and cloud services using resources from many public cloud providers.

Companies usually choose a hybrid cloud configuration for one of two reasons:

- They have made large purchases of hardware and on-site data centers.
- Rather than keeping and protecting their most sensitive data on the public cloud, they would prefer to retain control over it on local servers.

Hybrid cloud data management frequently places a greater emphasis on the following:

- Managing and integrating data among private cloud, public cloud, and on-premises services.
- Considering security and compliance requirements while deciding how to deploy apps and services among on-premises, private, and public cloud infrastructure.
- Securing private cloud or on-premises servers' sensitive data by securing the link between them and public cloud infrastructure.
- Multi-cloud data management, on the other hand, is typically focused on centralizing, securing, and analyzing data from across multiple public clouds.

Multi-cloud

- **Public cloud**: An environment where multiple organizations share computing resources is known as a public cloud. Google Cloud is one instance.
- **Private cloud:** A computing environment or cloud owned by or devoted to a single entity.
- **Hybrid cloud**: An organization's on-site combination of one or more public and one or more private clouds.
- **Multi-cloud**: Two or more public clouds, potentially with private clouds as well.

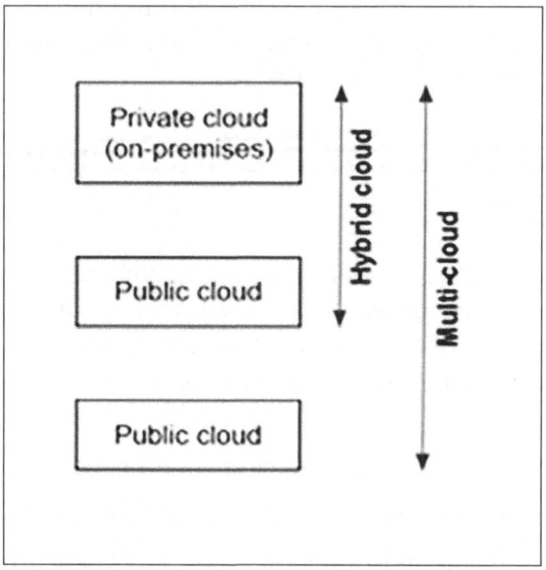

Figure 10.2: *Hybrid cloud and multi-cloud*

Database Application

A database is used by a database application to maintain its persistent state. It consists of the following elements.

- **User interface**: It is typically an installed client, a mobile client, or a browser client.
- **Application logic**: It works on any computing environment, including virtual machines, Kubernetes, Cloud Functions, Cloud Run, and so on, and implements the business logic.
- **Database**: A database application uses the database to maintain its permanent state and the database itself implements data management capability.

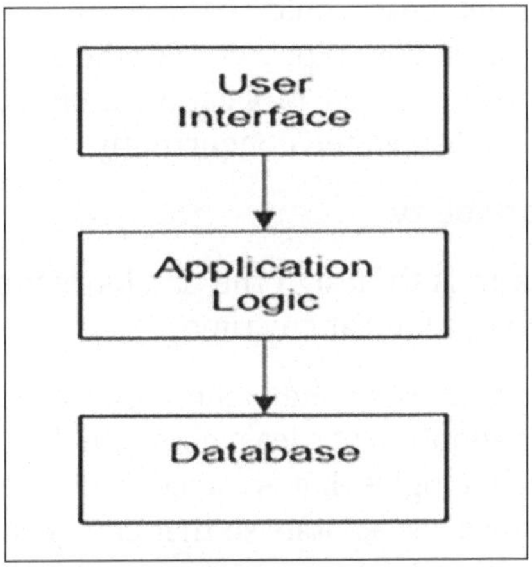

***Figure 10.3**: Database application*

Networking

It is implicitly believed that for an organization to adopt a multi-cloud arrangement, communication across the various clouds involved must be possible. Since the deployed apps exchange configuration metadata, management functionality, and business data, clouds are generally not used in isolation.

Multi-Cloud Use Cases

Database applications have a wide variety of use cases across multiple clouds. We will go into greater depth on a handful of them here to show the current spectrum. Later, a thorough and comprehensive list will be provided. Naturally, the focus will be on the database element (see Database Application Components earlier), with no further explanation provided for the application logic or client parts.

Use Case: Cloud Bursting

The application case of cloud bursting is significant. The hybrid cloud scenario is where this use case shines because a private on-premises data center can handle the fundamental, steady-state load.

Depending on the sector, a spike in customer activity can surpass a data center's capacity at specific times of the year. In these cases, the cloud offers the extra capacity needed to meet bursting demands.

To boost capacity during bursting, the application logic is also executed in the cloud. It's possible that the on-premises database can manage the bursting on the database side.

If that is insufficient, then a database is also put into the cloud; synchronization between two databases becomes crucial.

A distributed multi-master database would be the simplest to set up; data partitioning across two databases across clouds to prevent conflicts would be more challenging. The most difficult is a bi-directional replication approach that needs to resolve conflicts when the same data is updated concurrently.

Use Case: Cross-Cloud Portability

One tactic to prevent lock-in is to design the database and application logic so that they can be transferred to any cloud at any time.

This use case may necessitate using the same technology across all clouds in one variation. This requires the adoption of a least common denominator strategy because only cloud services and technologies that are accessible across all clouds can be used. From the standpoint of databases, a database that can be installed on all clouds must be selected.

An alternative approach is to define portability as the capacity to move models and patterns rather than the technology being used. For instance, in the case of databases, any database that can handle the relational model will do so, and portability can be achieved through the usage of either the relational or document model. However, this can only select model pieces that are supported by cloud computing technology. Rather than the technology, it will be a common denominator of the model.

Use Case: Disaster Recovery

By implementing a disaster recovery plan that facilitates failover and fallback between a primary and secondary cloud, downtime due to cloud failure can be avoided. A so-called "hot-hot standby deployment," which requires that the database and application logic be available and prepared to handle client traffic in all participating clouds, is necessary to achieve the lowest RPO and RTO.

Data should be proactively copied from the primary cloud to the standby cloud to reduce RTO and RPO from a database standpoint.

A database system that replicates asynchronously suffices if some transaction loss is acceptable. The optimum option if RPO should be zero is a master-master database system that replicates synchronously.

Database Sharding

Multi-instance sharding is a component of orthogonal distribution (distributing data across different dimensions, such as by geography or customer type). Managing (disjoint) data divisions is the foundation of sharding. A separate database instance is in charge of each partition. While extra shards can be created dynamically over time, this scales on the one hand and may prevent cross-shard queries on the other.

All distribution types mentioned earlier have the potential to facilitate sharding and function as a sharded system. But since many systems weren't made for sharding, not all of them offer it.

A database system can be chosen depending on the database deployment architecture and database distribution model for a certain use case, such as cloud bursting and the database management pattern decided for it.

Two different methods for cloud bursting are discussed independently in the following instances. The database management pattern is selected first, followed by the database.

Mixed Multi-Cloud Use Cases

Before beginning the database selection process in this example, an overall architecture choice must be made: will each use case have its own database system, or will one database system need to support them all?

The selection process will be guided by the use case with the most stringent requirements. The database that is chosen must support the completely synchronized use case, for instance, if have a partitioned use case and a fully synchronized use case. The partitioned use case will also be supported by this system by definition.

Database as a Service (DBaaS) Offerings and Management Tools

Software and/or services that let users set up, run, and scale databases without having to install software, set up physical hardware, or configure for performance are referred to as "Database-as-a-Service" (DBaaS). The user or application owner only needs to use and access the database because the service provider handles all administrative duties and maintenance. Of course, the degree of control can change based on the service provider's offerings and the user's preferences.

The following are primary concepts that are important to appreciate the usage of the DBaaS:

- **Availability**: It is how the users interact with the DBaaS that users have encountered web interfaces or automated APIs that facilitate simple management and manipulation of database operations.
- **Updating and maintenance**: The service providers take all the responsibility for such things as patching, upgrading, and updating all databases. They also ensure that the database operates on the latest safe version of the software.
- **Capability to grow**: With the on-demand scalability provided by DBaaS solutions, databases can grow to satisfy the demands of the users without the interference of the manual adjustments of storage and hardware.
- **Information security**: It is now a common practice to combine adequate data protection measures and reliable backups with regular disaster recovery services to achieve restoration of most systems even in cases of advanced failures.
- **Performance observation**: The provision of advanced database health and performance management tools has enabled enterprises to manage and optimize database resources more proactively.

The following are the key points to adopt the DBaaS system within an organization:

- Repetitive and time-consuming administrative procedures can be eliminated with DBaaS to automated one-click operations that simplify database management.
- It facilitates the initiation of projects and timely completion of workloads, hence helping organizations to improve business performance.
- The procedures needed to make information accessible via internet-based connections are made simpler.
- Migration of databases to the cloud is storage consolidation. For instance, a large company's databases from several departments can be merged online into a single hosted database management system.

Here are the key differences between DBaaS and a DBMS:

Parameters	**DBaaS**	**DBMS**
Service model	DBaaS is a cloud computing service model that offers database capabilities	A DBMS is a type of software that is installed and run locally on servers or other computers
Infrastructure management	The service provider oversees the hardware, networking, and storage infrastructure needed to host and run the database	The entity or individual is responsible for overseeing and maintaining the infrastructure of the database system

Scalability	It enables users to increase or decrease database resources based on their needs. Additionally, resource provisioning is handled by the service provider	Scaling up or down a database in a traditional DBMS usually involves human intervention and infrastructure modifications by the user or organization
Maintenance	Administrative duties such as software updates, security updates, performance monitoring, and database maintenance are performed by the service provider	Duties and responsibilities have to be performed by the organization or the user
Cost	Usually, cost includes maintenance, charges for software, and infrastructure costs which must be fixed at the time of subscription	The company normally manages the infrastructure and purchases or licenses the program, resulting in an initial payment and subsequent maintenance costs
Flexibility and control	DBaaS creates a level of ease that makes the users not restrain their efforts on the creation of data as well as applications. It can, nonetheless, be subject to some rules and restrictions from the provider	The organization has limited power and options with the type of database system since much of the database system control including the customization of the infrastructure, software version, and its configuration is limited with a database management system

***Table 10.1**: Difference between DBaaS and DBMS System*

Conclusion

DBaaS is a comparatively cheaper solution as the client company does not have to make huge investments in acquiring software and infrastructure, something which is expected deployed in the provision of the database on-premise. The costs can be kept at reasonable levels in slow seasons without compromising on service levels. Such flexibility encourages growth and ensures that database capacity expands without human effort or extensive cloud management. It creates a scenario where the databases are always running the newest and the most secure version of the software. This helps internal resources to refocus on innovations for the organization such as engaging on the roadmap of elevating the prioritization of products.

DBaaS is highly flexible, an application development process can be handled in a DevOps manner, which enhances the effectiveness of the continuous integration and deployment processes. It includes a wider range of compliance and many companies also conform to them making it less difficult for companies to be in compliance.

Organizations may utilize this to ensure their data is kept safe with security procedures that may be overly intricate. Procedures are in place so that there are backups of the data at any time and data can be restored in case of such factors, such as catastrophes, system damages, or even data corruption. High availability configurations ensure that databases are available, even during unscheduled downtime, system outages, or routine maintenance.

Questions

1. Explain the various Database backup and recovery procedures.
2. Analyze the performance tuning of a cloud environment and discuss the optimization in cloud environments.
3. Write a use case based on the various cloud deployment models in the context of a database.
4. Apply the cloud deployment models in database systems to optimize the performance using a case study.
5. Define and discuss multi-cloud and hybrid cloud strategies for database systems.
6. Explain the Database as a Service (DBaaS) offerings and management tools with the help of an example.
7. Using a case study apply the log-based recovery mechanism to recover the data in a cloud environment.
8. Explain the process of backup restoration testing with the help of a suitable example.
9. Define and discuss the various disaster recovery plans in a distributed database environment.
10. Explain database as a service (DBaaS) with the help of a suitable example and discuss the advantages of the DBaaS system over the other database environment.

Index

Symbols

A

B

C

G

H

I

J

L

M

N

O

P

Q

R

S

T

V